HIS
GLORIOUS
NAME

VOLUMES IN THIS SERIES

HIS
GLORIOUS
NAME

The Names and Titles of
Jesus Christ
T.U.V.W.Y.Z.

by Charles J. Rolls

LOIZEAUX BROTHERS
Neptune, New Jersey

FIRST EDITION, MAY 1975
SECOND EDITION, REVISED AND EXPANDED, SEPTEMBER 1985
THIRD PRINTING, MAY 1989

Library of Congress Cataloging in Publication Data

Rolls, Charles J. (Charles Jubilee), 1887–
   His glorious name: The names and titles of
Jesus Christ: T–Z. Revised edition.

   1. Jesus Christ—Name.   I. Title.   II. Series:
Rolls, Charles J. (Charles Jubilee), 1887–
Names and titles of Jesus Christ.
BT590.N2R59   1985   232   85-6926
ISBN 0-87213-735-X

PRINTED IN THE UNITED STATES OF AMERICA

Dedicated
to
my lifelong friends
Robert Alexander Laidlaw, C.B.E.
and Lillian, his devoted wife,
the kindness of whose generosity excelled.
Bunyan describes one of his Bible characters
as having boarded the Lord's servants
by the year, and who looked for payment
at the return of the good Samaritan.
This was my experience exactly
in their home

CONTENTS

T

U

V

W Y Z

FOREWORD

The incentive for writing an outline on some of the names, titles, and vocations of Christ was brought about through reading the life story of that famous scientist, Dr. George Washington Carver. This man prayed that he might be shown some of the chemical contents that God had put into peanuts. In answer to his request, he was enabled to produce three hundred and ten products from the same. The late Henry Ford was a great admirer of Dr. Carver and visited him frequently.

The present writer's interests were centered in the Scriptures and one morning, after reading through the book of the Revelation, he was deeply impressed with our Lord's repeated claim, "I am Alpha and Omega."

If it be possible for the mind to be directed to comprehend the chemical constituents of perishable peanuts, how much greater must be the spiritual values incorporated in our Lord's imperishable names. Shortly after praying for enlightenment on this subject, I was asked by the editor of a monthly magazine to write a series of articles for publication. The first consisted of eight of Christ's titles beginning with the letter A. The second eight commenced with B, and so they continued. By the time we reached the letter F the demand for the magazine had well-nigh doubled. The growing interest caused me to enlarge the outlines and increase the number beginning with each letter to twelve. The first volume covered A to G, which was well received and included eighty-four of our Lord's names, titles, and offices. When the second book was issued, one ministerial association chose it as the book of the year. Volume three was financed by the president of a large business, who also paid for the first three titles to be sent to the libraries of one hundred universities over the English-speaking world.

Many years ago one of the great artists in Europe decided to portray his conception of Christ on canvas. His best friends expressed their disappointment with his production. Later he made a second attempt and met the same disapproval. Undaunted, he visited a number of the leading art galleries and examined the famous presentations of former artists. With greater concentration than ever and over a longer period, he completed his third attempt, only to be told it was not as good as his first. Disheartened with his failure, he determined to give up painting altogether. In his disconsolation he visited a resort in the country. During the second night he dreamt that Christ came to him and asked why he was so disheartened. After he told of his grief, Christ said to him, "Did you not know that you cannot paint Me for anyone else?"

Of this the writer is fully aware, that his description of the Saviour will not be fully accepted by others. Peter had a revelation to his own heart (Matt. 16:17). The Apostle Paul likewise (Gal. 1:16). This is what each soul needs (Luke 10:21-22). Christ can suit Himself to the budding heart of a child or satisfy the capacity of a philosopher or scientist intimately and directly.

Book five is sent forth with the prayer that it may stimulate some to seek to develop a greater capacity for apprehending and appreciating the personal beauties, virtues, graces, and glories of the Lord Jesus Christ Himself.

C.J.R.

T

In tracing the timeless realities of Him who is the True Light and the Tree of Life, together with the immensities and immutables of His many administrations, we marvel that He should be made manifest as the Son of Man.

The TEACHER (John 3:2; Matt. 7:28-29)
    With full knowledge of the visible and invisible.
The TRUTH (Deut. 32:4; John 14:6)
    He is always and altogether perfectly accurate.
The TRUE LIGHT (John 1:9; II Cor. 4:6)
    He makes clear and interprets the vital and virtuous.
The TRUE BREAD (John 6:32,35,48-51)
    Christ personifies all that is essential to eternal life.
The TRUE VINE (John 15:1)
    With sufficiency of resource vital for fruitbearing.
The TABERNACLE (Exod. 25:8-9; John 1:14; Rev. 21:3)
    The features and functions of Christ foreshadowed.
The TEMPLE (John 2:18-22; Matt. 12:6; Rev. 21:22)
    The mediatorial ministry of Messiah in miniature.
The TRESPASS OFFERING (Lev. 6:6-7; Col. 2:13)
    The condescending compassion of His sacrificial love.
The TESTATOR (Heb. 9:15-17)
    The One who bequeaths the eternal spiritual inheritance.
The TRANSFIGURED SON (Mark 9:2-8)
    The superexcellence and superiority of the Son of Man.
The THUMMIM (Exod. 28:30)
    Perfections, the title expressing His supreme glories.
The TREE OF LIFE (Gen. 2:8-9; Rev. 2:7; 22:2,14)
    The source of infinite treasures of life immortal.

Whatsoever God doeth it shall be forever

His Light has an eternal effulgence
His Truth has an eternal effluence
His Word has an eternal eloquence
His Wisdom has an eternal excellence
His Work has an eternal existence
His Joy has an eternal exuberance
His Glory has an eternal endurance

"Thine is the kingdom and the power and the glory for ever"

The Highest Himself
(Ps. 87:5)

King of all that's kingly, King of life and light,
 Lord of all that's lovely, robed in raiment white;
Highest of the lofty, grandest of the great,
 Gentlest of the gracious, perfect is Thy state.
Prince of all that's princely, strongest in Thy might,
 Boundless in Thy bounty, brightest of the bright.

Kindest of the kindly, wisest of the wise,
 Morning Star most brilliant, Monarch of the skies;
Richest of the wealthy, of mankind the Head,
 Fairest of the friendly, First-born from the dead.
Famous in Thy vict'ry, foremost in renown,
 Righteous in Thy justice, matchless is Thy crown.

God of all that's godly, truly good and just,
 Noblest of the worthy, worthy of our trust.
Choicest of the comely, mighty, Thou, and strong,
 Gorgeous in Thy glory, valiant all along.
Wondrous in Thy wisdom, changeless in Thy love,
 Ageless in Thy goodness, so like God above.

Chiefest of the lovely, fragrant is Thy name,
 Reigning in Thy splendor, evermore the same;
Christ the Lord most precious, peerless is Thy grace,
 Matchless is Thy mercy, shown to every race.
Gracious, precious, holy, true and faithful friend,
 On earth, meek and lowly, yet Thy works transcend.

What amazing features! Visage superfine,
 Everlasting beauty, loveliness sublime;

Power, riches, wisdom unto Thee belong,
Hosts proclaim Thee worthy, in an endless song;
Every lip is praiseful, every voice upraised,
Christ is Lord triumphant, and forever praised.

I am Alpha and Omega (Rev. 22:13)

Christ is the founder and framer of all revealed truth, the innermost center and uttermost circumference of all wisdom and knowledge. In Him are hid all the treasures of wisdom and knowledge (Col. 2:3). He is most remote in ageless priority as the Ancient of days, He is most real as revealer of the Father, and He ever remains when all else recedes and passes into oblivion (Heb. 1:11). There is no such thing as knowledge before Him and there cannot be any beyond Him. The marvels of mediation and miracles of mercy are wholly within the bounds of His ministration. He is mindful of mankind and in His majestic ministry, has made and maintained the everlasting covenant, for the honor of God and well-being of man. Christ is the founder of all fidelity and the fountain of faithfulness, and more, He is file leader, forerunner, and the finisher of faith. He is likewise the spring and stream of sufficiency and sustenance to support and satiate the sheep of His flock, the saints of His fellowship, and the sons of His family forever. He is the author of all authority on earth, the arm of the Lord availingly at the present hour, and the apex of all administration in Heaven.

Christ is the sum and substance of greatest dimension and grandest dominion in abiding power and peace, love and light, grace and glory. He originates and ordains the orbits of the planets and comets and governs and guides the courses of starry constellations through space continuously. No decree exists prior to His determinate counsel, or before the good pleasure which He purposed in Himself with regard to creation and the Church (Eph. 1:9), and beyond His ultimate objective in these matters there can be no posterior plan, because He is the First and the Last.

Christ commenced and will conclude all time periods. He conceived the duration of the ages and will yet crown and consummate the ages to come. Every prerogative and potential is within the confines of His unwaning, unwearying, unwavering control. No event preceded the exercise of His will and none will succeed His determinate counsel, because He is the Beginning and the End. In Him dwelleth all the fullness of Godhead bodily; therefore outside of Christ there is no wider, broader, deeper, higher, greater, or vaster dimension known. Wherefore, He is well able to save to the uttermost all them that come unto God by Him. He orders and ordains, He originates and oversees the entire course of nature and national life, and His objective is sure of realization.

THE TEACHER

Rabbi, we know that Thou art a teacher come from God (John 3:2).

Master, we know that Thou art true, and teachest the way of God in truth (Matt. 22:16).

It is written in the prophets, and they shall be all taught of God (John 6:45).

When Jesus had ended these words, the people were astonished at His doctrine: For He taught them as one having authority, and not as the scribes (Matt. 7:28-29).

Universally, mankind stands in need of being taught. We all derive the greater part of our knowledge from those who have preceded us. Ninety-nine per cent of what we know has been derived from our predecessors. Man's first teacher was the Creator Himself, and humanity has never wholly lost sight of this fact. The mind is a wonderful witness to divine workmanship and requires to be instructed by its Maker. The Prophet Isaiah speaks of God as "thy Maker," and later in the same chapter states, "and all of thy sons shall be taught of the Lord" (Isa. 54:5,13). Wherefore in the New Testament, we are reminded that Christ is the Maker of all things (John 1:3), and He affirmed He was Teacher by stating, "And they shall be all taught of God" (John 6:45). Christ is man's highest source of wisdom and knowledge. "In whom are hid all the treasures of wisdom and knowledge" (Col. 2:3). Long after

King David's coronation he gratefully remembered his Instructor, "O God, Thou hast taught me from my youth. . . . Now also when I am old and grayheaded, O God, forsake me not" (Ps. 71:16-18). Let us recall that the words "teach, taught, teacher, and teaching" are used two hundred and forty times in the Bible, which gives the subject a place of great prominence and importance.

In this capacity, as in all vocations of value and virtue, Christ excels all other qualified teachers, whether they come from the ranks of the philosophers or physicists; scientists, specialists, or sages; legislators, logicians, or teachers; moralists, magnates, or mathematicians. The dignified abilities of Christ are exceptional and supernatural. His methods and material when teaching are eloquently distinguished, while His words of wisdom are unprecedented. He taught the truth of God plainly yet profoundly, simply yet sublimely, He Himself personifying the Truth He taught. Besides this being so, His message was magnified by His marvelous works, and verified by the Father's witness from Heaven. His life was in full harmony with His labor and these two combined to demonstrate divine loving-kindness.

When we examine the striking qualities of His sayings, the searching questions He submitted to the rulers, and the startling application He made of quotations from the Old Testament in defense of His claims, we must admit He is wholly incomparable. His teaching covered a widespread variety of subjects and was accompanied by a wholesome veracity and wondrous vitality. He avowed His sayings were spirit and life (John 6:63). He also affirmed that He had used similitudes in His discourses recorded by the Apostle John, "These things have I spoken to you in similitudes" (John 16:25).

Man is incapable of producing, in his finest woven fabric, a texture as delicately perfect as God makes in the petal of a fragrant flower. Likewise the profoundest teaching of which man is capable, can in nowise compare with the immortal words of the Son of Man. He is the Alpha of thought and truth, His lightest word outweighs the weightiest ever spoken by man. His very thoughts outsoar the starry sky. He

Himself is the author of faith and love, the anchor of hope and holiness, the arbiter of justice and mercy, and the Amen of all confirmation and certitude. His authority is authentic, absolute, and abiding; all He taught was in keeping with His sublime claim (Matt. 28:18). He taught them as one having authority (Matt. 7:29).

Never at anytime in His teaching did the slightest indication appear of inability or imperfection such as is apparent with all other instructors. No trace of uncertainty or taint of unreality is ever found in His speech. In the light of His presence the greatest, wisest, and cleverest of human teachers, however illustrious, must step aside. Christ as teacher stands alone in personal splendor; He has neither rival nor equal. He set forth the most precious elements of knowledge, He unlocked the door to the highest privileges of heritage, and He opened the highway that directs· humanity to the greatest advantage of all history, namely, access to the Father of Glory. John records that He made reference to the Father over one hundred times.

In real fact and resplendent truth Christ is God manifest. Only God in person could teach what He taught. Maps of the world were not in vogue in His day, yet He declared the gospel would be preached throughout the whole world. He was perfectly familiar with the beginning of creation and taught that time itself would terminate at the *last day,* an expression He used seven times in John's record.

Our beloved Lord made it quite clear that, as Son of Man, He was inescapable, for, said He, "All that are in the graves shall hear My voice and shall come forth, they that have done good unto the resurrection of life and they that have done evil unto the resurrection of judgment" (John 5:28). He plainly taught the truth concerning a life that was immune from the consuming and destructive laws of this world, and also demonstrated on the Mount of Transfiguration, that names and personalities that are known here, are continued beyond the veil. He likewise affirmed that Abraham, Isaac, and Jacob are living entities in the world unseen (Matt. 22:32).

When dealing with life's occupations, possessions, and relations in Luke 14, our Lord taught that in connection with these divinely bestowed associations, there was one supreme possession, one superior occupation, and one sublime relationship that concerned all mankind. His knowledge was full and complete, any reference He made to creation, history, prophecy, or destiny is perfectly accurate. With all the advance that has been made in learning during the more recent centuries, not one thing He taught concerning God, Heaven, angels, man, or the infernal realm needs to be amended or withdrawn. Who but He could have told us in detail of the conditions that would exist nationally and universally at the end of this age? Who knew as He did that national conflict, racial cleavage, class clash, creed controversy, and sex contention would ultimately cease, and a remaking of all things new would transpire? Or that death, the enemy's great master power would be destroyed? He taught us the divine design and deepest meaning of the Passover, that the judgment that fell on homes, where the blood of a slain lamb was not sprinkled on the doorposts, was not directed against behavior, but against birth. Space forbids more on this topic, wherefore in summing up we would say, how descriptive His references to the characteristics of His Kingdom! (Matt. 6:9; 7:21; 18:4)

How predictive His foreview of world conditions of violence and corruption at the close of the age! (Matt. 24:27-29; Luke 21:25-26)

How appreciative His kindly words of approval for companionship in the days of adversity! (Luke 22:28-29)

How positive His pledges of assurance and assistance to those who loyally serve Him! (Luke 12:32; Matt. 16:25)

How selective His choice when calling men of various occupations to serve Him! (John 6:70; 13:18; 15:16; Luke 6:13)

How instructive His clear-sighted presentation when commenting on unseen realities! (John 14:2-3; 17:24)

How comprehensive His teaching on the chief features

of the law pertaining to God and man! (Matt. 22:37-40)

How distinctive His ministry of healing the sick, cleansing the lepers, and casting out demons! (Matt. 8:2-3,7,16)

How attractive His winsome appeals when offering rest of mind and contentment of heart! (Matt. 11:28; John 7:35,39)

How inclusive His fervent prayer for the preservation of His people in an unsympathetic world! (John 17:9,17)

How extensive His range of administration in every realm of dominion and right of resource! (Matt. 10:1; 24:30)

How conclusive His final verdict either of commendation or condemnation! (Matt. 25:34,41)

How attentive His attitude toward all who come to Him seeking mercy! (John 6:37; 7:37)

How impressive His claim to all authority of every kind in every realm! (Matt. 28:18-19)

We can never overestimate the standards, quality, and value set forth by Christ as Teacher. His wisdom, knowledge, and discernment, combined with a complete understanding of all things in every realm — past, present, and future — determine perfect ability. Not a single thing He taught needs amending or qualifying to this very day. He never made a single misstatement and never minimized or misrepresented one syllable of truth. Mary of Bethany recognized the profound superiority of His character and sat at His feet and heard His word (Luke 10:39). She took time to let Him teach her, took heed to what He said, and took pains to let Him praise her devotion (Mark 14:9). Let us learn a lesson from her life. She loved Him, she listened to Him, she learned of Him. The result was she had a deeper, fuller appreciation of His message and mission than anyone else of her day.

THE TRUTH

He is our Rock. His work is perfect: for all His ways are judgment: a God of truth...without iniquity (Deut. 32:4,31).
Mercy and truth are met together (Ps. 85:10).

I am the way, the truth.... (John 14:6).

Howbeit when He, the Spirit of truth, is come, He will guide
you into all truth (John 16:13).

Sanctify them through Thy truth: Thy word is truth (John
17:17).

Comment has just been made on the fact that Christ is
the personification of the Word of God and the wisdom of
God. This is also true in the case of His being the personification of the Truth of God. His own claim is conclusive, I
am...the Truth (John 14:6). Truth is not truth because of age
but because of accuracy; truth is always and altogether
correct, consistent, and crystal clear. We should give rapt
attention to the character of Christ and the command of Christ
because He is the Truth and truth has no defects or deformities
that need to be eliminated. Truth has no retractions to make,
such as Augustine found necessary, and no apologies to offer,
such as the Apostle Paul expressed (Acts 23:5).

The character of Truth, as the Truth is in Jesus (Eph.
4:21). The Apostle John in the Gospel and Epistles written by
him makes reference to truth forty-eight times, and through
him the Spirit of God has given to us a comprehensive
presentation of the characteristics by which truth may be
identified. Let us remember that the treasures of truth's
treasury are everlasting, a familiar word in John's message.
The wealth of truth's riches cannot be weighed. The volume of
truth's virtues cannot be valued. The excellence of truth's
essence cannot be estimated. The range of truth's resources
cannot be reckoned. The magnitude of truth's ministries
cannot be measured, and the repleteness of truth's revenue
cannot be tabulated. Every detail of these abounding features
is embodied in the Person of Christ of whom it is written, "We
beheld His glory, the glory as of the only begotten of the
Father, full of grace and truth" (John 1:14).

If we gaze more intently and examine our subject more
intimately, we discover the preciousness of truth's celestial
character. For brevity's sake let us tabulate a few of the facts.

Truth is immaculate in stainless purity

Truth is immeasurable in dateless entity

Truth is invincible in endless victory
Truth is immutable in changeless reality
Truth is indestructible in ceaseless stability
Truth is immortal in deathless beauty
Truth is incorruptible in fadeless glory

We may substitute Christ in the place of truth in each case, for He is not merely a sample or specimen of such, but the whole truth.

> Truth is the Word, the Word is Christ;
> The Word is the Truth, the Truth is Christ;
> Truth is the Light, the Light is Christ;
> The Light is the Life, the Life is Christ.

Numerous parallels are given in Scripture of the experience of believers in relation to Christ and truth, which are identical. We shall mention three of these. "If ye continue in My Word...ye shall know the truth, and the truth shall make you free" (John 8:31-32). "Stand fast therefore in the liberty wherewith Christ hath made us free" (Gal.5:1).

"I rejoiced greatly, when the brethren came and testified of the truth that is in thee, even as thou walkest in the truth. I have no greater joy than to hear that my children walk in truth" (III John 3-4). "As ye have therefore received Christ Jesus the Lord, so walk ye in Him" (Col. 2:6).

"Sanctify them through Thy truth: Thy word is truth" (John 17:17). "To them that are sanctified in Christ Jesus" (I Cor. 1:2,30).

The sanctifying of His servants is one of the stateliest ministries of Christ's mediative priesthood and holds a central place in His high priestly prayer (John 17). All truth is given for our perfecting in beauty, purity, and glory and leads and directs toward holiness, which is the ultimate aim. "Christ in you, the hope of glory...perfect in Christ Jesus" (Col. 1:27-28). "That we should be holy and without blame before Him in love" (Eph. 1:4).

The Commandment of Truth, "as the truth is in Jesus" (Eph. 4:21).

"Thou art near, O LORD and all Thy commandments

are truth" (Ps. 119:151).

Wherefore Christ says,; "If ye keep My commandments, ye shall abide in My love. . . . This is My commandment, that ye love one another, as I have loved you. . . . Ye are My friends, if ye do whatsoever I command you. . . . These things I command you, that ye love one another" (John 15:10,12,14,17).

"The law was given by Moses, grace and truth came by Jesus Christ" (John 1:17).

Yes indeed, and Christ reveals truth as being more searching than law (Matt. 5:27-29).

Truth has a singular distinction because of the preciousness of its character, because of the pureness of its source, and because of the perfectness of its virtues. Truth pervades in the highest ranks of spiritual honor, predominates in the noblest courts of heavenly justice, and prevails in the greatest divine victories of saving grace. Truth's victories are without vindictiveness and the triumphs won are wholly devoid of tyranny.

In the nature of truth there is a total absence of all surliness, sourness, and sharpness; nothing that is unseemly, unlovely, or ugly mars truth's holiness, for remember, the Holy Spirit is the Spirit of truth (John 15:26; 16:13). "The Spirit *is* truth" (I John 5:6). Compare the Spirit of Christ (I Pet. 1:11), with the Holy Spirit (II Pet. 1:21).

Notice also the similarity of statement in connection with Truth and the Spirit abiding forever.

"Whom I love in the truth; and not I only, but also all they that have known the truth; For the truth's sake, which dwelleth in us, and shall be with us for ever" (II John 1-2).

"I will pray the Father, and He shall give you another Comforter, that He may abide with you for ever; the Spirit of truth. . . for He dwelleth with you, and shall be in you" (John 14:16-17).

So that within the riches of Christ's personal Being, the highest values, the choicest treasures, and the total wealth and weight of truth's authority reside in fullness. Wherefore, in disposition, in deportment, and in demonstrative example,

Christ is truth, and the truth He embodies constitutes the scepter of power which He wields over the hearts of men. Perfect truth embodied in human form exercises royal power over regenerated lives.

Christ witnessed a good confession before Pontius Pilate. He said, after affirming His kingly majesty, "For this end was I born and for this cause came I into the world, that I should bear witness to the truth. Every one that is of the truth heareth My voice" (John 18:37).

His confession was at once truthful, faithful, and forceful. Because He is the mainspring and mirror of all truth, we shall mention seven of the facets that flash their radiance from His personal glory.

Christ is Truth various. Many and varied are the graceful forms and gorgeous views of truth which we learn to admire as we consider His testimony and contemplate His teaching. Especially is this so in relation to the Father's fellowship and faithful friendship, His fervent love and fragrant kindness. Also the instruction He imparts concerning the Father's purpose in sending to the Church the Spirit of truth. Linked with this is the insight He initiates into the privileges and possibilities of prayer and the value therein of His own royal name and regal nature. We need but trace the use He made of the expression, "I say unto you," in the Gospel by Matthew, where it occurs fifty-six times, and take heed to the truth He taught. He prefaced twenty-nine of these expressions with the word "Amen" (rendered *verily* in the AV) and paved the way for the declaration of His notable name, "The Amen, the faithful and true witness" (Rev. 3:14). Without difficulty we might extend this first aspect into an entire volume.

Christ is Truth veracious. He Himself is the verification and confirmation of all He taught. All verity is verified by His flawless life and faultless labors. "Jesus Christ became a minister of the circumcision for the truth of God, to confirm the promises" (Rom. 15:8). "All the promises of God in Him are certified" (II Cor. 1:20). God has an inestimably strong reserve to discharge the obligations of every promise He has ever made. He could not have rendered it easier for man to trust than by impersonating truth for the verification of His purpose, in the attractive character of His beloved Son.

Christ is Truth virtuous. Here truth's full tide reaches high-water mark in sterling virtue, in which realm also Christ is magnificent. Lovers have described Him as altogether lovely, and this is the verdict of all the virtuous, the estimate of all the enlightened, and the opinion of all overcomers. The golden gleams of Christ's moral glory shine forth in their iridescent brilliance from His sympathetic service, from His Messianic ministries, and from His dynamic declarations of divine truth. He Himself is the quintessence of the highest qualities of spiritual graces and the very essence of all essential excellences. All that is lovely and loveliest, all that is comely and comeliest, all that is saintly and saintliest, all that is stately and stateliest, all that is worthy and worthiest, all that is lofty and loftiest, and all that is holy and holiest is enshrined in Him.

Christ is Truth vigorous. We are considering one who is spoken of in Scripture as retaining the dew of His youth, this signifies that the holy vitality of His eternal vigor is forever fresh and forceful. The Prophet Isaiah records that He is never weary, and that because of His almighty strength and omnipotent power which never wane or weaken, combined with His rich resources which never decrease or dwindle. In His vigor as a Shepherd He is characterized by sufficiency to sustain, as a Saviour by His power to protect, and as a Sovereign by His revenue to renew. A figure of the vigor of His energy is expressed in His bushy hair, black as a raven (Song of Sol. 5:11), also the vesture of His royalty in purple hair (Song of Sol. 7:5), and the virtue of His purity in snow-white hair (Rev. 1:14).

Christ exhibited a nobler kind of vigor associated with fervency of spirit, friendliness in service, forcefulness in speech, faithfulness in stewardship, and fruitfulness in saving grace. He harnessed all the faculties of His priceless life and, out of love for man, offered Himself as a sacrifice to God for a sweet smelling savor (Eph. 5:2).

Christ is Truth valorous. If the truth made men valiant (Heb. 11:34), much more is Christ valiant, who is the Truth. His valiance was continually expressed in genuine love which was often misinterpreted (Matt. 8:34), in generous acts which were sometimes misunderstood (Mark 6:52), and in gracious deeds which were frequently misrepresented (John 5:16). His valor was vividly shown when He cleansed the Temple courts (John 2:15-16), when He cured the man with the dropsy (Luke 14:1-6), and when He climbed the steep road leading up to Jerusalem to face the cross (Mark 10:33). He knew that truth would triumph and therefore with boldness and confidence He declared His mission and message, and never modified His words to gain public approval or popular approbation. Christ was always vigorous in promoting the cause of truth, zealous in advancing the claims of right, and strenuous in His demands that justice be done for all classes. He remained untarnished by the defilements of His day and undaunted by the distractions of the way.

Christ is Truth vicarious. "Who bewitched you, that ye should not obey the truth, before whose eyes Jesus Christ has been evidently set forth, crucified among you?" (Gal. 3:1) Truth on the scaffold, crucified. Truth is perfect in sensitiveness and therefore suffers more keenly when bearing the penalty for guilt. Truth like love, her constant companion, never, never fails. What a spectacle of sorrowful suffering Christ became. How astounding that He should stoop so low and allow Himself to be made sin for us. Amid the inhuman insult of hoarse laughter and coarse language, the soldiers mocked His royal claims. No ridicule more rude, no scorn more scorching, no mockery more menial, and no contempt more cruel was ever hurled at anyone. Yet under every possible disadvantage Christ was the first and only one who made platted thorns to become a princely crown. He transformed the gloom of human grief into the grandeur of heavenly glory. Yea, more, He transmuted a dishonored death into a dignified diadem of higher life, and via the steps of a painful crucifixion at the rough hands of haughty men, He ascended to a preeminent coronation at the right hand of the highest majesty in the Heaven of heavens.

Christ is Truth victorious. He wore the panoply of omnipotence and His loins were girt about with truth, He Himself, the embodiment of all that is noble, stable, and durable. He paid no honor to the phylacteries of Pharisee gowns. He stood unabashed and undeterred before the cold materialistic philosophy of the Sadducees, and confessed belief in the Word of God and faith in invisible spiritual realities. He trembled not at the threat of the Herodian, with his worldly politics, but sent him the message of the plan He had determined to fulfill in the two ensuing years. He met the great enemy of truth in the wilderness when physical energies were at their lowest ebb, and demonstrated that spiritual equipment from the Word of God was far superior to the infernal powers of evil. He overcame the world order, the sphere dominated by the prevalence of sin, with its modes, manners, and ministrations; with its customs, fashions, and laws. This whole system of things which is divorced from God and which offers position, possession, and power to those who serve its interests. Christ declined every overture made to Him and stated emphatically, "I have overcome the world" (John 16:33).

With the strongest insistence, He constantly affirmed His divine authority, but with equal persistence He consistently refused all offered positions in the community.

At the cross under the direst conditions of conflict, when everything was unfavorable, and the utmost power of evil arrayed against Him, He conquered the oppressor and vanquished the diabolical power of the foe. "Thanks be unto God, which giveth us the victory through our Lord Jesus Christ" (I Cor. 15:57). Here we meet with three in one in holy harmony, the victory of verity, the triumph of truth, and the conquest of Christ.

THE TRUE LIGHT

The true Light, which lighteth every man that cometh into the world (John 1:9).
The light of the knowledge of the glory of God (II Cor. 4:6).

The power of the Godhead is displayed primarily in the creation of the world, and appeals to the human reason. The purpose of the Godhead is declared particularly in the revelation of truth, which appeals to the human conscience. The presence of the Godhead is disclosed perfectly in the manifestation of the Son, and appears to the human heart. These facts express a personal Creator, a personal Revealer, and a personal Manifester. All three are realized and recognized in Christ.

The opening chapter of John's Gospel declares in no uncertain terms that Christ Jesus the Lord is the Creator.

"All things were made by Him.... The world was made by Him" (John 1:3,10). Creatorship is the mainspring of John's message. The word *made* is used on twenty-eight occasions. Christ wrought works and spake words that no one but the Creator is capable of doing or saying. His creatorship is also affirmed in Col. 1:16; Heb. 1:2; and elsewhere.

Christ is likewise the Revealer: "No one knoweth the Son but the Father, neither knoweth any the Father save the Son, and he to whomsoever the Son will reveal Him" (Matt. 11:27). He is both Revealer and Declarer of the Father (Luke 10:22; John 1:18). Christ Himself became the manifest presence of Deity on earth, bearing the name Emmanuel — God with us (Matt. 1:23). This selfsame person who creates, reveals, and makes manifest, is the True Light which lighteth every man that cometh into the world (John 1:9). This He does by implanting the lamp of conscience in everyone.

As being the True Light, Christ brought to mankind a full knowledge of God's name and will, a perfect demonstration of the Father's grace and love, and a final proof of God's omnipotence, omniscience, and omnipresence. All of these features are clearly expressed in the record of the Gospel as written by John. Therein God's beloved Son made a bold broad claim concerning Himself, when He affirmed, "I am the light of the world: he that followeth Me shall not walk in darkness, but shall have the light of life" (John 8:12). No such statement could be made by anyone save the Creator Himself. By this very declaration the blessed Lord makes Himself to be the explicit center and circumference, the sum and substance, the core and crown, and the fount and fullness of all truth, even to the extent of being the light of the knowledge of the glory of God (II Cor. 4:6).

If anyone else had the unblushing affrontry to make so prodigous a claim, he would encounter utter contempt and disgust. Man in himself is not capable of obtaining even a glimpse of the incomprehensible, infinite Godhead save through revelation and the medium of the incarnation. For the invisible God is out of range of human perception, until He assumes human form and appears in fashion as a man (Phil. 2:7-8). In other words, the underlying mystery of deity, which is beyond the capacity and capability of man's mind to grasp, may now be ascertained through the Son (John 1:18). Wherefore He stated, "If ye had known Me, ye should have known My Father also" (John 8:19). Being the True Light, He brought to mankind a knowledge of the only true God who gives us the true bread from Heaven (John 17:3; 6:32). This tremendous claim of being the Light of the world cannot be accounted for on any other ground than that of the Son's unmistakable deity. He said only what He had the divine right to say. Examine His life, no word He spake, no act He wrought, no thought of mind and no inward impulse of heart, but what was conducive to the glory of God and the good of man. In Him we view the admirable union of all spiritual values in active harmony and abiding unity. In Him all virtues and verities, promises and perfections, abilities and attributes, excellences and essentials combine. What a blending we behold of bounty and beauty, of all that is lofty and lowly, of supremacy and simplicity, of majesty and mercy, and of kingliness and kindliness!

The light of His life reveals new estimates, reflects new values, and with brightest rays illumines new aims and claims and brings into focus divine motives and ministries; making obvious the potentials of prayer and privileges of praiseful worship. His luminous life brought into visibility the highest standards of liberty and liberality, service and sacrifice, love and law, justice and justification, recompence and reward that were ever known. Christ lived and loved and labored in a manner that rightly represented and resembled God the Father. Wherever He went, whatever He did, whenever He spake, and whomsoever He addressed, was all in harmony with Heaven and glorifying to God.

The light of His life brought into being a variety of rich social benefits, including a wide circle of friendships and fellowships, relationships and stewardships, care for the sick, and provision for the aged. But greater by far is the volume of spiritual blessings, with access to the throne of grace, together with generous bestowments of spiritual gifts, and the earnest of an eternal inheritance. How very true of Christ are the words, "For with Thee is the fountain of life: and in Thy light shall we see light" (Ps. 36:9).

Let us notice that in the first ten chapters of the Gospel by John, Christ interprets Jacob's vision, the Temple, the brazen serpent, Jacob's well, the pool of Bethesda, the manna, the feast of tabernacles, the secret of Abraham, the pool of Siloam, and the divine Shepherdhood, all of which are recorded in the Old Testament. This is the True Light that never dims or diminishes. How vast the range of illumination and the scope of interpretation that is being constantly projected from the Sun of righteousness (Mal. 4:2)! How voluminous His light is, how resplendently radiant, and transcendently transparent, forever shining in glory everlasting!

By virtue of the incarnation, more light has been thrown on the character of God the Father and on the nature of man than through any other agency during the preceding centuries. In God's determinate counsels, which are according to the good pleasure of His will, He purposed to dwell with mankind, therefore the command was given to Moses, "Let them make Me a sanctuary; that I may dwell among them" (Exod. 25:8; see also Ps. 68:16-18). When this structure was completed the glory of the Lord filled the Tabernacle (Exod. 40:34). In course of time the Spirit of God bore witness to the fact, "The Word was made flesh, and dwelt [tabernacled, RV] among us, (and we beheld His glory, the glory as of the only begotten of the Father,) full of grace and truth" (John 1:14). The ultimate of this was made known to the apostle, John. He writes, "I heard a great voice out of heaven saying, Behold, the tabernacle of God is with men, and He will dwell among them, and they shall be His people, and God Himself shall be with them, and be their God" (Rev. 21:3). The True Light will then be recognized, "The city had no need of the sun, neither of the moon, to shine in it: for the glory of God did lighten it, and the Lamb is the light thereof" (Rev. 21:23).

In His ministry, during the manifestation, Christ declared He would build His Church. This habitation for God consists of living stones, a spiritual house, and is to be the medium by which the manifold wisdom of God is to be displayed to the heavenly hierarchies (Eph. 3:10).

The Wisdom of God has already been exemplified and amplified to mankind, by the True Light, in the profound plan of salvation. Also various wonderful phases of God's almighty power have been expressed. An enlarged conception of God's love has been given, of which Christ Himself is the gift. Enlightenment on the resurrection of the dead and reception into the Father's house, together with a clear explanation of divine judgment, is also given.

The true nature of man is clearly taught in Christ's own words. If man is a physical being only, he could be sustained by physical sustenance, but the Word of God declares he cannot be sustained by bread alone, nor can he be satisfied by material things. This proves that man has capacities and faculties that are spiritual.

"God, who commanded the light to shine out of darkness, hath shined in our hearts, to give the light of the knowledge of the glory of God in the face of Jesus Christ" (II Cor. 4:6). "This is the True Light."

Through centuries of brilliant shining, the light of His life remains undimmed, undiminished, and undespoiled universally. The agelong rays are verily present today, they are very pleasant alway, and vitally perfect eternally.

THE TRUE BREAD

Then Jesus said to them, Verily, verily, I say to you, Moses gave you not that bread from heaven; but My Father giveth you the true bread from heaven. For the bread of God is He which cometh down from heaven, and giveth life unto the world.... Jesus said to them, I am the bread of life: he that cometh to Me shall never hunger; and he that believeth on Me shall never thirst.

I am that bread of life. Your fathers did eat manna in the wilderness, and are dead. This is the bread which came down from heaven, that a man may eat thereof, and not die. I am the living bread which came down from heaven.... The bread which I will give is My flesh (John 6:32-35,48-51).

This wonderful dialogue arose as the outcome of a lad that gave his five barley loaves (John 6:9). The whole discourse refers to the subject of life, and in this case to eternal, or everlasting, life. Of the twenty-five references to eternal and everlasting life that occur in the four Gospels, seventeen are recorded by John. The apostle also specifies the eight oracular claims Christ made in His use of the great I AM title, and the eight obvious signs He wrought which constitute the full and complete evidence of His Messiahship (John 4:25). "Believest thou not that I am in the Father, and the Father in Me? The words that I speak to you I speak not of Myself: but the Father that dwelleth in Me, He doeth the works. Believe Me that I am in the Father, and the Father in Me: or else believe Me for the very works' sake" (John 14:10-11). His works occupy the first twenty-five verses of this chapter and His words the remainder. To the latter Peter refers in his reply, "Lord, to whom shall we go? Thou hast the words of eternal life" (John 6:68).

The miracle of feeding the multitudes in the wilderness is of immense importance because of the insight it gives as to the true character of Christ and the purpose of His mission and ministry. The reaction of the crowd was to make Christ king, a plan He definitely evaded. His purpose was not to establish a bread kingdom of a material order. His disciples were gravely disappointed that He did not approve of the public decision, for it would have meant promotion and honor for them. He dispatched His disciples and constrained them to take ship to the other side of the sea. He dispersed the multitude and sent them away. He then departed to a mountain to pray.

The disciples met with contrary winds and were in difficulty, as well as being disgruntled that their Master had not responded to the popular acclaim of the people to make Him king, which they were so anxious to see take place. Their mind would begin to wonder if He really had kingly power to rule and reign, and they may have discussed the matter. To dispel their misgivings He gave them a convincing demonstration of His kingly ability as Master of wind and wave. They gladly received Him into the ship and immediately they were at their desired destination. Still bewildered, they did not understand the events of the previous day (Mark 6:52).

Much people crossed the sea seeking Him, and in addressing these He told them plainly that their motive was to obtain material advantages and physical benefits. He urged them not to labor for perishable bread, but for that which endured everlastingly. Obviously they did not like what He said, and immediately attempted to minimize the sign He had given the previous day, which at the time had awakened their wonderment. They sought to detract attention from His stupendous act by rehearsing the fame of Moses, whom they said had wrought a greater service for the entire nation for a much longer period by giving the people bread from heaven. Christ disallowed their claim that the manna was bread from heaven, for they that ate of it had died.

Thereupon He uttered the first of the eight greatest statements of claim that were ever spoken by anyone anywhere. "I am the bread of life: he that cometh to Me shall never hunger; and he that believeth on Me shall never thirst" (John 6:35). When His words were questioned, He enlarged His claim with ever greater emphasis, "I am the living bread which came down from heaven; if any man eat of this bread, he shall live for ever: and the bread that I will give is My flesh, which I will give for the life of the world" (John 6:51). Physical bread is composed of material elements including a suitable proportion of calcium, silicon, iodine, iron, phosphorus, potassium, sodium, and such like. The living bread consists of spiritual elements such as righteousness, goodness, faithfulness, loving-kindness, preciousness, truthfulness, holiness, and all other virtuous graces which are imperishable and incorruptible. These immortal features in perfect balance combine in and constitute the person of Christ, who is the Word made flesh (John 1:14).

Christ incorporates in Himself and personifies every one of these spiritual features, each of which is from Heaven (John 6:32). The fascinating form of this true bread from Heaven, the features of its substance, expressed in fashion as a man, and the celestial qualities contained therein, should appeal and attract the heart of man. How desirable and acceptable is the nature of the life which this bread imparts. What, may we ask, is there in the personality of Christ that is unacceptable to real faith, undesirable to pure love, and unpalatable to true hope! In our Beloved's entire being there is not the slightest trace of a single thing that is repulsive to ethical courtesy or repugnant to moral decency. His excellences are exclusively exquisite, His perfections are preeminently precious, His virtues are vitally voluminous, His graces are genuinely glorious, and His attributes are admirable and abidingly attractive. All spiritual qualities are beautifully blended in Him who is the True Bread.

To believe Christ and receive Him is to appropriate and partake of the Bread of God which cometh down from Heaven. In so doing, the result is life everlasting, because these divine virtues are imperishable. Therefore, the gift of God is eternal life through Jesus Christ our Lord (Rom. 6:23). In answer to Christ's question, "Will ye also go away?" Peter well said, "Lord, to whom shall we go? Thou hast the words of eternal life" (John 6:68). "This is the record, that God hath given to us eternal life, and this life is in His Son" (I John 5:11). He "hath life in Himself" (John 5:26); He gave Himself (Gal. 2:20); He offered Himself (Heb. 9:14); He put away sin by the sacrifice of Himself (Heb. 9:26).

"All things were made by Him" (John 1:3). This included the material bread which He made to provide for the multitude. This act was a signpost to direct attention to Himself as being the true and living Bread, which came down from Heaven. Christ, as Maker, gives and sustains physical life on earth. He came in manifestation as the giver and sustainer of eternal life. Relative to this, John speaks of birth, breath, and bread, which are attached to the spiritual realm. The same conditions are prevalent today as then, many see the material sign in the wonder wrought and the power that made ample provision where none existed, without perceiving the real significance of what is signified by it. The True Bread from Heaven...the Bread of God, is available. Christ is the gift of God.

THE TRUE VINE

I am the true vine and My Father is the husbandman (John 15:1).

The Lord used the word "true" during His manifestation and after His ascension on twenty occasions. He referred to the true riches, the true worshipers, the true bread, the true vine, the true God; also in connection with His judgment, His words, and His sayings. He Himself is the true Light and the true and faithful Witness.

The various connections in which we find the word "true" used indicate the existence of that which is untrue and unreal. For instance, Satan himself is transformed into an angel of light to deceive and bear false witness. False gods and false worshipers are mentioned, also bread that perisheth. The same contrast is frequently stated in connection with the vine. "The vineyard of the LORD of hosts is the house of Israel" (Isa. 5:7). "I had planted thee a noble vine, wholly a right seed: how then art thou turned into a degenerate plant of a strange vine unto Me?" (Jer. 2:21) What a disclosure is made in these and other portions of the degrading of Israel's function. This resulted in "wild grapes," "sour grapes," and "grapes of gall."

Wherefore, our Lord's words stand in contrast, "I am the true vine," which bespeaks constancy, fidelity, and vitality. Because of the failure of the nation it is cut off and Christ replaces it and is true to all entrustments, assuring the full realization of the eternal purpose. By adopting the symbol of the vine, our Lord indicates that He is the source of all fruitful energy in spiritual productiveness. He plainly stated, in this very connection, "the branch cannot bear fruit of itself, except it abide in the vine; no more can ye, except ye abide in Me" (John 15:4). Then He added, "For without Me ye can do nothing." The very vitality of the genuine vine is the life energy of the branches, which is supplied most generously to all who abide and ask. The Lord repeatedly stressed these two words in His final discourse. What a wonderful honor He confers on the branches!

In declaring Himself to be the True Vine, He again adopts a common material figure of His own creation to express the finer, richer, fuller spiritual resources which He Himself continually supplies. This He does in complete submission to the Father's will. "My Father is the husbandman," said He. The Father sent Him (John 5:30), the Father sustained Him (John 6:57), the Father sanctioned His place and plan of service, yes, even the words that He uttered (John 7:46; 14:10).

As the True Vine His manner of life was to abide in the Father's love. Therefore He exhorts His disciples to abide in His love (John 15:10). In the space of nine verses He refers to love ten times. In doing so He uses one of the twelve correlatives mentioned in the Gospel by John, not one of which could possibly be adopted by anyone else. "*As* My Father hath loved Me, *so* have I loved you" (John 15:9).

To be true in the degree in which Christ is true, means to be genuinely correct, sincerely accurate, and faithfully loyal in everything. He is true in every pledge and promise, in every saying and statement made. He is true in every commitment and covenant, in every answer and assurance given. He is true in His teaching concerning the resurrection and the remuneration and retribution that follows; and true in His claims of affinity (John 10:30) and of authority (Matt. 28:18). He is true in His prediction that the gospel would be preached in all the world and to all nations before the end of this age (Matt. 24:14); likewise in His declaration that the Temple would be made desolate and not one of its great stones left upon another (Matt. 24:2). How true are His words that He would ascend to the realm from which He came (John 6:62). Not a single word of all that He ever spake is untrue, unreal, or unwise.

He is absolutely true. This is verified in the stainless sanctity of His sinlessness, in the peerless purity of His perfectness, and in the faultless fidelity of His faithfulness. Wherefore, as the True Vine, all the supply of strength and sustenance that He provides for the support of the branches is of a like character. By virtue of what He is, He enriches the soul, enlightens the mind, energizes the will, engraces the heart, and ennobles the entire life. This enables and makes possible fruit-bearing, so we need to remember that the fruit of the Spirit is love, more love, and much love, and love is the bond of perfectness (Col. 3:14).

Love is the most productive factor in the spiritual life. His divine love promotes joy and joy is love's cheerfulness. His love purchases peace, which is love's confidence. His love perfects patience, which is love's composure. His love prompts gentleness, which is love's considerateness. His love produces goodness, which is love's character. His love purposes fidelity, which is love's constancy. His love provides meekness, which is love's condescension. His love procures self-control, which is love's conquest. These eight features are the very constituents of love (Gal. 5:22-23). The love of Christ, the True Vine, enlarges horizons, expands hopefulness, engenders humility, enthuses heartiness, enjoins holiness, and environs Heaven itself. The Scriptures affirm that love never fails, but bears all things that can be borne and endures all things that can be endured. The heaviest and hardest of these was to endure the cross and to discount its shame. Christ has demonstrated, by

His submission to crucifixion, how real and true His love is. He did not say to His disciples, "Continue ye to love Me," but "Continue ye in My love" (John 15:9). This we may do by keeping His sayings.

All of the faithful and fruitful, the stewards and servants, the wrestlers and worshipers, and the warriors and workers that were animated for spiritual activities of every kind and in every sphere of the vast vineyard, were energized by the True Vine. The renowned ranks in this truceless warfare that were fortified and fitted by the True Vine included the virtuous, the courageous, the gracious, the lustrous, the zealous, the generous, the vigorous, the famous, the glorious, and the victorious overcomers throughout all the centuries. Each and every one derived their resources of energy to serve the Lord, obtained their eagerness to please God, and secured their essential armor to resist the foe from the True Vine. The almightiness of this expressive claim, I am the True Vine, expands the thought of the magnitude of Christ's resourceful vitality to an immeasurable degree.

When we consider the millions of martyrs, the myriads of missionaries and ministers of the Word of life that have borne witness in the world, the continual supply of vitality and strength they expressed emanated from the True Vine. Every Christian has received the qualities of the good character they exhibit and noble conduct they express from Christ Himself. He is the Author of all faith and the Originator of all the factors and facilities for bearing fruit. He it is that enlivens, enriches, and enthuses all that is vitally spiritual and of immortal importance, in the lives of multitudes of the godly. He imparts all spiritual vitality to believers and implants all spiritual virtue in the lives of the saints.

What consolation it is to know that we have a solid basis for our confidence, one we can completely trust. For Christ's word is true, His motive is pure, His love is real, His heart is kind, His ways are just, His aims are right aims, and His name is holy. The simile He uses of being the True Vine signifies that He is in possession of endless energy and is the fountain of ceaseless vitality. He everlastingly supports and sustains His people in vigorous, virtuous life. The final occasion on which He Himself uses the word "true" is most thrilling. "He that sat upon the throne said, 'Behold, I make all things new.' And He said to me, 'Write: for these words are true and faithful.' And He said to me, 'It is done. I am Alpha and Omega, the beginning and the end. I will give to him that is athirst of the fountain of the water of life freely'" (Rev. 21:5-6).

THE TABERNACLE

Let them make Me a sanctuary; that I may dwell among them. According to all that I show thee, after the pattern of the tabernacle, and the pattern of the instruments thereof, even so shall ye make it (Exod. 25:8-9).

The Word was made flesh, and tabernacled among us, and we beheld His glory (John 1:14).

Behold, the tabernacle of God is with men, and He will dwell with them (Rev. 21:3).

In the sphere of typology no figurative structure exists that expresses such a wide range of illumination and instruction as does the Tabernacle and its services. The highest and holiest resources of divine wisdom find expression in the multiplicity of parts and manifold ministries associated with it. The distinguished model was a miniature in material form of Messiah's many variegated ministries, and of the present creation which He redeems from the thralldom and bondage into which it lapsed.

The entire structure had to be most carefully erected according to the divine pattern. Not a single loop or tache, of which there were two hundred on the innermost curtain alone, was left to human judgment or arrangement. The Lord gave to Moses, in the plan revealed, a set of signs, symbols, and shadows which comprised a fascinating forecast of the true substance, for the entire structure signified Christ and His ministry. The ritual portrayed the function of the priest, king, and prophet, represented in the colors of blue, purple, and scarlet. The Son of Man discharged the obligations and responsibilities of these three offices as the royal priest, the righteous king, and the renowned prophet, mighty in word and in deed.

The purpose for which the Tabernacle was erected is stated as being a sanctuary for God to dwell with His people in their pilgrimage (Exod. 25:8). Immediately following this announcement the ark of the covenant is described in detail (Exod. 25:10-22). The ark clearly prefigures Christ. Notice that the mercy seat, which was made of pure gold, is mentioned seven times. Christ came to represent the God of mercy, in the character of a merciful and faithful high priest (Matt. 9:13; 12:7; Heb. 2:17). The mercy seat had two cherubim of gold on its opposite corners, with wings outspread and looking at each other face to face. The crown of gold above and content of the ark are very significant, the former denoting sovereignty and the latter sufficiency. Within was the rod that budded, the pot of manna, and the tables of the covenant. These witness to Christ as the resurrection and the life, the bread of life, and as the one that magnified the law and made it honorable.

By virtue of these three features, namely the mercy seat, the crown of gold, and the contents of the ark, Christ is prefigured in the sympathy of His mercy, the sovereignty of His majesty, and the sufficiency of His ministry. He is actually the covenant in person (Isa. 49:8), wherefore this sacred casket was called the ark of the covenant.

When Israel was stationary the ark within the Tabernacle was in the midst of the camp (Num. 2:17); when setting forward the ark led the way. "The ark of the covenant of the LORD went before them...to search out a resting place for them" (Num. 10:33). The counterpart of this finds its final expression when the Lamb, which is in the midst of the throne, feeds and leads unto living fountains of waters (Rev. 7:17). The Tabernacle was pitched in a different setting with each encampment. This is suggestive of what we find in relation to the true Tabernacle, Christ, and His manifold ministry as recorded in the Gospels.

We may view Christ in the prophetical setting. He went into the synagogue on the Sabbath day and stood up for to read: "The Spirit of the Lord is upon Me, because He has anointed Me to preach the gospel to the poor" (Luke 4:15-22; Isa. 61:1). What a striking and fascinating portraiture this is, as predicted by the Prophet Isaiah. We view Him also in the sphere of His preaching, "Galilee of the Gentiles" (Matt. 4:14-17), predicted in Isaiah 9:1-2. To Him give all the prophets witness (Acts 10:43). Christ was able to expound in all the Scriptures the things concerning Himself (Luke 24:27). Instead of forty-two differing encampments of Israel (Num. 33), Christ is pictured in more than five times that number of prophetical settings that clearly portray the many aspects of His manifold service and sacrifice. Every minute detail of His life is seen to be in full conformity to the will of God.

We may behold Christ in His official setting, which is presented in over forty positions which He fills perfectly. These include the background of His Apostleship as sent by the Father to reveal and represent Him. His Messiahship, to make known spiritual realities, in relation to which He averred, "I that speak unto thee am He" (John 4:26). His Sonship, in exercise of all divine prerogatives, "Jesus...said...Dost thou believe on the Son of God? He answered and said, Who is He, Lord, that I might believe on Him? And Jesus said to him, Thou hast both seen Him, and it is He that talketh with thee" (John 9:35-37). His Lordship, in the administration of spiritual privileges and blessings, "If I then, your Lord and Master, have washed your feet; ye also ought to wash one another's feet" (John 13:13-14). "What think ye of Christ? Whose Son is He? They say...of David...He said...How then doth David in Spirit call Him Lord, saying, The Lord said unto my Lord, sit Thou on My right hand, till I make Thine enemies Thy footstool?" (Matt. 22:42-45) His Judgeship, to condemn and sentence or commend and compensate, "The Father judgeth no man, but hath committed all judgment to the Son. As I hear, I judge, and My judgment is just; because I seek not Mine own will, but the will of the Father which hath sent Me" (John 5:22,30). Space forbids our dealing with His Mediatorship, Headship, Leadership, Suretyship, and forty other of His official settings.

Nor are we able to include the ministerial, vocational, governmental, and sacrificial viewpoints, each of which incorporates scores of aspects.

When visiting the town of Cochin on the Malabar coast of South India, I was the guest of a business manager who had married one of Sir Robert Stanes' daughters. His wife was away in a city further north visiting her parents. My host produced a photo album, which, he said, he had received from his intended during their courtship. On opening it, my eyes alighted on photographs of Maud in different postures. Neatly printed beneath each picture, of postcard size, was a participle descriptive of the setting, namely reading, writing, gardening, baking, knitting, sewing, entertaining, motoring, fishing, cycling, golfing, and so it continued through the fourteen pages. The album was cleverly compiled, and brought to mind the many aspects in which Christ is presented in the four Gospels.

We may visualize Him under a manifold variety of environments, each one with a differing presentation — that of preaching, teaching, commanding, healing, praying, reading, journeying, predicting, revealing, sitting, eating, providing, warning, commending, foretelling, thirsting, suffering, dying, rising, promising, appearing, ascending, interceding, and scores of other viewpoints, far more numerous than the varied settings of the Tabernacle. The vocations, functions, ministries, services, and activities of Christ are beyond comprehension (John 21:25). "The Word was made flesh, and tabernacled among us, and we beheld His glory" (John 1:14).

During the public ministry of Christ, recorded in the first twelve chapters of John, it is not difficult to behold forty of the settings in which He is portrayed. The baptismal setting, the Son of God identified and manifested (John 1:31-34). The sacrificial, "Behold the Lamb of God" (v.36). The mediatorial, "angels of God ascending and descending upon the Son of Man" (v.51). The institutional, at the wedding in Cana. The ceremonial setting, present at the Passover. The instructional, a teacher come from God. The antitypical setting, "As Moses lifted up the serpent. . . even so must the Son of Man be lifted up." This is an enlightening exercise to write out the many settings in which the Son of Man is seen during His ministry as being the true Tabernacle which the Lord pitched and not man (Heb. 8:2). Christ is the greater and more perfect tabernacle not made with hands (Heb. 9:11).

The many figures and features of the interior of this earthly sanctuary are too numerous to be included here, so we shall mention a few of the more prominent. The very elements of the elaborate sacrificial and sacerdotal system of services set forth the matchless splendor of Christ's manifold priestly ministry. The intricately woven veil, with its combination of bright colors, was designed to express the official characteristics of Christ in manifestation (Heb. 10:20). The effulgence of the incandescent flame, which flooded the Tabernacle with light, denoted the brightness of His personal glory (Heb. 1:3). The arresting aroma of the incense signified the fragrant merit of His precious name. The beautiful blue robe illustrated the faithful constancy of His heavenly priesthood. The golden lampstand with its seven lamps throwing light on the central shaft (Num. 8:2) was to represent the Revealer and what He revealed (Rev. 1:13). The main teaching of the laver was to set forth regeneration, the laver of regeneration (Tit. 3:5). In this province also Christ is the Regenerator. No mention is made of the size of these two vessels, for the lampstand and laver emphasize the magnitude of Christ's administration as Revealer and Regenerator, both of which are boundless and measureless in their range and searchless and reckonless in their scope. The revelation of the infinite Father and of immutable truth, and the unveiling of perfect wisdom and of absolute power, has no boundaries. His work in the regeneration of millions of lives is without limits. The One to whom the Tabernacle bears witness is from everlasting to everlasting and every detail of its gorgeous interior of glistening gold contributed to the praise of His glory.

THE TEMPLE

Then answered the Jews and said to Him, "What sign showest Thou to us, seeing that Thou doest these things?" Jesus answered and said to them, "Destroy this temple, and in three days I will raise it up." . . . He spake of the temple of His body (John 2:18-21).

But I say unto you, That in this place is one greater than the temple (Matt. 12:6).

The Lord God Almighty and the Lamb are the temple of it . (Rev. 21:22).

Many of the figures that are used in Scripture to set forth Christ in His various vocations are of His own selecting from His works in creation. But in the case of the Temple He identifies Himself with an edifice that man erected. The pattern of this wonderful sanctuary was received by revelation (I Chron. 28:12). The Spirit of God, who imparted to David the plan and purpose, had a perfect understanding of what the magnificent structure was to prefigure, namely the function and vocation that the Son of Man would fulfill as Mediator, on behalf of mankind.

Although the Temple built by Solomon was the most costly building ever erected on earth, man has not given it a place in his selection of the seven wonders of the world.

In preparation for Christ's manifestation in fashion as a man, the Lord forwarded plans and specifications beforehand of a Tabernacle for dwelling, a Throne for ruling, and a Temple for blessing. These miniature models were revealed in order that the mind of man might be instructed to grasp the magnitude of the divine purpose for humanity and the manifold grace of Heaven's beneficent design.

The Temple, when built in Jerusalem, made offer of the privilege of access to God in prayer, irrespective of origin, whether it be a difference of caste or community, tribe or territory, race or religion, nation or nature (Matt. 21:13). Christ came to transplace the function of the Temple and is most certainly far greater. The Temple was confined to a locality; Christ is universally accessible because He is omnipresent. The Temple was of temporary advantage; the privileges Christ secures eternally abide. The Temple was limited in its capacity; Christ is limitless in His capability. The Temple was built of materials and metals; Christ is the Creator of all such and of the builders who built it, and therefore He is greater than all that He made.

For a thousand years the Temple stood as a meeting place between the soul and God. After the manifestation, Christ drew attention to Himself as being the way of access to the Father (John 14:6). The truth of this is confirmed by the statement, "There is one...Mediator between God and men, the man Christ Jesus" (I Tim. 2:5). Having transplaced the Temple, He uttered the appealing words, "Come unto Me...and I will give you rest" (Matt. 11:28). He "is nigh to all them that call upon Him."

The method we are free to adopt in our present meditation is to take that of comparison, which Christ sanctions by His claim, "In this place is one greater than the temple." The Temple was a storehouse of wealth. Christ is greater in wealth.

Never before nor since was such prodigious wealth accumulated for building a sacred edifice. The total offering exceeded four thousand million dollars, in present day gold standard values. In addition to this enormous wealth of material, the Temple contained the treasure chambers wherein the wealth of the nation was stored (I Chron. 9:26). Placing all this far below in the scale of values, we ascend to much greater and imperishable wealth in Christ, "In whom are hid all the treasures of wisdom and knowledge" (Col. 2:3). By virtue of His omnipotent might and majesty, these superlative treasures are forever secure. Boaz, of royal nature, who redeemed Ruth, was a mighty man of wealth (Ruth 2:1). Christ is mightiest among the wealthy and wealthiest among the mighty. One glimpse of the immeasurable wealth and unsearchable riches of Christ assures us that we may be enriched unto all bountifulness (II Cor. 9:11). The wealth of

Christ's love is greater in volume than the strength and warmth of an unsetting sun. The wealth of His kindness and mercy is more extensive than the whole planetary system.

What inestimable ability He demonstrated during His manifestation! What riches of resource in both wisdom and knowledge He expressed! What treasures of truth He taught concerning the invisible and infinite realities, which are everlasting! What intimate relationship and resemblance He claimed with the eternal Father, which was confirmed by the voice from Heaven!

During His earthly ministry He was accessible to all. His sympathetic heart and strong hands were ever ready to help. He regarded the aged, protected the feeble, strengthened the disabled, delivered the enslaved, healed the sick, blessed the young, enriched the guileless, enlightened the inquirers, engraced the devoted, endowed the sincere, and beautified the meek. Of His fullness have all we received. The wealth of the Temple has long since departed; His treasures have not diminished one iota. The privilege of access to the Temple was denied to many of the defiled and diseased, whereas Christ affirmed, "Come unto Me *all* ye." Whosoever will may come to Him, and He said, "Him that cometh to Me I will in no wise cast out" (John 6:37). The Temple was a shrine of witness. Christ is greater in witness.

This wonderful sanctuary as a structure was a creditable witness to the wisdom of God who planned it. But the Oracle of this house of the Lord was a cardinal proof of the holy character of the One who established it. God spake in times past through the prophets, priests, and kings.

One of the distinctive avenues of communication was the voice of the Lord from between the cherubim (Num. 7:89). The messages received were wholly reliable and fully dependable, and their absolute veracity proved that they were of divine origin. The Temple and its function was a type. When Christ came as the great antitype, it was displaced. God never reverts back to reestablish a type when the antitype has appeared. To do so in this case would be detrimental to the honor of His Son. Christ fully, finally, and forever having fulfilled the function of a material Temple, replaced it, and is the living, loving, and lasting Oracle of God.

Christ is the actual mouthpiece of Heaven. He affirmed, "I have not spoken of Myself; but the Father which sent Me, He gave Me a commandment what I should say, and what I should speak" (John 12:49). The very Word of the Oracle became flesh and dwelt among us. His Word is light to enlighten, life to enliven, and love to environ. "God has spoken to us by His Son" (Heb. 1:2). He Himself, after His resurrection, declares to John on Patmos that He is "the faithful and true witness." So fully and accurately did He disclose the counsel of the Father's will, that He exclusively is worthy of the title, "The Amen" (Rev. 3:14). No saying Christ ever uttered needs amending, no word He used at any time requires to be withdrawn. With all the discoveries man has made and the advances of scientific investigation, not one statement of His requires correcting. No one else exists whose words abide the centuries in verity and vitality, in both accuracy and authenticity, and in fervor and freshness. The truth He taught is eternal, His testimony is absolutely faithful and altogether true (Rev. 21:5). The Temple was a sanctuary of wisdom. Christ is greater in wisdom.

The wisdom of God was conspicuously set forth in the design of the building, the method of its erection, the significance of its furnishings, and the nature of its ritual. But divine wisdom was the more prominent in the instruction received through the messages that were revealed. The entire structure was a magnificent monument to the divine mind that originated its design, purposed its function, and engraced it with the glory of the divine presence. The interior was the most exquisite of any sanctuary ever built in this world. The adornment consisted of glistening gems, the purest gold, the richest colors, the choicest fabrics, the sweetest fragrance, the costliest furnishings, and the brightest radiance.

Yet all the material things in the Temple were perishable and have long since ceased to exist. The entire pattern was revealed in order to set forth in costly figures the excellent features of Messiah's perfections. The temple of His perfect body, in which the Father's glory was made manifest, is age-abiding (John 1:14). He is the everlasting Temple (Rev. 21:22). The body that was prepared Him is now exalted in peerless splendor, adorned in matchless grace, perfumed with priceless fragrance, beautified in fadeless grandeur, and magnified in endless glory. All spiritual blessings are dispensed from this bodily Temple. Whether it be revelation, He is Revealer; or redemption, He is Redeemer; or reconciliation, He is Reconciler; or regeneration, He is Regenerator (Eph. 1:3). The counsel of the eternal Father determined that the riches of infinite wisdom should be centered in the person of His Son. Wherefore, Christ is the wisdom of God (I Cor. 1:24). The ever-blessed God could not have given us the evidence of His divine wisdom more conclusively than by directing our attention and drawing out our affection to admire and adore His Son, whom He sent and in whom are all the treasures of wisdom. The Son could not more effectively have constrained and captivated our love than by laying down His unforfeited life to save us.

By coming to this Temple we realize that the three wonderful capacities the Creator implanted in man may be fully met. These comprise the intellectual, the volitional, and the emotional; of the mind, will, and heart. Christ is the answer to the investigation of man's mind, which requires a subject that can be comprehended and appreciated, but never exhausted. He meets the insistence of the will that seeks an authority which governs and guides but never proves tyrannical or oppressive. He, too, satisfies the impulses of the heart that longs for a perfect love that never changes in its consistency and constancy. To God only wise be glory forever for sending His beloved Son to adequately meet these capacities. We can contemplate more of Christ than we can assimilate. The supreme honor of His royal majesty, the sublime splendor of His regal beauty, and the supernal grandeur of His eternal glory exceed the bound of our human capacity to grasp. The Temple metals were of specified weight. Christ is greater in weight of worthiness.

On eighteen occasions the word "weight" is used in

reference to the gold, silver, brass, and iron employed in the building of the Temple. On three occasions these metals and the many vessels made of them are spoken of as being "without weight." This implies that the prodigious quantity was virtually incalculable, which reminds us that the superlative treasures of the riches of Christ are unsearchable (Eph. 3:8), and the stupendous wealth of God's gift unspeakable (II Cor. 9:15). King David amassed enormous riches for the work of God's house. The gold and silver were worth over four billion dollars, in the light of today's values (I Chron. 22:14,16). The fathers, princes, and captains gave millions more (I Chron. 29:6-9). Pure gold and silver and precious gems were contributed by the ton.

Listen attentively to Christ's words, "I say unto you that in this place is one greater than the temple" (Matt. 12:6). Messiah's weight of merit as the one Mediator for mankind is far greater than all material wealth. His weighty words of abiding authority remain when Heaven and earth pass away (Matt. 24:35). His work is more weighty in value, with the redeeming and transforming of millions of lives, than any that is wrought by human skill. The magnitude of this Mediator's mercy and the magnificence of His glory outweigh and outshine all other values and virtues. The spacious splendors of His superior sovereignty and the gorgeous grandeurs of His absolute authority in Heaven and earth, have not staunched the sweetness of His sympathy, the gentleness of His grace, the tenderness of His touch, the preciousness of His pity, the considerateness of His care, the graciousness of His gifts, or the perfectness of His love one iota.

Let us therefore labor to enter (Heb. 4:11). Let us therefore come boldly...that we may obtain mercy (Heb. 4:16). Let us draw near with a true heart (Heb. 10:22). Let us offer the sacrifice of praise to God continually (Heb. 13:15).

Whatever may have been the incentive that caused people to go to the Temple, we know that the constraining love of Christ, His assurance of a real reception and warm welcome is far greater. We shall make mention of one other comparison. The Temple had a significant way of ascent by which

Solomon went up to the house of the Lord, but Christ is greater in His way of ascent to the right hand of the Majesty on high.

The city of Jerusalem was built on two historic mountains, Mount Moriah and Mount Zion. These were immortalized by Abraham's sacrifice and David's sovereignty. Moriah was chosen as the site for the erection of the Temple and Zion was selected for the establishment of the throne. Separating the two mountains was a deep valley of over one hundred and twenty-five feet. Solomon built a causeway of ascent from his palace on Mount Zion to the Temple. The bases of the seven great pilons were excavated by Professor Robinson, who described the huge blocks of stone as weighing about one hundred tons, all marked with Phoenician characters. The great spring of the arch may still be seen on Mount Moriah. When the Queen of Sheba saw this massive viaduct she was overcome with amazement (I Kings 10:5).

Christ referred to the Temple as "My Father's house" (John 2:16). He used this expression also in relation to the eternal abode (John 14:2). If the Queen of Sheba was so amazed at Solomon's way of ascent to the Father's house on earth, what are we to say of Christ's way of ascent to the Father's house in Heaven? Miracle of miracles, marvel of marvels, wonder of wonders, that the body that was prepared Him, in which He offered Himself in voluntary sacrifice, through the eternal Spirit, was raised out of death by the glory of the Father (Rom. 6:4), raised from the silence of the sepulcher, from the sealed tomb, from the sentinels the Roman authorities placed on guard, and enthroned at the right hand of the Majesty on high. Those who discount the resurrection have not considered "the glory of the Father." This is a thrilling statement, vibrant with all the might and majesty of Godhead. The Father's glory consists in the perfect harmony of the forty-two revealed attributes, all of which are immutable and in absolute accord. Wherefore the Father's righteousness demanded that Christ should be raised, His goodness demanded it, His graciousness demanded it, His kindness demanded it, His faithfulness demanded it, His truthfulness demanded it, His holiness demanded it, His justness demanded it, and so we might record the entire range of these intrinsic perfections and the inherent virtues that are so perfectly blended and mysteriously combined to express the Father's glory. The glory of the Father assures us that the resurrection and ascension of Christ are both beyond controversy.

The Temple in Jerusalem was not built merely as a place of worship, but to be a paragon that eloquently expressed the greater riches and glories of the Son of Man in all His delectable and equitable graces. Our Temple is the person of the Lord Jesus, in whom dwelleth all the fullness of the Godhead bodily. Our Mediator is altogether lovely, in His personal loveliness as the brightness of God's glory and the express image of His person (Heb. 1:3). In His official loveliness, with a more excellent ministry...the Mediator of a better covenant, established on better promises (Heb. 8:6). In His regal loveliness, the Prince of the kings of the earth (Rev. 1:5). In His symbolical loveliness, greater than the Temple (Matt. 12:6). In His celestial loveliness, like a jasper and sardine stone in the midst of a rainbow encircled throne (Rev. 4:3). Our Mediator is without a peer in personal dignity, without compare in judicial authority, without a challenger in final victory, without rival in moral beauty, without equal in royal majesty, without parallel in supernal constancy, and without sequel in eternal glory.

THE TRESPASS OFFERING

He shall bring his trespass offering unto the LORD, a ram without blemish out of the flock...and the priest shall make an atonement for him before the LORD: and it shall be forgiven him for any thing of all that he hath done in trespassing therein (Lev. 6:6-7).

Quickened together with Him, having forgiven you all trespasses (Col. 2:13).

A fivefold expression of the sacrificial work of Christ is

presented in the opening seven chapters of the book of Leviticus.

The burnt offering indicates the completeness of His perfect life being offered to God, which secured acceptance and atonement (Lev. 1:4). "It shall be perfect to be accepted," is the stipulated condition for all sacrifices (Lev. 22:21).

The meal or gift offering displayed the character of Christ. Twice it is referred to as most holy of the offerings of the Lord; "most holy" is a term which is elsewhere rendered "holy of holies." Such a character affirms the adequacy of the offering for providing assurance. Also, the fourfold use of "fine flour" points to the evenness and consistency of Christ's character, which we need to apprehend if we are to appreciate His holiness.

The peace offering suggests that He is the covenant by whom we are brought into agreement, to enjoy association with divine persons. Can two walk together, except they be agreed? (Amos 3:3)

The sin offering reveals His compassion, identifying Himself with our state, and as a substitute, being made sin for us (II Cor. 5:21). To acknowledge this results in absolution from all sin, wherefore in Christ we are justified (Rom. 5:1).

The trespass offering expresses Him as complying with all divine standards of conduct and answering for our misconduct, in regard to which we are guilty on seven counts.

Unawareness in a common fault, through contact with ought that defiles, a breach of relationship (Lev. 5:2-4).

Unconcernedness in a ceremonial observance because of ignorance, a breach of fellowship (Lev. 5:14-16).

Unwatchfulness in a commitment of land or otherwise, a breach of stewardship (Lev. 6:2).

Untruthfulness in a contract of what is entrusted to be kept, a breach of partnership (Lev. 6:2).

Unlawfulness in a claim taking anything by force, a breach of ownership (Lev. 6:2).

Unrighteousness in a clever deception, misrepresenting a matter, a breach of citizenship (Lev. 6:2).

Untruthfulness in a casual find, possessing an article

somebody lost, a breach of citizenship (Lev. 6:2).

In any or all of these that a man doeth (Lev. 6:3), he is guilty and a trespass offering is required of him. James declares that in many things we all offend (Jas. 3:2). Where are we to turn for deliverance from our plight? Where may we find one to befriend us, who is entirely free from all trespasses? There is but One who is qualified and capable of undertaking for humanity, who is both princely and holy. But to expect one so distinguished in personal dignity and moral glory to deign to become a trespass offering for the guilty, seems too unreasonable to contemplate. Let us consider for a few moments the perfect character of the One who offered Himself. We are fully aware of how impossible it is to estimate the value or calculate the worth of such an offering.

In the negative aspect, Christ is entirely exempt from the slightest semblance of blemish, devoid of all defects, and free from the slightest trace of fault or failure. Scripture describes Him as being the brightness of God's glory and the express image of His person (Heb. 1:3). Therefore in the presence of Christ we stand face to face with transparent truth, One whose character is crystal clear, the very embodiment of perfect purity and immaculate integrity. The values of His gracious love are measureless, the virtues of His glorious excellence are priceless, yea, and all estimates of His worth and worthiness fall far short of expressing His infinite fullness. What latent spiritual wealth is involved in His perfect love, which is so evident in His sacrificial ministry, so fervent in personal intensity, so permanent in celestial constancy, so radiant in crystal purity, so resplendent in regal dignity, so preeminent in moral integrity and so effulgent in eternal glory! All such features are delicately blended in the balanced perfections of Him who is altogether lovely. In the Son of Man reside the choicest graces, the noblest virtues, the holiest designs, the richest values, the purest motives, and the worthiest desires and designs.

For such a person to leave the environment of holiness amid the splendor of perfected praise and enter an atmosphere permeated with malignant envy and insolent hate, so as to become a trespass offering for the guilty, is more than the finite mind can fully comprehend. Furthermore, the great enemy at first sought to allure Him by appeals, and when these failed, sought to assail Him by attack and frustrate His designs. This caused Him to say, "Be ye come out, as against a thief, with swords and staves? ... But this is your hour, and the power of darkness" (Luke 22:52-53). Diabolical enmity marshaled its forces to deter and disrupt His intentions. But He spoiled principalities and powers, made a show of them openly, triumphing over them in His cross. By so doing He also took away the handwriting of ordinances that were against us. Wherefore we are quickened, that is, made alive, in Christ and are forgiven all trespasses (Col. 2:13-15).

When our Lord undertook to become manifest in human form, in order to glorify God by obedience unto death, and to meet human need by sacrifice, He displayed His divine love in its unparalleled pity, its unprecedented preciousness, and its unsurpassed purpose. Why should He so love humanity? For He is totally independent of man and derived nothing of His wonderful name, His worthy fame, and His weighty claim from any human source whatsoever. Scripture gives expression to His motive in the words, "For the joy that was set before Him, He endured the cross and despised the shame" (Heb. 12:2). He determined and decided to do this, according to His own good pleasure, which He purposed in Himself (Eph. 1:9). Therefore we love Him because He first loved us (I John 4:19).

When making recompense to rectify a trespass, the offender was required to add twenty per cent to the value of whatever had been misappropriated or misused. Zacchaeus, the wealthy taxgatherer of Jericho, resolved to restore four times the amount of any overcharge he had made. This would indicate that Christ not only answered for man's guilt, but the honor He also brought to God's name far outweighed the dishonor man had wrought by his offense. Both estimates are considered from the divine standpoint, not the human viewpoint.

Christ, by His sacrifice, overpaid the enormous debt,

proving the strength of His love. Scripture affirms that love is strong as death, and many waters cannot quench love (Song of Sol. 8:6-7). The lion is strongest among beasts (Prov. 30:30); this Lover is the Lion of the tribe of Judah. Another symbol of strength is the great rock; this Lover is the Rock of ages. Yet another is the sun (Rev. 1:16); this Lover is the Sun of righteousness (Mal. 4:2). In the light of such figures, how amazingly strong is His holy love!

We also behold the sympathy of His love. "Love suffereth long, and is kind" (I Cor. 13:4). The kindness and love of God toward man has appeared (Titus 3:4). King David made the request, "Show me Thy marvellous lovingkindness ... keep me as the apple of the eye, hide me under the shadow of Thy wings" (Ps. 17:7-8). The kindness of His sympathetic love was vividly expressed when He wept over Jerusalem and said, "How often would I have gathered thy children together, even as a hen gathereth her chickens under her wings, and ye would not" (Matt. 23:37). What a dramatic portrayal of gentleness and tenderness is shown in the attitude of a mother hen toward her brood! How much more marvelous is our Saviour's affectionate attention, considerate care, and favorable friendship which He lavishes upon those for whom He hath given Himself as an offering and sacrifice to God for a sweetsmelling savor (Eph. 5:2). We must pass by the sufficiency of love, which beareth all things ... and endureth all things; also the stability of love, for love never faileth (I Cor. 13:7-8). All of these choice features are expressed in the perfect offering of Himself. Let the memory of His wondrous love become the monitor of the soul, to instruct and to inspire ceaseless gratitude, which He is so worthy to receive.

THE TESTATOR

For this cause He is the mediator of the new testament, that by means of death, for the redemption of the transgressions that were under the first testament, they which are called might receive the promise of eternal inheritance. For where a testament is, there must also of necessity be the death of the testator. For a testament is of force

after men are dead: otherwise it is of no strength at all while the
testator liveth (Heb. 9:15-17).

The further we advance with our investigation of our
Lord's names, titles, offices, and vocations, the more we are
impressed with the magnificent range of His amazing ability
and astounding authority. Deeper insight into the nobility of
His personal character, a clearer comprehension of the majesty
of His perfect control, and a greater conception of the
capability of His preeminent power, greet us with every
designation we consider.

We should take more time to study the Biblical similes,
comparisons, metaphors, correlatives, and superlatives that
are used in Scripture to declare and describe Him.

In the present instance we meet with the term "testator"
for the first time. When a will and testament is made by a
testator, it does not become operant until after the testator's
death. In the matter of a covenant, this can be made without
requiring a death, for instance the covenant made by David
and Jonathan (I Sam. 20:16).

Two clearly defined differences are expressed in the use
made in Scripture of the words "covenant" and "testament." A
covenant is a mutual agreement or compact in which at least
two persons must act, whereas a testament is a bequest made
by one.

A covenant may be dissolved by one of the parties
involved not fulfilling its conditions. Zechariah predicted that
Christ would do this in connection with the covenant made
with the people of Israel. "And I took My staff, Beauty, and
cut it asunder, that I might break My covenant which I had
made with all the people. And it was broken in that day: and
so the poor of the flock that waited upon Me knew that it was
the word of the LORD" (Zech. 11:10-11); whereas, a
testament does not become operative until the death of the
testator.

A covenant may be concluded without necessarily
having an inheritance implied in it (Gen. 26:28; I Sam.
23:18).

A testament implies property and possessions; a person

who has nothing cannot bequeath a legacy.

A covenant existed between God the Father and His beloved Son from everlasting, which can never break down because of either one failing to fulfill the agreement.

Christ is spoken of as being the Messenger of this covenant. "The Lord whom ye seek, shall suddenly come to His temple, even the Messenger of the covenant whom ye delight in" (Mal. 3:1). This designation, messenger, is rendered "angel" ninety-six times in the Old Testament. It is always distinguished by use of the definite article in the RV, "The Angel of the LORD" (see Gen. 22:11,15 and Exod. 3:2-6, where He is the Messenger of the first covenant). Never before nor since did a testator make known a will, and after establishing it by death, come back to be the sole executor in the administration of the same. Never before in the whole range of human knowledge was a messenger sent on such an important issue for mankind which involved, besides other supreme matters, the gift of eternal life, the bequest of an everlasting inheritance, and the legacy of immortal blessedness. More than all this, the person of the Messenger Himself by far exceeds the exceptional mission and ethereal message on account of which He came. Heaven's chiefest and choicest in the whole celestial hierarchy came in manifestation, to convey the glad tidings and to confirm the covenant. The pure motive of His precious message and the perfect magnificence of His personal majesty are unrivaled in world history. How strange it appears that everyone's attention is not arrested and attracted by the manifestation of such a delegate, with so wonderful a purpose from the celestial court.

This supreme Testator came from the confines of the eternal throne of everlasting authority, with all the credentials of Godhead, to declare and confirm God's age-abiding agreement through the blood of the covenant (Heb. 13:20) Himself, the president of principalities in the heavenlies, "far above every principality and authority" (Eph. 1:21). The kingliest of kings (Rev. 17:14), the princeliest of princes (Dan. 8:25), the loftiest of leaders (Isa. 55:4), the worthiest of worthies (Rev. 5:9), the friendliest of friends (Prov. 17:17; Luke 7:34), and the loveliest of lovers (Song of Sol. 5:16), He stands alone in the solitary grandeur of His preeminent regality, the mightiest in majesty and the meekest in mercy, the stateliest in sovereignty and the strongest in sympathy, the chiefest in competency and the choicest in constancy. No wonder that on the memorable night of His betrayal, after having celebrated the ordinance and ceremony of the Passover (Luke 22:15-17; Num. 9:2-3,14), He diverted the interest of the disciples to Himself and substituted the memory of His own vicarious death in place of it. No one else had the right to lay aside the annual commemoration of the most miraculous national emancipation that ever occurred and to replace it with the memory of His personal action of establishing the new covenant. "He took bread, and gave thanks, and break it, and gave to them, saying 'This is My body which is given for you: this do in remembrance of Me.' Likewise also the cup after supper, saying, 'This cup is the new covenant in My blood which is shed for you' " (Luke 22:19-20). The bread was always present. It was called the continual bread (Num. 4:7) and was to be renewed every week. "Every sabbath he shall set it in order before the LORD continually, being taken from the sons of Israel by an everlasting covenant" (Lev. 24:8). A special assignment was made to carry out this order (I Chron. 9:32). Christ took the bread and interpreted it to be a symbolical figure of His body given in sacrifice. In the Old Testament it is spoken of as the bread of the plan, and the bread of the presence, while in the New Testament it is called the bread of the purpose, or purpose bread.

The rite Christ instituted to be a continual reminder of the covenant He confirmed has seven clear-cut features associated with it.

Firstly, a command, "This do." His own will determined and His wisdom designed the best way to promote a continual remembrance of Himself and His substitutionary death. He chose that of eating and drinking, which is a universal feature, as a means of keeping the memory of His personal love and ministry fresh and fragrant. He said in the upper room, "Ye are My friends, if ye do whatsoever I command you" (John 15:14).

Secondly, a commemoration, "In remembrance of Me." He may well have added, not only in remembrance of My personal preciousness, friendly faithfulness, and majestic meekness; not merely to keep before you My promise and passion, but to hold Me in remembrance as the Revealer of the Father, the Ratifier of the covenant, the Redeemer of the enslaved, the Reconciler of the alienated, the Regenerator of the degenerate, and the Recorder of the kingdom of Heaven. No one else has such a wealth of merit and such a weight of honor to be remembered. The Man Christ Jesus is the most worthy of all men to be remembered because of what He has been. "His ways have been from of old, from everlasting" (Mic. 5:2). As set up from everlasting from the beginning, or ever the earth was (Prov. 8:23), He was able to say, "O Father, glorify Thou Me . . . with the glory I had with Thee before the world was" (John 17:5). From being in the form of God, He took on Him the form of a servant and was made in the likeness of men, and being found in fashion as a man He humbled Himself and became obedient unto death (Phil. 2:6-8).

He is worthy of remembrance because of what He has done. "He hath done all things well" (Mark 7:37). He has done works that none other ever did (John 15:24). "Know ye what I have done to you? . . . I have given you an example, that ye should do as I have done to you" (John 13:12-15). Following the thousands of love deeds of His virtuous life came the supreme love deed of His vicarious death. "Hereby perceive we the love of God, because He laid down His life for us: and we ought to lay down our lives for the brethren" (I John 3:16). "He died, the just for the unjust, to bring us to God" (I Pet. 3:18). "Greater love hath no man than this" (John 15:13). "As My Father hath loved Me, so have I loved you" (John 15:9).

He is worthy of remembrance because of what He is doing. He fills the highest office as an unchangeable Priest, wherefore He is able to save them to the uttermost that come to God by Him, seeing He ever liveth to make intercession for them (Heb. 7:24-25). He is preparing a place for His people in the Father's house (John 14:3). He is constantly adding to the Church, which He continues to build, such as receive His salvation (Acts 2:47). He is still accompanying His servants who obey His commission and is working with them (Mark 16:20), for He affirmed, "I am with you alway" (Matt. 28:20). He continues His transforming work of regenerating those who believe and receive Him (John 1:12).

He is worthy of remembrance because of what He will yet do. He said, "I will not drink henceforth of the fruit of the vine, until that day when I drink it new with you in My Father's kingdom" (Matt. 26:29). The Father's kingdom is the generous gift of the good pleasure of His gracious will. The blessed Lord said to His disciples, "Fear not, little flock; for it is your Father's good pleasure to give you the kingdom" (Luke 12:32). This is the sphere of "treasure in the heavens that faileth not" (v.33). The Lord hath established His throne in the heavens and His kingdom ruleth over all (Ps. 103:19). To demonstrate this objective Joseph was empowered to unify all Egypt under one scepter. Likewise, when the kingdom is manifested unification will have taken place (Eph. 1:9-10). Christ gave the assurance that He would raise the dead, for He said, "The hour is coming, in the which all that are in the graves shall hear His voice, And shall come forth" (John 5:28-29). None but Christ is capable of fulfilling this divine purpose. This kingdom brings in harmony for national disharmony; unity for racial disunity; parity for social disparity; and unanimity for theological diversity. If we consider the present dilemma of the grave division between Jew and Arab, black and white, bond and free, rich and poor, English and Irish, Chinese and Japanese, Buddhist and Brahman, and a score of other wide diversities, only the Almighty Shepherd can repair the damage caused by sin and reduce these diversities to one flock (John 10:16). In view of His character being essentially righteous, His word is entirely reliable and what He says He will do shall most surely be done. "Hath He said, and shall He not do it? or hath He spoken, and shall He not make it good?" (Num. 23:19)

He is most worthy of remembrance because of what He is. The Lord's personal perfection transcends His noblest work, exceeds His greatest deeds, and eclipses in virtue His most renowned victory. He is the blessed and only Potentate, the King of kings and Lord of lords, who only hath immortality (I Tim. 6:15). He is the Faithful Witness, the Fountain of Life, in Him dwelleth all the fullness of the Godhead bodily. He is far above all heavens that He might fill all things, yea the fullness of Him that filleth all in all. He is altogether lovely in disposition and altogether lofty in dominion. In Headship and Heirship He is supreme, in lowliness and loftiness preeminent, and in friendliness and faithfulness sublime.

Thirdly, a celebration to proclaim the Lord's death (I Cor. 11:26 marg.), thus contemplating a triumph over the great adversary. "Having spoiled principalities and authorities, He made a show of them openly, triumphing over them in His cross" (see Col. 2:15). Christ's death was not defeat but the victory of verification in the confirming of the new covenant. "This cup is the new covenant in My blood" (Luke 22:20; Matt. 26:28). In Gethsemane, when the chief priests, captains, and elders came with swords and staves to arrest Him, He said, "This is your hour, and the authority of darkness" (Luke 22:53). Although assailed by the sinister forces of evil and attacked by the infernal powers of darkness, He prevailed gloriously by submitting to death and destroying its power. Christ's death is the master stroke of divine mercy toward mankind, the conquest of compassionate love, the triumph of personified truth, and the victory of virtuous might. No personal act is more worthy of celebration. "Thou art worthy . . . Thou wast slain, and hast redeemed us to God by Thy blood out of every kindred, and tongue, and people, and nation" (Rev. 5:9).

Fourthly, a communion, the cup of blessing which we bless, is it not the communion of the blood of Christ? (I Cor. 10:16) The emblems signify a spiritual presence of the One whose love sacrificed all for our reconciliation. To Him we may convey our thanksgiving, praise, and gratitude and voice our adoration. Here also we may have converse and worship the Father in spirit and in truth, expressing our appreciation for the great love wherewith He loved us, and gave Himself for us.

In the presence of one so royal and majestic, so loyal and realistic we feel subdued with a sense of our unworthiness, that one of such worth should be willing to die for us. Let us not tire of telling Him how much we revere His loving-kindness, relish His tender mercy, and revel in His gracious compassion. Our beloved Lord has given us the guarantee of His presence, for He said, "Where two or three are gathered together in My name, there am I in the midst of them" (Matt. 18:20). Being assured of His presence makes the memorial tokens of fellowship fragrant with the sense of nearness.

Fifthly, a contribution, the rendering of a tribute of thanksgiving. Thankfulness is one of the choicest of virtues. In the Psalms, the book of praise and worship, there are thirty references to the giving of thanks, and in almost all a reason is appended. Twice we are exhorted to give thanks at the remembrance of His holiness (Ps. 30:4; 97:12). On ten occasions in the Psalms the word *for* is used when giving the reason for thanksgiving. "Give thanks to the LORD; for He is good; for His mercy endureth for ever" (Ps. 106:1). "It is a good thing to give thanks unto the LORD, and to sing praises unto Thy name, O most High.... For Thou, LORD, hast made me glad through Thy work" (Ps. 92:1,4). We have a much greater cause to bring an offering of thanksgiving by virtue of the greater work Christ has wrought for us. The word the Lord used when He gave thanks is *eu-charist,* which marks the occasion as the feast of good grace, or good thanks.

Sixthly, a confession, are not they which eat of the sacrifices partakers of the altar? (I Cor. 10:18) Participation in the Lord's Supper is therefore a solemn commitment. To eat of the bread means to become identified with the altar, which is the cross of Christ. As the apostle stated, "I am crucified with Christ" (Gal. 2:20). "For in that He died, He died unto sin once: but in that He liveth, He liveth unto God. Likewise reckon ye also yourselves dead indeed unto sin, but alive to God through Jesus Christ our Lord" (Rom 6:10-11). "Ye are not your own, For ye are bought with a price: therefore glorify

God in your body" (1 Cor. 6:19-20). "If ye be risen with Christ, seek those things which are above, where Christ sitteth at the right hand of God" (Col. 3:1; see also 2:12).

Seventhly, a confirmation, confirming the covenant for the remission of sins, and in contemplation of the kingdom (Matt. 26:28). This kingdom of righteousness, peace, and joy cannot be moved (Heb. 12:28). The hosts of the redeemed will be welded together in a united tribute of wonderful worship and adoring admiration. A unified service will be rendered in perfect obedience and full submission to the King of kings. A unity of spirit will pervade with harmony of heart and oneness of mind. The Lord stipulated the character of the kingdom without a shadow of uncertainty and described, as among its many fadeless features, the liberty of life eternal, the society of love immortal, the stability of peace indestructible, the ecstacy of joy invariable, and the beauty of glory ineffable.

The Testator and Messenger of the New Covenant instituted the most distinctive and delightful of all memorial celebrations. The Lord's Supper clearly sets forth the loving-kindness and tender mercy of God the Father, who sent His Son to be the Saviour of mankind. "We have seen and do testify that the Father sent the Son to be the Saviour of the world" (I John 4:14). This impregnable rock of revealed truth which is Christ Himself — the covenant (Isa. 49:8) — is the stronghold of our confidence and the secret of our complacent trust. The confirming of the covenant by the Son secures to us blessings that are invaluable, innumerable, and imperishable, for He fits us to be partakers of the inheritance of the saints in light.

THE TRANSFIGURED SON

And after six days Jesus taketh with Him Peter, and James, and John, and leadeth them up into a high mountain apart by themselves: and He was transfigured before them. And His raiment became shining, exceeding white as snow, so as no fuller on earth can white them. And there appeared unto them Elias and Moses: and they were talking with Jesus. ... And there was a cloud that overshadowed them: and a voice came out of the cloud, saying, "This is My beloved

Son: hear Him." And suddenly, when they had looked round about, they saw no one any more, save Jesus only with themselves (Mark 9:2-8).

Of the seven mountain experiences recorded of the Saviour during the manifestation, this one is perhaps the best known. The very grandeur of the mountainous elevation and the gorgeous panorama of the scenic outlook appear to be the most suitable setting for this memorable display. In a few masterful strokes the thrilling description is given of God's beloved Son transfigured. Hereby we are furnished with a foreview of the glory in which He will appear, when the final kingdom is manifested. The Apostle Peter, when writing of this momentous event, describes it as the power and coming of the Lord Jesus Christ in which he and others were eyewitnesses of His majesty, and also heard the Father's voice from the excellent glory (II Pet. 1:16-18).

Matthew, Mark, and Luke vividly record the mysterious movements that occurred. They each mention the white radiance of His glistening raiment, the wonderful resonance of the Father's voice, and the worshipful resplendence of the Son's personal glory. We are assured from this threefold account that in the kingdom Christ fills every office in the magnificence of His everlasting merit in Lordship; in the munificence of His majestic mediation in Kingship; and in maintenance, by virtue of His masterful might, in Governorship. In the presence of such preeminent dignity and ability Moses, the most powerful legislator, and Elijah, the most prominent reformer, fade from view, and no one in the field of administration remains but "Jesus only." On the mount, the beloved Son is forever identified by the eternal Father, who is Himself the originator and overseer of omnipotent authority, which He warrants His Son to exercise. The Father's voice, resounding from the excellent glory, speaks forth the immortal injunction commanding all mankind to "hear Him" (Mark 9:7).

This exclusive and superlative honor is not conferred on any other personality, for it constitutes the highest approval ever expressed in speech. No declaration ever made is more thoroughly trustworthy, coming as it does from the Father of lights with whom is no variableness. Wherefore the words of Christ are supremely weighty in authority and demand the utmost reverence and confidence, for He is Truth personified (John 14:6). Let us therefore consider His words which are infallible and cannot be disputed; let us contemplate His wisdom which is immutable and cannot be displaced; let us carefully weigh His teaching which is irrefutable and cannot be dispelled; let us concentrate on His statements which are irrevocable and cannot be disproved. The stately grandeur and lofty splendor of His authority is age-abiding. "If so be that ye have heard Him, and been taught by Him, as the truth is in Jesus" (Eph. 4:21). Nothing ever spoken by sage or philosopher can match or compare herewith, "as truth is in Jesus." This refers to that which is as lasting as it is sublime.

Luke assures us that when the disciples were fully awake they saw His glory and the two men that stood with Him (Luke 9:32 RV). Many people are so soundly asleep in relation to invisible spiritual realities they are wholly oblivious as to the scintillating glory of Christ. On the mount His glory was momentarily and magnificently displayed. The fashion of His countenance was altered, the form of His raiment was changed to an inexpressible whiteness, so much so, the disciples were overwhelmed with the marvelous and mysterious display. We must remember that the genuineness of Christ's glory is real, the greatness of His glory is replete, and the grandeur of His glory is radiant in splendor, surpassing human knowledge. The greatest characters of Bible history who were permitted a glimpse of that glory, from Abraham down, had their souls ravished. These included Moses, Isaiah, Ezekiel, Daniel, John, and others. One of the final requests in our Lord's great and gracious prayer is, "Father, I will that they also, whom Thou hast given Me, be with Me where I am; that they may behold My glory" (John 17:24).

The value of this event on the holy mount cannot be overestimated or overstated. Jesus transfigured confirms and certifies conclusively every claim the Son of Man made. Likewise the final unveiling in the book of the Revelation ratifies forever His full Deity. We should mark the fact that each of the three evangelists, in concluding their record of what transpired when Christ was transfigured, refers to the one solitary person. The disciples saw no one save "Jesus only," states Matthew and Mark; "Jesus alone," writes Luke. This expression signifies absolute adequacy, complete capability, and supersufficiency in every sphere, every realm, and every rank of honor. Jesus stands highest, chiefest, and choicest, the only and alone, in headship and heirship, in mediatorship and Messiahship, in Lordship and leadership, in authorship and advocateship, in progenitorship and proprietorship, in suretyship and statesmanship, in governorship and guardianship, in worship and workmanship, in creatorship and counselorship, in friendship and fellowship. There is no supreme office that He does not hold, no stately rank He cannot fill, no royal scepter He cannot sway and no regal crown He cannot legitimately and appropriately wear.

"Jesus only," "He only is my rock and my salvation" (Ps. 62:2,6). "The only begotten of the Father, full of grace and truth" (John 1:14). "The blessed and only Potentate, the King of kings, and Lord of lords; Who only hath immortality" (I Tim. 6:15-16).

Christ clearly affirmed, "All authority is given unto Me in heaven and on earth." "The Father loveth the Son, and hath given all things into His hand" (John 3:35). All supremacy, all sovereignty, and all sufficiency, finally and eternally, is in His hand. He is foremost in faithfulness, the uppermost in princeliness, and the uttermost in loving-kindness. Jesus only constitutes enough to gratify, satisfy, and glorify forever. How entirely becoming it was that He should be tranfigured while here in manifestation, for He is so inherently precious, so intrinsically gracious, so immaculately righteous, and so immortally glorious.

THE THUMMIM

Thou shalt put in the breastplate of judgment the Urim and the Thummim (Exod. 28:30).

We drew attention previously to the fact that "im" appended to a word in the Hebrew language changed the singular into the plural number. Examples were given, such as cherub and cherubim, seraph and seraphim, ur—light, and urim—lights. In this title of Christ, the Thummim, He is, in all totality, perfections. All the attributes, virtues, and excellences, in complete perfection, constitute His very essence. Wisdom is a transcendent excellence that lends luster to every other divine perfection and to all the exquisite qualities of the divine nature. The Lord's personal beauties and glories in the radiance of their effulgence, eclipse all other brightness combined. Not a single spot mars or blemishes the crystal clearness of His ineffable splendor. No defect nor deficiency in any wise dims the burnish of His immaculate purity. The resplendence of His perfect beauty and the transcendence of His preeminent glory exceed the range of our vocabulary to depict or describe. The perfection of His immortal loveliness never declines, the repleteness of His immutable goodness never decreases, and the immensity of His infinite wisdom never varies.

King David desired to dwell in the presence of the Lord to behold His beauty (Ps. 27:4), the beauty of His lofty dignity, His lowly deportment, and lovely disposition, yea, the beauty of His wholesome, handsome, winsome countenance. The perfections concentrated and incorporated in the title Thummim outweigh all our known means of reckoning and outrange all our codes of calculating. In majesty He is indescribable; in energy He is inexhaustible; in capability He is incalculable; in mercy He is immutable; in sympathy He is inestimable; in purity He is incorruptible; in sufficiency He is illimitable; in beauty He is inexpressible; in sovereignty He is inconceivable; in stability He is impregnable; and in glory He is incomprehensible. The accumulated excellencies, the aggregate of all perfections, and the amalgamated virtues of Deity dwell bodily in Christ Jesus the Lord (Col. 2:9).

Professor McGregor expressed the truth of this accurately and concisely in the McMaster University hymn, "Jesus, all perfections rise and end in Thee." In other words,

He is the source and summit, yea, the sum total, fully and finally, of all divine attributes. No other one word in Scripture so completely expresses the entire character of Christ as does the title "Thummim," perfections. We have cause to bless God for providing such a Saviour who possesses the prerogative to impart that same perfection to His redeemed people. David said, "The LORD will perfect that which concerneth me" (Ps. 138:8). The Spirit of God reminds us that, having begun a good work in us, He will perfect it (Phil. 1:6 RV). The Apostle Paul labored in order to present every man perfect in Christ Jesus (Col. 1:28). Of the first creation the statement is made seven times in Genesis 1, that it was good. The new creation is to be perfect. The perfect Saviour perfects forever them that are sanctified (Heb. 10:14). The spirits of just men are made perfect (Heb. 12:23). The prayer of desire is that we should be made perfect (Heb. 13:21). There are thirteen observations in Hebrews which commence with the words "we have," and thirteen obligations commencing with "let us," one of which exhorts, "Let us go on unto perfection" (Heb. 6:1), while the words perfect, perfected, and perfection appear twelve times.

　　We need to meditate more on the person of Christ who is titled Thummim—perfections. Think of the grandeur of His goodness, graciousness, and greatness. Consider His friend-liness, faithfulness, and fullness. Dwell on His loving-kindness, lowliness, and loveliness. Spend time ruminating on His brightness, bountifulness, and blessedness. Employ the spare moments recounting His helpfulness, His holiness, and His highness (Job 31:23). Recall His mightiness, meekness, and mercifulness. Remember to include His comeliness, cheerfulness, and changelessness. Add another twenty-one of these characteristics which constitute His complete character and rejoice to know that in every one of them He is absolutely perfect. We may quote that "He is altogether lovely," "He is the chiefest among ten thousand," that He is the blessed and only potentate, or that He is Lord of lords and King of kings, but listen! This is a greater personal title, *"Perfections."* Christ stated in His teaching, "Be ye therefore perfect, even as your Father which is in heaven is perfect."

THE TREE OF LIFE

The LORD God planted a garden eastward in Eden; and there He put the man whom He had formed. And out of the ground made the LORD God to grow every tree that is pleasant to the sight, and good for food; the tree of life also in the midst of the garden, and the tree of the knowledge of good and evil (Gen. 2:8-9).

To him that overcometh will I give to eat of the tree of life, which is in the midst of the paradise of God (Rev. 2:7).

In the midst of the street of it, and on either side of the river ... the tree of life, which bare twelve fruits, and yielded her fruit every month (Rev. 22:2).

Blessed are they that have washed their robes that they may have access to the tree of life, and may enter in through the gates into the city (Rev. 22:14).

The book of Genesis contains the foundations in point of fact or figure for all that follows in the revelation of truth. One of its many features consists of twelve conspicuous contrasts: two spheres—heaven and earth; two symbols—light and darkness; two signs—sun and moon. Two standards expressed in two trees. Two sentences—thorns, sweat, and death for man; sorrow, travail, and subjection for woman. Two seeds—Cain and Abel; two securities—the covenants as related to the heritage and the heirs; two sympathies, set forth in two mothers, Hagar and Sarah, which represent bondage and freedom (Gal. 4:22-31). Two societies—earthly, Babel; and heavenly, Jerusalem; And two sequels—Jacob and Esau, setting forth the spiritual and carnal, dealt with in Galatians, a message in which the words "flesh" and "spirit" are each referred to sixteen times. The undesirable aspects of these twelve finally depart, therefore the problem of the tree of the knowledge of good and evil is solved and the tree of life remains, which yields twelve fruits every month (Rev. 22:2). This is a perfect figure of Christ as the maintainer of the eternal social order, which is presented as a garden city of bridal character (Rev.21:2). The Bible opens with a marriage that took place before sin came in, and it closes with a marriage that takes place after sin goes out forever. What an inheritance is this! The inheritance of the saints in light (Col. 1:12). An inheritance incorruptible and undefiled and that fadeth not away, reserved in Heaven for you (I Pet. 1:3-4). They which are called might receive the promise of eternal inheritance (Heb. 9:15).

The perfections of eternal life in Christ are expressed in the tree of life in a twelvefold manner, assuring maintenance to the redeemed of the Lord from His immortal resources. The maturing of the twelve fruits every month presents the twelve times twelve of manifold sufficiency, to maintain the twelve times twelve of bond-servant requirements to sustain (Rev. 7:4). The statement is made, "His bond-servants shall serve Him: And they shall see His face; and His name shall be on their foreheads" (Rev. 22:3-4).

The great objective of sonship is worship and service. Christ, the beloved Son, was perfect in worship, and twelve of the aspects of the service He rendered are expected of us: in apostleship, as the sent one (Heb. 3:1); in discipleship, "the tongue of the disciple" (Isa. 50:4 RV); in workmanship, as the mighty worker (Mark 6:2); in friendship, as the friend of publicans and sinners (Luke 7:34); in fellowship, as God's fellow (Zech. 13:7); in heirship, heir of all things (Heb. 1:2); in Lordship, "Ye call Me Master and Lord: and ye say well; for so I am" (John 13:13); in stewardship (John 18:9) He is surely "that faithful and wise steward" (Luke 12:42); in citizenship, "Zion ... city of God ... this and that man was born in her, the highest Himself shall establish her" (Ps. 87:5; Heb. 12:22-24); in Sonship, the beloved Son did always those things that pleased the Father (John 8:29); in Kingship, "That thou sayest, I am, a King" (John 18:37); in Judgeship, "My judgment is just, because I seek not Mine own will, but the will of the Father which hath sent Me" (John 5:30).

The service Christ rendered in all of these relationships is perfect. Under the New Covenant, with its amazing privileges, He makes these features of service possible to the redeemed. The Scriptures affirm that Christ is Himself the Covenant, "I will ... give Thee for a covenant of the people"

(Isa. 49:8). Therefore He is the everlasting Covenant (Heb. 13:20) whose blood redeems (Col. 1:14), reconciles (Col. 1:2), justifies (Rom. 5:9), makes nigh (Eph. 2:13), cleanses (I John 1:7), looses from sins (Rev. 1:5 RV), and assures peace (Col. 1:20).

The spiritual blessings of the covenant are indicated by the meaning of the names of the twelve tribes that are on the twelve gates of entrance to the city. Let us refer to these names in the same order as they are listed in Revelation 7. We may suggest that they represent the following: Judah, worship; Reuben, sonship; Gad, kinship; Asher, friendship; Naphtali, discipleship; Manasseh, headship; Simeon, fellowship; Levi, workmanship; Issachar, stewardship; Zebulon, companionship; Joseph, apostleship; and Benjamin, heirship. Space forbids our enlarging on these features. Maybe if we state why Joseph is a figure of apostleship it may suffice. Apostle means "a sent one." Christ was sent by the Father. His apostleship is mentioned in Hebrews 3:1. Joseph declares, "God did send me before you.... God sent me. ... It was not you that sent me but God" (Gen. 45:5,7-8). Christ said, "As Thou hast sent Me into the world, even so I also send them into the world" (John 17:18). The name Joseph means "to add," and the result of the disciples being sent was that the Lord added to the Church daily such as should be saved (Acts 2:47).

These twelve precious privileges are dealt with in the teaching concerning the Church from the book of Acts to Jude. They are not merely of a temporary nature, but comprise the character of the service in the inheritance of the saints in light (Col. 1:12). The magnitude of Christ's merit in establishing these services is inconceivable, and our attention is attracted by the apostle's prayer that He would grant, according to His riches in glory, that we be strengthened with might by His Spirit in the inner man, that Christ may dwell in our hearts by faith; that being rooted and grounded in love, we may be able to comprehend with all saints what is the breadth and length and depth and height, and to know the love of Christ which surpasseth knowledge, that we might be filled with all the fullness of God. (See Eph. 3:14-21.)

The range of these dimensions is beyond all human capacity to explore. They are spoken of as the unsearchable, or untractable, riches of Christ. From these infinite resources in glory He is well able everlastingly to maintain the unblighted purity, unblemished beauty, and unbroken harmony and unity of myriads of the redeemed in their worship, sonship, fellowship, and heirship, etc. This replete resource from the Tree of Life is likened to twelve fruits, luscious and luxurious, pleasant and plenteous, sumptuous and satisfying. We are reminded in the Word of God that the fruit of the Spirit is love, and love is the very environment of this realm of righteousness where eternal enjoyment, enlightenment, and enlargement abound.

The redeemed are occupied in the exercise of the faculties of the twelve relationships which Christ established by making us sons, daughters, citizens, priests, kings, heirs, stewards, brethren, saints, epistles, disciples, friends, and servants. The tree of life furnishes the facilities for the sustaining of all of these spiritual blessings, and the twelve gates of access thereto are never shut (Rev. 21:25). He who secured them is abundantly able to maintain them in undiminishing freshness and fullness, to the complete satisfaction of all the citizens of the Holy City or society. Of the twenty figures that are used in Scripture of Christ in connection with life, we shall mention seven. He is the Way of Life (Prov. 15:24; Jer. 21:8; John 14:6); the Light of Life (John 8:12), the Bread of Life (John 6:35,48), the Word of Life (Phil. 2:16; I John 1:1), the Fountain of Life (Ps. 36:9), the Promise of Life (II Tim. 1:1), and the Tree of Life (Gen. 2:9, Rev. 2:7; 22:2,14).

A tree, as illustrating a personality, is used elsewhere in Scripture. The Prophet Daniel, when interpreting the dream of King Nebuchadnezzar, said to him, "The tree that thou sawest . . . it is thou, oh king" (Dan. 4:20-22).

In the golden age of Egypt's grandeur, Ezekiel the prophet, when describing Pharaoh, said, "Nor any tree in the garden of God was like unto him in his beauty" (Ezek. 31:8-9). These celebrities have perished, but the Person who is designated the Tree of Life in the midst of the paradise of God, abides forever and the riches of His resource never fail.

Christ is the great and glorious maintainer and sustainer of all relationships in the celestial realm. He multiplies the expressions of His worthiness through the lips of adoring multitudes in the praise of spiritual worship. He magnifies the prerogatives of Sonship by conforming the redeemed to His own perfect image (Rom. 8:29). He expands the values and virtues of kinship by implanting His very likeness in every soul (I John 3:2). He enhances the joy unspeakable of friendship with the happy cheerfulness of divine love, to promote spiritual vigor and vitality for acceptable service in the heavenlies (Rev. 22:3-4). These are suggestions of the first four fruits of the Tree of Life.

Christ served perfectly in all twelve relationships as holiest in worship, highest in sonship, noblest in kinship, staunchest in friendship, keenest in discipleship, greatest in headship, choicest in fellowship, wealthiest in workmanship, wisest in stewardship, nearest in companionship, chiefest in apostleship, and loftiest in heirship. As the Tree of Life He will sustain and maintain His people who are yet to function in these very activities in the celestial realm. As we have borne the image of the earthly we shall also bear the image of the heavenly (I Cor. 15:49).

Daniel was told that he would rest and stand in his lot at the end of the days (Dan. 12:13). The Lord is the portion of mine inheritance and of my cup, Thou maintainest my lot (Ps. 16:5).

U

Every vital symbol and virtuous figure known is requisitioned to interpret Christ as the Son of Man. From every realm of nature, from the entire scope of Scripture, yes, and from the heavenlies also, imagery is utilized to describe Him.

The URIM (Exod. 28:29-30; Lev. 8:8)
>Love discerned in the great gift of the Father of Lights.

The UNCHANGEABLE PRIEST (Heb. 7:23-25)
>Altogether consistent, constant, and compassionate.

The UNSPOTTED LAMB (I Pet. 1:18-19)
>A person without defect, deficiency, or disability.

The UNSEARCHABLE (Rom. 11:33; Eph. 3:8)
>Nothing we may say exaggerates His merit.

The UNDERSTANDING (Prov. 8:12-15)
>He who foreknows and foreordains is able to foretell.

The UNDIVERTED (Ps. 16:8-9)
>Wholly steadfast in integrity, loyalty, and fidelity.

The UNIFIER (John 10:16; 17:21; Eph. 1:10)
>All present disparities He coordinates into harmony.

The UNDERMOST (Matt. 11:11; Luke 9:48)
>From loftiest in honor He became lowest in humility.

The UNDEFILED (Heb. 7:26)
>He touched disease and death without defilement. (Luke 5:13; 7:14)

The UPBRAIDER (Matt. 11:20)
>Doubt and disinterest in His Word and work He censures.

The UPHOLDER (Heb. 1:3; Ps. 119:116-117)
>No title adequately expresses His majestic power.

The UNVEILED (Rev. 1:1)
>The eternal Father identifies and interprets the Son.

Great is the Mystery of Godliness

The Son of Man, His Identity
The Son of Man, His Intimacy
The Son of Man, His Integrity
The Son of Man, His Infallibility
The Son of Man, His Intrepidity
The Son of Man, His Immortality
The Son of Man, His Infinity

God Was Manifest in the Flesh

Ancient of Days, radiant hope of peace
    Expected long, to bring divine release,
Portrayed in every phase of power and love
    Christ our Saviour, sent from Heaven above.

Of Judah's Tribe, with David's royal fame
    His purpose — to declare the Father's Name,
Creation's Lord, the Maker of the stars,
    Controller of the stormy sea, and Mars.

Before all time, Designer of the years,
    Molder of world history and the spheres;
Dividing nations, limiting their bounds,
    Ordaining kings, who wear their golden crowns.

The Covenant Maker, and the Faithful God,
    Who lives to sway the everlasting rod;
Foretold by prophets to appear on earth,
    Submits and enters by a virgin birth.

Wondrous thought! Emmanuel, God with men!
    Such condescension lies beyond our ken.
The Glorious God assumes a human form,
    And in our midst, the Prince of Peace is born.

His life and labors verify His claim,
    His many conquests certify His name,
The Son of God, the Son of Man 'tis He,
    Who gave Himself to set the prisoners free.

Behold in faith a coming fadeless day
    The many diadems His head array;
Who rideth forth intrepid as the Sun,
    His final victory and His reign begun.

Most worthy to receive the greatest Name,
    Above all names, He gained the highest fame;
He triumphed over Satan's power and might,
    Subdued all foes, Great Champion for the right.

Awake my soul and bow in rapturous praise,
    With anthem, hymn, and psalm thy voice upraise,
The Saviour conquers death and cancels sin,
    Earth's final battle He is sure to win.

I am Alpha and Omega (Rev. 22:13)

The threefold claim with which this title is connected sets Christ forth as being lonely in His exclusive grandeur as Revealer, lofty in His excessive splendor as Creator, and lovely in His expressive honor as Mediator. Following His ascension to the right hand of the majesty in the heavens, Christ combined these three great vocations in a sentence when He was communicating His message to the churches through the Apostle John. By so doing He made known the administrative authority of His Lordship in the incorruptibility of its virtue and resource, in the immensity of its volume and range, and in the immutability of its value and right. Man has no natural means of estimating the deity of Christ as Revealer, Creator, and Mediator. The degree and dimension of these administrations are wholly outside the province of human capacity, for they deal with infinite sublimities.

The matchless merging of these imponderable spiritual realities in one person assures forever the establishment of the eternal purpose which God purposed in Christ Jesus our Lord (Eph. 3:11). Therefore, the Word of God, the work of God, and the will of God are by Him fully and finally expressed and exhibited. Christ Himself is the certifying evidence of the wisdom of God's Word in revelation; He is the confirming exhibition of the wisdom of God's work in creation; and the conclusive exemplification of the wisdom of God's will in mediation. The vastness of range of these three great verities is wholly and fully incorporated in the unprecedented claim which Christ made when He said, "I am Alpha and Omega, the beginning and the end, the first and the last" (Rev. 22:13).

The substance of the message within these pages relates mainly to the first of the three statements, "I am Alpha and Omega." Wherefore, each group of titles dealt with is preceded by a brief comment under this heading, in order to keep before the reader the fact that Christ is the whole alphabet, from whom the entire vocabulary for expressing revealed truth is derived. The entire embodiment of all the treasures of wisdom and knowledge is incorporated in one who bears the Name that is above every name.

We must attribute to the Revealer and Personifier of all truth, perfect wisdom, infinite knowledge, and complete understanding. James discloses that the character of divine wisdom is both pure and good (Jas. 3:17). This is certainly true of the Word of the Lord (Ps. 12:6; 119:140; Prov. 30:5). Christ personifies both the Wisdom of God and the Word of God (I Cor. 1:24; John 1:14). Wherefore He it is who decides what is noblest and just, He determines what is purest and right, He reveals what is wisest and best, and He directs our attention and affection to the Father's house, so radiant with rest, joy, and peace, which are the evergreen features of unwithering beauty and fadeless delight.

In order to assure to mankind the fulfillment of the eternal purpose, the Father has committed all authority into the hands of the Son of Man. During His manifestation in manhood, He fully demonstrated His unvarying capacities and unfailing capabilities, whereby He is able to subdue all things unto Himself. In the realm of celestial status, the Son of Man is the highest of the holy and mightiest of the strong. Yea, He is the loftiest of the lordly and princeliest of the royal, forever preeminent in power. He is abidingly the Alpha in His priority and supremacy, and enduringly the Omega in His stability and superiority, His precedency and finality.

Because the mystery of the divine will has been made known (Eph. 1:9), we may rest assured that all that Heaven has determined will be carried through to completion. Let us, therefore, rejoice in the divine counsels and relish the restful hope of their glorious fulfillment. Our present meditation is directed to a choice of names, titles, and vocations beginning with the letter "U."

THE URIM

And Aaron shall bear the names of the sons of Israel in the breastplate of judgment upon his heart, when he goeth in unto the holy place, for a memorial before the LORD continually. And thou shalt put in the breastplate of judgment the Urim and the Thummim; and they shall be upon Aaron's heart, when he goeth in before the LORD: and Aaron shall bear the judgment of the sons of Israel upon his heart before the LORD continually (Exod. 28:29-30).

Urim and Thummim — the lights and the perfections. How grandly these words befit our blessed High Priest and beloved Mediator. In view of such designations as Ancient of Days, Anchor of Hope, Balm of Gilead, Chief Cornerstone, Corn of Wheat, Door of the Sheep, Ensign of the People, Fountain of Life, Alpha and Omega, Beginning and End, First and Last, and such like, we are not exceeding the bounds of propriety in applying the Urim and the Thummim as personal titles of our blessed Lord and Saviour, Emmanuel.

The Hebrew word in the singular for light is — *ur*; the plural form is *urim* — lights. Maybe we are more familiar with this matter in the Bible use of cherub and cherubim, or seraph and seraphim. Therefore the Urim and the Thummim mean "the lights and the perfections." The purpose of the breastplate is stated to be for judgment, that is, in the sense of discernment. For instance, this feature is expressed in the apostolic prayer for the church at Philippi, "That your love may abound yet more and more in knowledge and in all judgment" (Phil. 1:9), and the reason is also given, "Because I have you in my heart" (v. 7). Notice the heart is thrice mentioned in the portion with which we are now dealing.

We esteem it possible to say that in all the symbolism portrayed in the Tabernacle, Temple, and throne, no figure suggesting Christ's superlative virtues in their manifold beauty and purity, grace, and glory, is more sublime than what is set forth in the Urim and the Thummim of the breastplate.

This applies even in a material sense, apart altogether from the higher spiritual verities therein contained. For we are introduced to jewel beauties, color varieties, metal values, fabric specialties, design intricacies, floral symmetries, and perfume qualities of the rarest and richest kinds, all of which and much more is involved in the symbolism.

On the occasion when Moses prepared his brother to officiate in the high priestly ministry, he adorned Aaron with the coat, the girdle, the robe, the ephod, the curious girdle of the ephod, the breastplate containing the Urim and the Thummim, and the miter (Lev. 8). This sevenfold apparel had a definite relationship to the seven articles which we refer to as the furnishings of the Tabernacle. These consisted of the brazen altar, the laver, the golden incense altar, the table of shewbread, the lampstand, the veil, and the ark of the covenant. Then again, these two groups of seven held an important relationship to the seven set feasts recorded in Leviticus 23. In connection with these festivals each garment and each article in turn were associated. Our present interest concerns the sixth feature of the priestly apparel, which was the breastplate of the ephod, with its Urim and Thummim, the sixth article was the veil, which was made of the same material as the ephod; while the sixth feast was that of the atonement.

Moses was given very explicit directions concerning the breastplate; sixteen verses are occupied with instructions (Exod. 28:15-30), and fourteen, telling of how precisely they were discharged (Exod. 39:8-21). The breastplate was a bag or pouch, made of blue, purple, and scarlet and white linen, embroidered with threads of gold. The cloth was made twice as long as broad and, when folded, measured a span each way. A gold chain was attached to the two upper corners and fastened to the two onyx stones on the shoulders. Two rings of gold were in the lower corners, and a ribbon of blue fastened the breastplate to the curious girdle of the ephod. The two were united by ties that were not to be detached. The twelve jewels, bearing the names of the twelve tribes, were to be on the heart of the high priest continually. This indicates that the Lord's people cannot be separated from His love (Rom. 8:39).

No creature has the capacity to comprehend how fully and fervently, how fondly and faithfully Christ loves. His love outvies all the dimensions as we know them, of length, breadth, depth, and height, and surpasses the most profound knowledge of the greatest minds (Eph. 3:17-19). Christ is disposed to love, He desires to love, yea, He determines to love, because love is the very nature of His infinite Being. His love is age-abiding, without change, without limit, and without end. Or to state the same positively, His love is changeless, limitless, and endless. Christ displayed and diffused the sunshine of Heaven's perfect love throughout His ministry.

> His light of love transfigures and transforms
> And fortifies the soul to face life's storms.
> Her incandescent flame makes clear the way,
> Shines more and more unto the perfect day.
>
> Dimensions as we know them all break down;
> The love of Christ is virtues' greatest crown.
> In worth and worthiness His love transcends
> A stream of preciousness that never ends.
>
> No love like His, of such immensity,
> That loves with ever deep intensity.
> The Lord IS love in kingly royalty,
> Immortal in His changeless loyalty.
>
> His love endures, enlightens, and excels.
> In beams that bless and brighten He foretells
> Reception in the Father's house above,
> The very atmosphere of perfect love.

The Urim and the Thummim consisted of twelve precious stones set in a gold framework. On each stone the name of one of the twelve tribes of Israel was engraved, but not in the order of birth, as in the case of the two onyx stones of the ephod (Exod. 28:9-10). The gems were placed in the bag or pocket of the breastplate at the front of the ephod. The mounting of the jewels, and the colorful light scintillating their beauties, was exquisitely lovely, and we might refer to it as the covenant light of the sanctuary. "Every good ... and every perfect gift is from above, and cometh down from the Father of lights" (Jas. 1:17). Of all the gifts, the Well-Beloved Son is the most precious and perfect, and He incorporates and assures all the others (Rom. 8:32).

He Himself is the Revealer of lights. He is the true light that lighteth every man that cometh into the world (John 1:9).

He is the light of the world (John 8:12).

He is the light of life (John 8:12).

He is the light of Israel (Isa. 10:17).

He is the light of the Gentiles (Isa. 42:6).

He is the light of the knowledge of the glory of God (II Cor. 4:6).

In all of these features, He is the light unfading and unfailing, "For the LORD shall be thine everlasting light" (Isa. 60:20).

No other light illumines and instructs like the true light that lighteth every man. No other light glistens and gladdens like this light of the world. No other light is as colorful and cheerful as this light of life. No other light informs and interprets as does the light of Israel. No other light is as bright and beneficent as the light of the Gentiles. No other light is as clear and consoling as the light of the knowledge of the glory of God. No other light is as radiant and reliable, as true and trustworthy, as the everlasting light.

A beautiful illustration of this is given in the golden lampstand of the Tabernacle. The seven lamps thereon had a specific service to render; they were so arranged as to throw light on the central stem of the lampstand, which was of pure gold (Num. 8:3-4).

In the first chapter of the unveiling of Jesus Christ in the book of Revelation there are seven lampstands, with Christ walking in the midst. In this case there are forty-nine lights bearing their witness. Let us make a suggestion or two in this relation. We noted that the Hebrew word for light is *ur*; one of the titles for God is *el*. In the name *Uriel* these two are put together, so the name means "God is light." In the Old Testament there are forty-nine names with this title of God appended as an affix, each one of which, in its meaning, expresses a characteristic of Deity. For example, Daniel—God is judge; Uriel—God is light (I Chron. 15:5); Immanuel—God with us (Isa. 7:14); Pethuel—enlargement of God, more literally, Openhearted God (Joel 1:1). The Apostle Paul

expresses the sense of it when he says, "Our mouth is open unto
you, our heart is enlarged.... Be ye also enlarged" (II Cor.
6:11,13). In other words, we are openhearted, be ye
openhearted. Light is thrown on the divine nature by each of
these names, but fully, entirely, and supremely by Him whose
Name is above every name, the true light. Did He not appear
in His manifestation to reveal, resemble, and represent the
Father? In Thy light shall we see light (Ps. 36:9).

We might also draw attention to one other instance
without comment: Ur—light, Jah—God, Urijah—"God is
light." Elijah—God is God, which He exemplified before the
prophets of Baal. There are likewise forty-nine occasions in
which the title *Jah* occurs in the Old Testament, twenty-six of
which appear in the word *Hallelujah*.

Christ is light essential, He lit all other lights that shine.
He is light's essence, excellence, and effulgence eternally. The
enlightening rays, that emanate from the light of His countenance, enlarge our conceptions of the greatness and
graciousness of the Godhead, expand our comprehension of
the everlasting kingdom of the Son of Man, and enrich our
minds with a clearer understanding of the treasures of truth.

Inasmuch as Christ personally is Urim—lights, let us
note four of the great lights that now shine clearly before us as
the outcome of His manifestation.

He is the embodiment of the Will of God. "A body hast
Thou prepared Me.... I come ... to do Thy will, O God"
(Heb. 10:5-10). Christ declared that the purpose of His
coming was to do that will. "I came down from heaven, not to
do Mine own will, but the will of Him that sent Me. And this is
the Father's will that sent Me" (John 6:38-39; 5:30). Christ
has illumined and interpreted the mystery of God's will and
made it clearly known (Eph. 1:9-10). He assured us during His
ministry, that there would be one flock and one Shepherd
(John 10:16). He made use of the word *one* repeatedly,
referring to it six times in His profound prayer of John 17. By
these statements He confirmed that the divine purpose was the
unification of all things.

He is the personification of the Word of God. "The

Word was made flesh, and dwelt among us, (and we beheld His glory, the glory as of the only begotten of the Father), full of grace and truth" (John 1:14). He is the only person ever to bear this name, "The Word of God" (Rev. 19:13). Not only the Will but the Word also is embodied in a person. Christ is the everliving certitude and confirmation of the everlasting Word. What wonderful avenues of enlightenment Christ, Himself the Word of God, opens to us. This He does by revealing the true character of the Godhead, full of grace and truth; in resembling the Father's glory faultlessly by the wisdom of His words and work (John 1:14); by representing the Father's claims and rights, He who seeks the tribute of spiritual worship (John 4:23); by rehearsing the reality of the generous and imperishable gifts of God (John 3:16; 4:13-14); by reporting on the resurrection of all that are in the graves (John 5:28-29); by recording the spaciousness of the Father's house (John 14:2); and by reassuring that He would return and receive His people into everlasting habitations. Christ, the incarnate Word of God is the living expression of the vitality and veracity of the written Word. David wrote the statement, "Send forth Thy light and Thy truth." The Father sent the Son who said, "I am the light of the world," "I am...the truth" (John 8:12; 14:6). The Scriptures of truth are the only writings that reveal these invisible realities, and Christ, the true light, is the only one who visibly and vocally expressed the truth, for He is truth incarnate (John 14:6).

He is the manifestation of the Wisdom of God. "Christ the power of God, and the wisdom of God" (I Cor. 1:24). "Who of God is made unto us wisdom" (I Cor. 1:30). Thummim means perfections, and all of the infinite attributes of God in perfection are displayed in their brightest luster in the person of God's beloved Son. These glorious virtues of deity shine forth in undiminished splendor, and their pure rays of luminous light emanate in undimmed grandeur from His radiant countenance (Rev. 1:16). The effulgence of His illuminative countenance is referred to on four occasions in the Psalms, "the light of Thy countenance" (Ps. 4:6; 44:3; 89:15; 90:8). The wisdom of God is expressed in Christ's capacity and ability to bring all matters into focus, view them in their right relationship, and to plan and work accordingly for a right aim, in a faultless manner, with perfect knowledge and flawless precision.

He combines in Himself the wisdom of God's purpose and the might of God's power in confirming the everlasting covenant. Although the magnitude of His imponderable wisdom and immeasurable power is demonstrated in the starry constellations above, in the laws governing the planetary system, and in the placing of the earth, with its weight of trillions of tons, in orbit and maintaining it at the exact distance from the sun to make it habitable for man; all this does not constitute Wisdom's supreme display. But Christ Himself is the most perfect and complete manifestation of the wisdom of God. There is no such display of the attributes and perfections of Godhead, in the entire universe, that in any way compares with the disclosure that is made in the Son of Man.

Behold the Son of Man! Behold His amazing and astounding qualities. These include His inexpressible beauty, His incorruptible purity, His incalculable ability, His impregnable stability, His indescribable majesty, His incomparable mercy, His imperishable constancy, His immeasurable authority, His inestimable sympathy, His inimitable humility, His illimitable sufficiency, His inexhaustible energy, His immutable memory, and His ineffable glory. Who, but one infinitely wise, could determine that all of these characteristics in perfection be manifested to mankind in one person? Yet these constitute but one-third of the list of qualities and capacities of the Son of Man, that I have written on a spare page of my Bible. Add to these the forty-two official ranks the Son of Man fills, and before each one append the words *supreme* and *sublime*: His supreme Headship, Lordship, Heirship, Leadership, Kinship, Judgeship, Mediatorship, Suretyship, Governorship, Messiahship, Progenitorship, Workmanship, Authorship, and Friendship. In all of these dignified offices and in the remaining of the twenty-eight, Christ is absolutely superior and preeminent. We cannot elaborate here on the fact that

His person centers and constitutes the forty-two revealed attributes of deity. It is not after the manner of a departmental store, where certain commodities are placed in different sections.

The whole of Christ is unblemished righteousness. The whole of Christ is unsullied holiness. The whole of Christ is unimpared goodness. He is the embodiment of all the attributes. We must also pass by the forty-two features relative to His obedience, patience, prudence, diligence, and so forth. Christ is infinite Wisdom's greatest masterpiece. He illumines with divine light every vocation of virtue, every position of power, every rank of renown, and the very highest stations of honor. He is fully, wholly, and totally all the fullness of the Godhead bodily, in whom are hid all the treasures of wisdom and knowledge (Col 2:3,9).

He is the exhibition of the perfect Work of God. Never before in the entire universe was there a more perfect presentation of the work of God than what is set forth in the moral glories and spiritual graces of the Son of Man. The Beloved Son's manifestation in human form constitutes God's most marvelous work and could not have been done more wisely, lovingly, and perfectly. Five witnesses had their eyes opened to behold His majestic loveliness and the beauty of His holiness when they were with Him on the holy mount (II Pet. 1:16-18). Not one of those eyewitnesses of His transfiguration ever questioned His perfect humanity. During the whole of His ministry the Son of Man demonstrated that His life was untainted, unmarred, and unspotted.

In addition His own work is altogether perfect. Nothing He did could have been done in a better way, nothing He said could have been expressed more wisely. The multitude were so impressed that, on one occasion, they made the inquiry, what shall we do, that we might work the works of God? (John 6:28) Jesus answered, "This is the work of God, that ye believe in Him whom He hath sent" (v. 29).

Christ is indeed the Thummim—the perfections. Professor McGregor has expressed the idea in the line of his beautiful hymn, "Jesus all perfections rise and end in Thee."

This implies that Christ commences all as being the source of perfections, and He completes all as being their summit and crown. His activities bear witness to this: "Having begun a good work in you He will perfect it" (Phil. 1:6 Newberry). The same was the aim of Paul's ministry, "This also we wish, even your perfection" (II Cor. 13:9). To this end he labored, "That we may present every man perfect in Christ Jesus" (Col. 1:28).

In view of these things we say, Urim and Thummim, the lights and perfections, constitute Christ Himself, who is the visible image of the invisible God (Col. 1:15). He is complete in comeliness, replete in radiance, brilliant in beauty, perfect in purity, graceful in gentleness, glorious in holiness, and gorgeous in glory. The light of His life and the luster of His love are sublime. The intrinsic values of the moral perfections of His beauty and the inherent virtues of the spiritual perfections of His glory defy description. Such an one is entirely without predecessor to rival Him, without successor to equal Him, and without superior to excel Him. The Lord Himself speaks through the Prophet Isaiah and declares, "There is none else, none beside Me." He uses the expression "none else" six times in the space of two chapters (Isa. 45–46).

There is none else who speaks of the Father's house, the Father's holiness, and the Father's honor.

There is none else who is able to command the dead to come forth, to cancel sins, and conquer death.

There is none else who gives light on the kingdom to come, the world to come, and the ages to come.

There is none else that ever demonstrated the character of everlasting life, everlasting light, and everlasting love.

There is none else that could ever claim to be the Alpha and Omega of revelation, the beginning and the end of creation, and the first and the last in mediation.

The Scriptures portray the Son of Man as being pure and holy, true and lovely, meek and lowly, warm and friendly, good and kindly, high and lofty, strong and mighty. As physical light produces all the colorful beauties of this terrestrial world, so the spiritual light emanating from Christ, the Sun of Righteousness, adorns with divine graces and glories the myriad hosts of the entire celestial world. "The city had no need of the sun, neither of the moon, to shine in it: for the glory of God did lighten it, and the Lamb is the light thereof" (Rev. 21:23).

The twelve precious stones of the Urim and the Thummim are seen finally as the twelve foundation stones of the city of God, which comprise the eternal society of saints, as constituting the Bride. They no longer bear the names of the twelve tribes, but those of the twelve apostles. The profound teaching connected with this extensive and expansive display of the precious jewels is beyond the range of our present aim.

Suffice it to say that Christ is the expression of celestial lights in all their variegated variety. He makes plain the realities of the unseen realms, and sheds light on His own supreme administrative authority (Matt. 28:18). This stupendous claim He confirmed after His ascension by revealing to John the amazing presentation of holding seven stars in His right hand (Rev. 1:16). The greater picture of this majestic might is given in the prophecy of Amos, "Seek Him that maketh the seven stars and Orion" (Amos 5:8). In the book of Job the reference is to the Pleiades (Job 38:31).

The Light of His Perceptive Authority. Notice that this is referred to thrice: "His eyes are as a flame of fire" (Rev. 1:14; 2:18; 19:12).

The Light of His Executive Authority. "The prevailing Lion of Judah is the only one worthy to take and open the Book of Title-Deeds entitling possession of the whole world" (Rev. 5:5).

The Light of His Redemptive Authority. "A Lamb as it had been offered in sacrifice.... Thou hast redeemed to God by Thy blood men of every kindred and tongue and people and nation" (Rev. 5:5,9).

The Light of His Mediative Authority. Signified in the figure of the angel, offering the prayers of all saints upon the golden altar (Rev. 8:3). *See* Malachi 3:1—the messenger or angel of the covenant.

The Light of His Adjudicative Authority. "The Father ... hath given Him authority to execute judgment ...

because He is the Son of Man" (John 5:26-27). "And I saw a great white throne ... and the dead were judged" (Rev. 20:11-13).

The Light of His Creative Authority. "He that sat upon the throne said, Behold, I make all things new" (Rev. 21:5).

The Light of His Consummative Authority. "And there shall be no more curse: but the throne of God and the Lamb shall be in it; and His servants shall serve Him: And they shall see His face; and His name shall be in their foreheads" (Rev. 22:3-4). His Light has an eternal effulgence and He is altogether luminous in beauty, altogether lustrous in purity, and altogether lovely in majesty. "His countenance as the sun shineth in His strength" (Rev. 1:16).

THE UNCHANGEABLE PRIEST

> And they truly were many priests, because they were not suffered to continue by reason of death: But this man, because He continueth ever, hath an unchangeable priesthood. Wherefore He is able also to save them to the uttermost that come unto God by Him, seeing He ever liveth to make intercession for them (Heb. 7:23-25).

In every vocational office and in every functional service, Christ is supremely superior because He ever lives. The reality of His age-abiding life assures us that His Priesthood, His Kinghood, His Saviourhood, and His Shepherdhood are linked with incorruptible virtues and inexpressible values. The continuity of His mediatorial ministry is without cessation, He is a Priest forever. We are informed that His life is endless, His Priesthood is changeless, His intercession is ceaseless; wherefore the salvation He provides is established forevermore and is therefore described as eternal salvation (Heb. 5:9).

This underived office that Christ fills is untransferable and the unbreakable continuity of His intercession permits of no substitute and admits of no successor. The revelation of these wonderful invisible realities which describe our Lord's perpetual ministry at the right hand of the Majesty on high, should grip our attention and beget our adoring worship.

The manifestation of Christ in human form is

miraculous, His mission in coming to save is marvelous, but His mercy in continuous intercession is the most momentous feature of His present ministry. We should determine to exercise every faculty, and utilize every facility available for concentrating thought on the supernatural ministry of this majestic Mediator.

What delightful comfort is derived from understanding that He knows and loves and cares. He has a complete knowledge and personal love for everyone on whose behalf He intercedes. He is touched with the feeling of our infirmities and is familiar with the trials and temptations of the way. He is fully aware of the tactics and'deceptions of the enemy. He maintains an individual interest in every one of His people, to safeguard them against the foe. He is thoroughly conversant with everything of the past, present, and future in the lives of all. He takes the full responsibility before the Father to fulfill all obligations on behalf of His redeemed people.

His faithfulness is worthy of our confident trust. His friendliness is expressed in His kindly regard, which warrants our complete reliance on His mercy.

No infirmity of age mars the work of this Priest, or shrivels His compassion. No inability through lack of strength weakens His service. No insufficiency of merit depletes His requests or disallows His petition. No incapacity of mind causes Him to disregard His people's needs. No inconstancy of love ever quenches His kindness of heart. No insecurity can ever unsettle His steadfast purpose. What exceptional provision has been made for both shielding and sustaining the redeemed of the Lord!

No one but Christ is characterized by the dignity of deity, and the form of humanity, so as to be God's representative toward man and man's representative toward God (Phil. 2:6-7). God's righteousness demands a perfect sacrifice to deliver from the guilt and penalty of sin. God's holiness requires a perfect Mediator to intercede, for maintaining the acceptance of all who come to Him. In the person of this Mediator there can be no diminution of His power which saves to the uttermost. This is assured because He abides the everliving, everloving, and everlasting Saviour. The character of His capacities and capabilities make Him foremost and final in priestly mediation.

Because He is almightily invincible in His omnipotence, He is perfectly able to utilize His power to deliver and defend. He clearly understands the needs of His people, and purposes ultimately to perfect them forevermore.

He is absolutely inestimable in His omniscience and is fully aware of everything and everybody everywhere. He is altogether inseparable in His omnipresence and always abides in faithfulness, helpfulness, and changelessness. Such an High Priest became us (Heb. 7:26). The superiority of His Holy character is most suitable and satisfactory to insure His unchangeable Priesthood in mediation.

THE UNSPOTTED LAMB

> Forasmuch as ye know that ye were not redeemed with corruptible things, such as silver and gold, from your vain behaviour received by tradition from your fathers; but with the precious blood of Christ as of a lamb without blemish and without spot (I Pet. 1:18-19).
>
> How much more shall the blood of Christ, who through the eternal Spirit offered Himself without spot to God, purge your conscience (Heb. 9:14).

Of no other personal being in all the world has it ever been written that he was without spot. The statement denotes one who is of unblemished character, of untainted conduct, and of unimpeachable consistency in every detail of life. This picturesque figure of Christ is used of set purpose to convey the perfect suitability of His character to be made an offering and sacrifice to God for a sweet-smelling savor (Eph. 5:2). The Father commanded Him to obey even to death. When addressing His disciples in the upper room, He told them of His approaching departure, and referred to the devil as attempting to divert Him from obeying to the death. Then said He, "That the world may know that I love the Father; and as the Father gave Me commandment, even so I do" (John 14:30-31).

Christ would not have submitted to a crucial death for anyone but the eternal Father; no more than Isaac would have permitted anyone but Abraham, his father, to bind him for sacrifice on Mount Moriah. When Christ repaired to Gethsemane with His disciples, and the rabble crowd came to take Him, Peter attempted to prevent His arrest; whereupon Christ rebuked him, saying, "Put up thy sword into the sheath: the cup which My Father hath given Me, shall I not drink it?" (John 18:11) Even in obeying to the very extreme, namely, that of a distasteful death of shame, He is the Lamb without spot.

In manifestation as Son of Man, His subjection and submission to the Father's will, by virtue of their mutual love for each other, defies and amazes our comprehension.

The suitability and acceptability of the Son's offering Himself in sacrifice is the greatest and grandest proof of implicit obedience known, in the whole realm of knowledge.

When we pause to consider the Son's perfection in detail, we are overwhelmed in wonder and admiration. His beauty and purity are without defect. His sincerity and sympathy are without blemish. His name and fame are without taint. His loveliness and lowliness are without tarnish. His kingliness and kindliness are without fault. His vesture and virtue are without stain. His ministry and mercy are without blame. His disposition and deportment are without detriment. His life and labors are without spot. Moreover, His diligence in service is proverbial; He said, "I must work the works of Him that sent Me, while it is day." His reticence in suffering is profound, "as a lamb led to the slaughter and as a sheep before her shearers is dumb, so He opened not His mouth" (Isa. 53:7). His patience in sacrifice is astounding, "I waited patiently for the LORD" (Ps. 40:1). Let us take particular notice of the conditions under which these latter words apply.

Psalm 40 explains that the one who waited patiently was in a horrible pit amid miry clay, awaiting deliverance. Later in the psalm it is written, "Sacrifice and offering Thou didst not desire ... burnt offering and sin offering hast Thou not required. Then said I, Lo, I come: in the volume of the book it is written of Me, I delight to do Thy will, O My God" (vss. 6-7). The pronoun "I" occurs seven times in four verses. Christ replaced compulsory offerings with a voluntary one. (Read Heb. 10.) He is depicted in deep mire, and is described as "laid in the lowest pit" (Ps. 69:2; 88:6).

The four great sorrow psalms constitute four descriptions of Christ's experiences in relation to His crucifixion, as recorded in the four Gospel records. Book one covers Psalms 1 to 41, in which the King is described in His superior majesty. Twenty-two is the sorrow psalm of this section and Christ is pictured as a babe upon a mother's breast, unable to act in self-defense, a figure of abject weakness.

Book two includes Psalms 42 to 72, depicting the Heir of the inheritance. Sixty-nine is the sorrow psalm of the section, and the rightful possessor of all things is described sinking in deep mire (vs. 2), without even a foothold, a figure of absolute helplessness.

Book three covers Psalms 73 to 89, which disclose the Priest of the sanctuary. Eighty-eight is the sorrow psalm in which the one who loves and befriends is portrayed without a lover or friend (vs. 18). The figure indicates a state of amazing friendlessness.

Book four comprises Psalms 90 to 106, wherein the Maker is described. "Maker," "make," and "made" occur twenty-eight times, a like number as in John's Gospel message. The sorrow psalm is 102, in which the I AM, the Maker, describes His unenviable position: "I am like a pelican of the wilderness: I am like an owl of the desert. I watch, and am as a sparrow alone upon the housetop" (vss. 6-7). Despised, deserted, and disregarded; all picturing His astounding loneliness.

"I looked on my right hand, and beheld, but there was no man that would know me: refuge failed me; no man cared for my soul" (Ps. 142:4). Even Peter said, "I know not the man." They all forsook Him and fled. What a plight is this! Fastened to a brutal cross, prostrate in utter weakness; nailed hands and feet in absolute helplessness; deeply conscious of a state of amazing friendlessness; and subjected to an astounding loneliness. While enduring such tragic circumstances, listen to the words (Ps. 40:2) He uttered, "I waited patiently for the Lord.... He brought me up also out of an horrible pit," a pit of corruption, for He had been made sin for us. "Out of the miry clay," not of mud, but malice and malignity, hate and enmity, scorn and ridicule.

There is no parallel to the patience of Christ in all history. Moses, the meekest of men, acted impatiently. Jeremiah, the prophet, with his enlarged heart of sympathy spake impatiently. When complaining he said, "Know that for Thy sake I have suffered reproach... Wilt Thou be altogether unto me as a deceitful brook whose waters fail?" (Jer. 15:15,18 Newberry) When in bitterest agony, bearing the heaviest burden and God-forsaken, Christ said, "But Thou art holy" (Ps. 22:3), and vindicated the character of God in forsaking Him. The durable character of the holiness of Christ as being without spot, and the desirable nature of His graciousness expressed as the Lamb, combine in displaying the virtues of His incorrupt suitability to be the Redeemer of mankind. In this winsome designation His dignified honor and distinctive humility are blended with the constancy of His care, the mercy of His meekness, and the gentleness of His grace. All beauty and purity, goodness and kindness, compassion and tenderness are personified in His sacrificial character as the unspotted Lamb.

THE UNSEARCHABLE

> O the depth of the riches both of the wisdom and knowledge of God! how unsearchable are His judgments, and His ways past finding out (Rom. 11:33).
> The unsearchable riches of Christ (Eph. 3:8).

No one can by any means diminish the universal range of divine discriminative judgment committed to the Son of Man. "The Father judgeth no man, but hath committed all judgment unto the Son.... And hath given Him authority to execute judgment also, because He is the Son of man" (John 5:22,27). His judgments are a great deep (Ps. 36:6), which intimates they are unfathomable. "True and righteous are His judgments" (Rev. 16:7; 19:2), a statement which indicates they are unalterable.

The Christ of God is the legislator of all the laws of the universe, both of the animate and inanimate, of the moral and material realms, also of all spiritual and physical spheres. Therefore He has the right to exercise jurisdiction to the utmost bound. Possessed of a perfect knowledge, He discerns "the thoughts and intents of the heart. Neither is there any creature that is not manifest in His sight: but all things are naked and laid bare to the eyes of Him with whom we have to do" (Heb. 4:12-13). The death of Christ on the cross confirms His right of jurisdiction to execute "the judgment of this world: now shall the prince of this world be cast out. And I, if I be lifted up from the earth, will draw all unto Me" (John 12:31-32). The word *men* is not in the text. The context shows that the drawing of all of everything referred to is for judgment, not salvation. "We shall all stand before the judgment seat of Christ" (Rom. 14:10).

In John's message of the gospel, perfect love is linked with perfect justice, these two divine attributes are not in conflict. Along with the fifty references to "love" and "lovest," the word "judge" appears twelve times, while "judged" and "judgment" occur twenty-one. At Calvary justice stands with her furbished sword triumphant; for it is written, "Awake, O sword, against My Shepherd" (Zech. 13:7). But mercy's sovereign scepter is also present, regnant, and radiant in sublimest splendor. Believers are said to be reconciled to God by the death of His Son and justified by His resurrection (Rom. 4:25; 5:10). Wherefore, the cross of Christ becomes both the touchstone of justification, and the tribunal of judgment for condemnation. In other words, a savor of life unto life, or of death unto death; so that God is honored in those that are saved and in those that perish (II Cor. 2:14-16).

Let us remember that the divine judgments are not limited to time-future. Judgment to come (Acts 24:25) is assured on the basis of judgments that have already occurred. The first mention of the word "judge" in the Bible is when the Lord told Abraham that He would judge Egypt (Gen. 15:14). Later He made known that He would destroy Sodom, whereupon Abraham said, "Shall not the Judge of all the earth do right?" Christ declared, "Abraham rejoiced to see My day ... he saw it, and was glad" (John 8:56). This statement should startle us, for Christ, who in manifestation preached the gospel to the poor (Luke 4:18), had centuries before preached the gospel to Abraham (Gal. 3:8-9). Afterwards he was assured of an everlasting inheritance, of which the Promised Land was a type. For he could not have an eternal inheritance in this earth, which is to be clean dissolved (Isa. 24:19; II Pet. 3:11). Christ pledged to Abraham a physical and spiritual posterity, revealed to him the divine purpose of an everlasting covenant, and made known by demonstration His universal plan of judgment against sin and wickedness. To confirm this we have the Lord's own interpretation, "Likewise also as it was in the days of Lot ... the same day that Lot went out of Sodom ... fire and brimstone from heaven ... destroyed all. Even thus shall it be in the day when the Son of man is revealed" (read Luke 17:28-30).

Abraham was given a panoramic foreview of the divine redemptive plan to prepare him for the final supreme test. "Take now thy son, thine only son Isaac, whom thou lovest ... and offer him ... for a burnt offering" (Gen. 22:2). This demand was unaccompanied by a single word of comfort, unrelated to any stated reason, and unconnected with any mention of promise. By virtue of this heartrending demand, he understood the very foundation on which the fulfillment of the divine purpose was to be based. All would ultimately be fully accomplished by judgment against man's guilt falling upon God's beloved Son. "O ye seed of Abraham His Servant. . . . He is the LORD our God: His judgments are in all the earth" (Ps. 105:6-7). The seven great world empires during Israel's history, from the Egyptian to the Roman, were visited with divine judgment. Each of these in turn dominated Palestine. The Prophet Amos in the two opening chapters of his message records another seven nations thus visited, and states the reason for it. The Lord selected a tenfold means to minister judgment on Egypt because of her tyranny. Assyria was famous for her cruelty and Babylon for her idolatry. God has repeatedly used famines, pestilences, epidemics, plagues, earthquakes, hurricanes, floods, and wars as judgments on nations and peoples.

To the Apostle John on Patmos God fully identified the Son of Man as being the Executor of judgment. He is described in His judicial capacity as the one who is and was and is to come, the Almighty. As executor He is full of eyes before, behind, and within. This figure signifies that He is fully aware with perfect understanding of the complete range of all that has been, is now, and ever shall be. Such knowledge of all the facts entitled Him to say, "I judge and My judgment is just." When to John had been disclosed the final judgment, he described the judgment seat as a great white throne, which symbolizes the steadfast righteousness of the tribunal. The one who sat thereon he depicted earlier as having head and hair white like wool as white as snow, indicating His mature wisdom, pure mind, and immaculate knowledge and understanding. In the previous chapter to this scene of the white throne, the judge is on a white horse in battle, signifying that His ministration of justice is in righteousness, harmonizing fully with His character of holiness. The display is awe-inspiring and amazingly sublime. In grandeur and greatness, in stateliness and splendor, in magnitude and magnificence the scene depicted is altogether incomparable.

The judgment of this Judge is unsearchable. He is the valuer of all virtuous service rendered in His name by millions of workers and witnesses. He is the appraiser of all sacrificial labors wrought for His sake by multitudes of missionaries and martyrs. He is the estimator of all deeds of kindness and love expressed, by myriads of disciples and followers, toward His redeemed people. No worthy work will be overlooked. When in manifestation He appreciated the gratitude of a leper who returned to thank Him for cleansing, He commented on a widow who cast two mites into the temple treasury, and also pledged a reward to those who gave a cup of cold water to a thirsty soul. He is just the same today and forever, perfect in His appreciation.

As to our Lord's unsearchable riches, space forbids their mention. The riches of His goodness (Rom. 2:4) are numberless in temporal mercies and terrestrial benefits. The riches of His grace (Eph. 2:7), are reckonless in spiritual blessings and imperishable virtues. The riches of His wisdom (Rom. 11:33) are measureless, as demonstrated in the plan and purpose of salvation, redemption, reconciliation, and regeneration. The riches of His glory (Eph. 3:16; Phil. 4:19) are traceless in that they are ageless, ceaseless, and changeless in their transcendent perfectness and effulgent holiness. We may extend, enlarge, and expand to a point of exasperation our attempt to describe the riches of His grace and glory, without the slightest fear of exaggeration. The wealth of these spiritual treasures cannot be weighed; the value of these celestial virtues cannot be voiced, and the preciousness of these personal perfections cannot be priced. Christ the Son of Man, who is the repository of all, is truly in Himself the Unsearchable. "Canst thou by searching find out God? canst thou find out the Almighty unto perfection?" (Job 11:7)

THE UNDERSTANDING

> I wisdom dwell with prudence. . . . Counsel is mine, and sound wisdom: I am understanding; I have strength. By me kings reign, and princes decree justice (Prov. 8:12-15).

Understanding refers to a status of knowledge. Christ in person is not only Wisdom, but also Understanding. This includes a complete comprehension of all matters and movements, an exact estimate of all values and virtues, and a clear conception of everyone and everything everywhere. Notice that in the chapter from which we derive this designation, the pronoun I occurs fourteen times in verses 12 to 30. As a further mark of identification, our attention is drawn to the way, the truth, and the life (vss. 7,20,35). Christ verified these words as referring to Himself by affirming, "I am the way, the truth, and the life: no one cometh unto the Father, but by Me" (John 14:6).

What an impressive and all-inclusive statement of personal claim is indicated in the words, "I am Understanding." The range of magnitude in the declaration cannot be calculated by the finite mind, for the Scriptures declare, "His understanding is infinite" (Ps. 147:5). This indicates an inherent comprehension of all that is visible and invisible in every sphere and in every creatorial, official, legal, moral, judicial, spiritual, and celestial realm.

Isaiah, the prophet, portrays the massive mind, majestic ministry, and manifold mercy of this marvelous Shepherd. Chapter 40 of the prophecy opens with a message of divine comfort, "Comfort ye, comfort ye My people, saith your God." Immediately following, three voices are mentioned: the voice of the herald in witness, preparing the way. The voice that affirms man's mortality, "all flesh is [as] grass." Then we hear the voice of testimony to the coming Shepherd, who gently leads His flock and safeguards the lambs with tender care (Isa. 40:3,6,9-11). This same Shepherd has measured the waters which cover one hundred million square miles of the earth's surface to the proportion of H_2O. He has meted out heaven with a span and comprehended the dust of the earth. He created the stars, tells their number, and calls them all by name by the greatness of His might; not one is omitted.

In the light of all this He asks the question, "Why sayest thou, O Jacob, and speakest, O Israel, My way is hid from the LORD?" (Isa. 40:27) Did not this Shepherd demonstrate at the brook Jabbock that He knew Jacob's deceit? The Lord was aware of the occasion when Jacob told his blind father that he was Esau the firstborn. Twenty years had elapsed since then and Jacob considered that two hundred and forty months had hidden the matter. But the first question the divine Shepherd asked, startled him, "What is thy name?" Read carefully the summing up of the message.

"Hast thou not known? hast thou not heard, that the everlasting God, the LORD, the Creator of the ends of the earth, faintest not, neither is weary? There is no searching of His understanding" (Isa. 40:28). Besides comprehending the billions of stars and calling them by name, He fully understands each individual sheep in His flock.

The reality of all this is confirmed in the record of the Gospel by John. The Creator who made all things is the Good Shepherd who calls His own sheep by name (John 10). In chapter 1 of the Gospel, He interprets Jacob's dream and applies it to Himself. In chapter 2 He is cognizant of the Passover history, and explained to the ruler in Israel that the judgment in Exodus 12 was not against human behavior, but natural birth, and therefore emphasized the need of a new birth as necessary to enter the kingdom of God. He had a clear understanding of the Temple, the brazen serpent, Jacob's well, the Bethsaida pool, the manna, the feast of tabernacles, the divine Shepherd of Israel in the wilderness, yea, the entire Old Testament record. He knew personally the seven historic personalities mentioned, Abraham, Jacob, Joseph, Moses, David, Solomon, and Isaiah. As the Good Shepherd His inexhaustible strength and inexpressible sympathy were accompanied by the background of His inscrutable understanding. "Thou knowest my downsitting and mine uprising, Thou *understandest* my thought afar off. Thou compassest my path and my lying down, and art acquainted with all my ways" (Ps. 139:2-3).

Absolutely faithful, altogether true,
Understanding all things, understanding you,
Infinite in knowledge, intimately near,
This is Christ our Shepherd, why have care or fear?

THE UNDIVERTED

I have set the LORD always before Me: because He is [on] My right hand, I shall not be moved. Therefore My heart is glad, and My glory rejoiceth: My flesh also shall rest in hope. For Thou wilt not leave My soul in hell, neither wilt Thou suffer Thine Holy One to see corruption (Ps. 16:8-10; Acts 2:25-27).

The pronoun "My" appears fourteen times, "I and Me" twelve times in this brief psalm, and these direct our attention definitely to the person of Christ. At Pentecost, the Spirit of God fully confirms that He fulfills this predictive statement. The loyalty and conformity of Christ to the Father's will assured to Him deliverance from (*ek*) that is, out of death (Heb. 5:7). His attitude stands in broad contrast to that of the devil. He, in the covetousness of his ambition, determined to exalt himself and be as God (Isa. 14:13). Lucifer as an archangel kept not his first estate. The originating power of evil from within prompted him to move from his sanctioned princedom. On the other hand, Christ Jesus set Jehovah, the supreme one, always before Him. Therefore He did not move from His ordained position. He did not think the devil's aim of equality with God a thing to be grasped at (Phil. 2:5 Newberry). The mind of Christ determined to obey the sovereign will of the Father unto death. "Wherefore God hath highly exalted Him, and given Him a name that is above every name: that in the name of Jesus every knee should bow, of things in heaven, and things in earth, and things under the earth; and that every tongue should confess that Jesus Christ is Lord, to the glory of God the Father" (Phil. 2:9-11).

In both deportment and design the devil was the exact opposite. He said in his heart, "I will ascend into heaven, I will exalt my throne above the stars of God" (Isa. 14:13-14). How exquisitely different is Christ's own description of Himself, "I am meek and lowly in heart" (Matt. 11:29). His attitude is expressed in the words, "I came down from heaven, not to do Mine own will, but the will of Him that sent Me" (John 6:38), and in the grave crisis of Gethsemane, "O My Father, if it be possible, let this cup pass from Me: nevertheless not as I will, but as Thou wilt.... Thy will be done" (Matt. 26:39-42). No one else ever obeyed to the same degree of submission as He did as the Son of Man. He lived and labored in full subjection to the will and Word of God. He was made sin for us, He who knew no sin (II Cor. 5:21). He was made a little lower than the angels for the suffering of death. He was made a surety of a better covenant (Heb. 2:7; 7:22). He was made a curse for us

(Gal. 3:13). Christ glorified not Himself to be made a High Priest (Heb. 5:5).

The disciples were frequently discussing among themselves whose lot it would be to have position and prominence in the kingdom of God. One of the commendable features prominent in the life of Joseph was this very matter; he never maneuvered to gain position or prominence in Egypt. Christ Himself sought not, from the leaders of His day, one spark of fame, of light one single ray. He replied to the criticism of His accusers by living a blameless life. When referring to the Father, He alone could say without fear of contradiction, "I do always those things that please Him" (John 8:29). The Father verified His claim from Heaven by affirming, "This is My beloved Son, in whom I am well pleased" (Matt. 3:17).

How sedulously and persistently the enemy sought to deflect Him from His mission, directly by subtle temptation offering Him all the kingdoms of the world for an act of homage, without including the kingdom of the world which he himself held. When this attempted persuasion failed, he next tried to dissuade Christ from His purpose indirectly through the affection of His earthly relationships, and even used Peter, to whom Christ said, "Get thee behind Me, Satan ... for thou savourest not the things that be of God" (Matt. 12:46-48; 16:22-23). Take particular notice of the Lord's use of the word "temptations" in the plural: "Ye are they which have continued with Me in My temptations" (Luke 22:28). He did not call His disciples until after His temptation in the wilderness, and He made this statement before His temptation in Gethsemane. This indicates that He was tempted throughout His ministry.

In the final attempts to prevent Christ from rendering obedience unto death the devil marshaled all his forces for attack. The chief priests and captains of the Temple, with the elders, all combined in a terrific onslaught, even while the overwhelming pressure and agonizing struggle of Gethsemane convulsed Him to bloodlike sweat. Said He, "This is your hour, and the power of darkness." At this stage He was tempted to appeal to the Father who would have dispatched more than 288,000 angels to deliver Him from their wicked hands (see I Chron. 27:1). Then He added, "how then shall the Scriptures be fulfilled, that thus it must be?" (Matt. 26:54)

> Many trials He had endured,
> To pain and sorrows' grief inured;
> Had manifold temptations met,
> But faced the sorest trial yet.
>
> Gethsemane! He's so distraught,
> The hardest battle must be fought.
> The conflict of the ages raged;
> The strongest powers were here engaged.
>
> When David's glory reached its crest
> Twelve legions were at *his* behest.
> Christ had the right to intercede,
> Receive response to meet His need.
>
> More than legions twelve would come
> If He requested such a sum,
> To save Him from their wicked hands,
> And take Him back to heavenly strands.
>
> To yield, would undermine His Love,
> And grieve the Father's heart above.
> He triumphed! God's obedient Son,
> Thy Will, not Mine; the Battle's won.

The enemy completed his diabolical attempts to deflect by hurling reproaches at Him in the hour of His excruciating pain on the cross. "If He be the King of Israel, let Him now come down from the cross, and we will believe Him. He trusted in God; let Him deliver Him now, if He will have Him: For He said, I am the Son of God. The thieves . . . cast the same in His teeth" (Matt. 27:42-44). He had power to vacate the cross, power to destroy those that mocked Him, but He endured the cross and despised the shame, although the reproach broke His heart (Ps. 69:20). The Father requested it; nothing could divert His conformity to the Father's will, cost what it may. Having glorified the Father in His obedience unto death, the Father glorified Him in resurrection. He was raised from the dead by the glory of the Father (Rom. 6:4). Christ went into death both gladly and rejoicingly, we are told, because He had already gained a twofold victory over evil, in both its originating energy and alluring power. Therefore He was confident of victory when bearing evil in responsibility on man's behalf.

As Dr. Bonner wrote:

Here we may rest midway as on a sacred height
The darkest and the brightest day gleaming before our sight,
From that dark depth of woe, wherein His feet have trod,
We rise to heights of blest repose, His Love prepares with God.

By the perfect obedience of His undeflected service He defeated the devil, magnified the Law, glorified the Father, and confirmed His own worthiness in relation to Lordship, Heirship, Mediatorship, and Judgeship, as presented in the four visions of the Revelation given to the Apostle John on Patmos. He is the undeflected, undefeated, undefiled Holy One. Hallelujah, what a Saviour!

THE UNIFIER

Other sheep I have ... them also I must bring ... there shall be one flock and one Shepherd (John 10:16).

That they all may be one; as Thou, Father, art in Me, and I in Thee, that they also may be one in Us (John 17:21).

In the dispensation of the fulness of times He might gather together in one all things in Christ (Eph. 1:10).

Till we all arrive unto the unity of the faith (Eph. 4:13 Newberry).

One place (Gen. 1:9). One flesh (Gen. 2:24).

The Scriptures reveal the unification of all things as being God's great and gracious purpose. He made known the mystery of His will, which determines the gathering together in one of all things in Christ (Eph. 1:9-10). Christ Himself is the Unifier, "That ... He should gather together in one the children of God that were scattered abroad" (John 11:52).

This pictures the complete establishment of an age-abiding unity in love and loveliness. Yea, it presents an eternal peace in purity and perfectness, and indicates absolute harmony in holiness and happiness forever.

The Scriptures refer to the word "one" over two thousand times from the first chapter in Genesis to the last but one in Revelation. Four hundred and sixty of these occur in the first five books, Genesis to Deuteronomy, and among the many expressions we find one flesh, one people, one Tabernacle, one law, one ordinance, and one Lord. In the first five books of the New Testament there are four hundred and forty-four occurrences of the word "one"; these include one Master, one God, one Shepherd, one Flock, one Son, one Lord, one Father, one accord, and one place. The prominent objective Christ's ministry has in view is to establish oneness for the glory of God. This constitutes a unified society under a perfect and permanent government, as pictured in the New Jerusalem adorned as a bride. Wherefore, He has made known the mystery of His will, to gather together in one all things in Christ (Eph. 1:9-10). The Scriptures abound with the facilities that contribute to the realizing of this before-ordained objective.

The book of the Acts of the Apostles presents a fascinating picture of the ascended Lord operating from the position He holds at the right hand of God. He wields the sword of truth, sways the scepter of righteousness, holds the balance of power and exercises the might to subdue all things to Himself. His inconceivable power and incomparable love leaps all barriers, surmounts all obstacles, subdues all resistance, and will yet weld a friendly fellowship that abides forever.

To the philosophers of Greece, the cross of Christ is presented as the supreme expression of divine wisdom, for the unification of mankind. Therein may be seen the highest exhibition of heavenly love to attract, the greatest demonstration of divine grace to appeal, and the brightest ray of celestial hope to arrest attention, and cause acceptance of God's plan. Christ, who is the power of God and the wisdom of God, has the ability to baptize Jew and Gentile into one body.

The body is one and hath many members...for by one Spirit are we all baptized into one body (I Cor. 1:24; 12:12-13).

In view of all the different languages, diverse customs, racial and religious disparities, the fetters of legalism, the ritual of ceremonialism, and the breaches in racialism, who but Christ can from these worldwide conditions create harmony, amity, and unity? Christ is the solution to every universal problem. There is in Him neither Jew nor Greek; there is in Him neither bond nor free; there is in Him neither male nor female; for ye are all *one* in Christ Jesus (Gal. 3:28 Newberry). To this we may add, there is neither Barbarian nor Scythian; neither circumcision nor uncircumcision; but Christ is all and in all (Col. 3:11). Therefore, we are assured that Christ will remove national conflict, remedy class clash, rescind sex contention, rectify racial cleavage, and remit religious controversy. These are the five main avenues of strife and contention throughout the world. Christ Himself is to be manifestly the sole Administrator of nations; the only accomplished Arbitrator to end all class disparity; the one prevailing authority to terminate sex contention; the Advocate supreme to counteract all racial discrimination; and the Almighty who will destroy every phase of religious disputes. He will finally and forever abolish all discord, divided opinion, and disaffection, and unify the regenerated hosts in harmony and holiness forever. Little wonder that poets have been enraptured, musicians captivated, and artists in every age entranced when contemplating Christ and His eternal purpose of unification.

The Ephesian message depicts the harmonization of all things in Christ, and illustrates the aim under the figures of the structure of a body controlled by one head; the sanctuary of a building constructed upon one foundation; the society of a bride in the companionship of one bridegroom; and the soldiers of a battalion under the command of one lord. Christ stands in relationship to the body as the one Head for unanimity, to the building as the one Constructor for uniformity, to the bride as the one Bond for unity, and to the battalion as the one Lord for universality of control.

The Philippian record deals with the mind of Christ in service under four specific aspects in the four chapters: these are the mind of unity, the mind of humility, the mind of constancy, and the mind of capability.

We are bidden to stand fast in one spirit with one mind (Phil. 1:27). Be like-minded having the same love of one accord of one mind.... Let this mind be in you which was also in Christ Jesus (Phil. 2:2,5). One-mindedness leads to one objective, "This one thing I do" (Phil. 3:13). Christ, by offering Himself in sacrificial service, demonstrated the loveliness of His unselfish mind, the lowliness of His understanding heart, and the limitlessness of His good and perfect will.

The magnitude of Christ's supernatural work, reflected in all this, is incomprehensible. He transforms the natural into the spiritual, He translates from the temporal to the eternal, and He transmutes from the mortal to the immortal. Among the many profound declarations Christ made, this one stands out majestically, "Behold, I make all things new" (Rev. 21:5).

THE UNDERMOST

Verily I say to you, Among those that are born of women there hath not risen a greater than John the Baptist: notwithstanding he that is *least* in the kingdom of heaven is greater than he (Matt. 11:11).

He that is *least* among you all, the same shall be great (Luke 9:48).

Never! never! never before nor since, has there ever been such a demonstration of love displayed! The one highest in honor becomes lowest in humiliation. "Thou hast laid Me in the lowest pit, in darkness, in the deeps" (Ps. 88:6). Although the most blessed in Heaven (Ps. 72:19), He is made a curse for us on earth (Gal. 3:13). He who is richest in glory, becomes poverty-stricken for our sakes, that we might be rich (II Cor. 8:6). The strongest becomes weakest, "My strength is dried up like a potsherd" (Ps. 22:15). The perfectly sinless one is made sin for us (II Cor. 5:21). He that is inconceivably lovely, yea, altogether lovely, is disfigured beyond recognition. "His visage was so marred more than any man, and His form more than the sons of men" (Isa. 52:14). He descended from the glory He had with the Father before the world was, to be nailed in the midst of thieves to a brutal cross (John 19:18). From the majestic sovereignty of a celestial manhood on the throne of the universe (Ezek. 1:26), to the insignificant state expressed in the words, "I am a worm, and no man; a reproach of men, and despised of the people" (Ps. 22:6). This figure describes the very features of manhood as having been obliterated.

When the disciples were discussing who should be the greatest, Christ said to them, "He that is *least* among you all, the same shall be great" (Luke 9:48). "Shall be great" are the words used of Him in the angelic announcement, "He shall be great, and shall be called the Son of the Highest" (Luke 1:32). Wherefore the word "least" refers to Himself.

Jonathan, the eldest son of King Saul, stepped down from his right and title to the throne of Israel for David's sake, because he loved David as his own soul. In so doing in very deed he acted chivalrously, but in this case, the Son of the Highest stoops to become the least and demonstrates His matchless love to mankind, in that while we were yet sinners, He died for us. He that is uppermost in superior sovereignty became the undermost in sacrificial suffering, that He might save to the uttermost them that come unto God by Him (Heb. 7:25).

The Spirit of God draws our attention to the fact that He that ascended to the right hand of the Majesty on high, first descended into the lower parts of the earth (Eph. 4:9); down to darkness and the deeps, to the deep mire, the deep waters, which prompted the prayer, "let [not] the deep swallow Me up" (Ps. 69). When Daniel the prophet was given a glimpse of our Lord's personal splendor, he declared in the light of it, that what he had previously regarded as comeliness was turned to corruption. From these topmost heights of dignified grandeur, our Saviour descended to the deepest depths of shame and ignominy for He said, "Thou hast known My reproach, and My shame, and My dishonour" (Ps. 69:19). The Jews even insinuated that He was born out of wedlock (John 8:41). Furthermore, in place of receiving the admiration and

adoration of millions of angels, in both praise and worship, He
became the song of the drunkards, and the curse word of the
wicked (Ps. 69:12; 102:8). The cross is spoken of as His grave,
which He made with the wicked and with the rich in His death.
For Joseph of Arimathaea was rich and provided a new tomb
for His body.

The birthplace of the Son of Man was not considered
least in importance among the dignified of Judah, but He was
(Matt. 2:6). No king received less of the nation's regard, they
esteemed Him not (Isa. 53:3). No governor was so little
respected and obeyed, and no prophet was taken less notice of
by the rulers of the land. Although as the Christ He fulfilled to
the letter the laws laid down in Israel for the selecting of
prophet, priest, and king, He was least esteemed. A king's
tribute money was never paid to Him; a governor's residence
was not provided; and a retinue of servants was never marshaled to assist in His many activities.

Notice in Mark's record, when the disciples were discussing who should be greatest, Christ said to them, "If any
... desire to be first, the same shall be last of all, and servant
of all" (Mark 9:35). His use of first and last is a further mark of
His identity, for He used it in reference to Himself five times in
the book of Revelation. He also stressed humility as one of the
supreme essentials of greatness. The perfect excellence of this
feature was never expressed more fully by any but Himself.
Think of the Lord of creation washing the feet of His disciples
and affirming, "If I then, your Lord and Master, have washed
your feet; ye also ought to wash one another's feet" (John
13:14).

His teaching was always clear and plain. Said He,
"Whosoever will be great among you, let him be your
minister; And whosoever will be chief among you, let him be
your servant: Even as the Son of man came not to be
ministered unto, but to minister, and to give His life a ransom
for many" (Matt. 20:26-28). In the doing of this He humbled
Himself and became obedient unto death, even the death of
the cross (Phil. 2:8).

Christ was defamed, discredited, and dishonored more

than any other God-sent messenger. His words were misconstrued and misinterpreted by many. The kindly deeds of His delivering power were attributed to His being in league with devilry, while His claim of having power on earth to forgive sins was termed blasphemy. The descriptions figuratively expressed of His sufferings are terrible in the extreme. Withered like grass; scorched like a potsherd; consumed like smoke; stricken by rulers; scandalized by priests; smitten of God; and afflicted. His wondrous love constrained Him to descend from the greatest position in the glory of Heaven to become the least and lowest in human esteem. This is the greatest evidence of real love in world history. "He hath looked down from the height of His sanctuary; from heaven did the LORD behold the earth; To hear the groaning of the prisoner; to loose those that are appointed to death; To declare the name of the LORD in Zion" (Ps. 102:19). What a descent it meant for Him, who was seated at the uppermost pinnacle of celestial honor, to come down to the lowest strata of society among publicans and sinners, and a multitude of impotent folk: amazing pity, astounding mercy, and love beyond degree.

> Loved, by the Highest in Glory
> Who stooped to be least in esteem;
> Whose gospel tells us the story
> Of love so intensely supreme.

THE UNDEFILED

Wherefore He is able to save them to the uttermost that come to God by Him, seeing He ever liveth to make intercession for them. For such a high priest became us who is holy, guileless, undefiled, separated from sinners and made higher than the heavens (Heb. 7:25-26).

These words describe the holiness of character and heavenly state of Christ as High Priest, in the distinguished dignity of His moral perfectness. He is the most suitable, acceptable, and admirable person to officiate in the presence of God for mankind. The added note of assurance that follows should hearten every believing soul. We have such a High Priest, who is set on the right hand of the throne of the Majesty in the heavens (Heb. 8:1).

We have great cause to rejoice, because the perfections of His person can never know defilement. The faithfulness of His friendly love is without defect and the constancy of His considerate care is without decline. Our High Priest can never be dislodged or deposed; He is ordained in office forever (Heb. 7:21). His merit can never be denied or diminished, as the Lamb once slain, nor His mercy depleted. For "the mercy of the LORD is from everlasting to everlasting upon them that fear Him," that is, revere Him (Ps. 103:17). As the High Priest, how very indispensable He is for our maintenance, sustenance, and guidance. Who is able to evaluate His wonderful wisdom and worthiness? No one can calculate the wealth of His riches in spiritual virtues and the weight of His resources in spiritual gifts. How impossible it is to estimate the values of His sacrificial merit or tabulate the treasures of His loving-kindness which He dispenses constantly to millions of the redeemed. An aroma of sweet spices and a lovely savor of fragrant perfume emanate from the spotless robes of this immortal High Priest. Beauty is combined with purity, comeliness with sincerity, and grace with glory.

One of the radiant predictions in one of the most precious psalms declares: "The LORD God is a sun and shield: The LORD will give grace and glory: no good . . . will He withhold from them that walk uprightly" (Ps. 84:11).

Remember the regency of our High Priest is a throne of grace to which we are bidden to come boldly and to obtain mercy and grace (Heb. 4:16). The same is pictured as encompassed by a rainbow which is the covenant token (Rev. 4:3; Gen. 9:12). This iridescent iris of light is often seen as a worldwide arch, spanning the watery clouds. What an assurance of His precious, generous, gracious LOVE! The rainbow is the radiant expression of grace in color. All color mingles and meets in the rainbow in iridescent splendor; likewise all beauties merge in Christ who is the Angel of the covenant (Gen. 22:15-18). He is identified in the Messenger of the Covenant (Mal. 3:1). The word "messenger" is the same as rendered "angel" elsewhere. The final mark of identity is given in Revelation 10:1 where He is displayed as the mighty angel with the rainbow on His head.

Red is the color of redemption, the Redeemer elucidates and clarifies for us the true nature, purpose, will, and love of God. The ultrared ray enables the commander of a liner to see ahead in a fog. Red speaks of *lucidity,* making the obscure obvious. "After that the kindness and love of God our Saviour ... appeared" (Tit. 3:4-5; Eph. 1:6; 2:5). Jacob said: "The angel which redeemed me from all evil" (Gen. 48:16), wherefore the Redeemer is called the mighty One of Jacob, and the mighty One of Israel (Isa. 49:26; 1:24).

Yellow expresses repossession. Golden wealth is seen in the flower world where there is a predominance of yellow flowers. Abraham was very rich and perceived the promise of an everlasting possession (Gen. 17:8). So are we, according to His abundant mercy—for He hath begotten us again to a living hope—to an inheritance incorruptible, undefiled, which fadeth not away (I Pet. 1:3-4). Ye know the grace of our Lord Jesus Christ, though rich, for your sakes He became poor, that ye might be rich (II Cor. 8:9). Yellow bespeaks *luxury.* Boaz, the redeemer of Ruth, made luxurious provision for his bride whom he purchased, for he was a mighty man of wealth (Ruth 2:1).

Our Redeemer is both wealthy and mighty, the possessor of Heaven and earth, heir of all things, who purchased the Church, His bride, with His own blood (Acts 20:28). The luxuries our Redeemer provides for the present life are evidenced in the use made of the words "abound," "abundance," and "abundantly," which occur twenty-five times in Second Corinthians. Notice the far more exceeding and eternal weight of glory (II Cor. 4:17), also the exceeding riches of His grace (Eph. 2:7).

Orange is liberation (Titus 2:11). Remember July 12, 1689, the Orangeman's day, and what it suggests. Christ is the Liberator, wherefore let us "stand fast in the *liberty* wherewith Christ has made us free" (Gal. 5:1). "Where the Spirit of the

Lord is, there is liberty" (II Cor. 3:17). Zechariah the priest blessed God for redemption and the mercy of deliverance from the hand of enemies (Luke 1:68-72). Christ preached deliverance for the captives (Luke 4:18). "If the Son therefore shall make you free, ye shall be free indeed" (John 8:36).

Green is satisfaction. My grace is sufficient for thee (II Cor. 12:9). With long life will I satisfy him, and show him My salvation (Ps. 91:16). Green predominates in this world and is the most restful color. So it does in heaven's rainbow which in sight is like to an emerald (Rev. 4:3). *Longevity* is expressed in this evergreen display. Your heart shall live forever (Ps. 22:26). The Living Bread sustains everlastingly (John 6:51). Listen to this: "Now our Lord Jesus Christ Himself, and God, even our Father, which hath loved us, and hath given us everlasting consolation and good hope through grace" (II Thess. 2:16).

Blue is devotion. The high priest's robe was all of blue, the figure of loyalty. He is "a merciful and faithful high priest in things pertaining to God" (Heb. 2:17). Christ is our High Priest and in His fidelity He is unchanging, unvarying, and undeviating in loyalty. In Him mercy and truth meet, righteousness and peace kiss each other (Ps. 85:10). "God is able to make all grace abound toward you; that ye, always having all sufficiency in all things, may abound to every good work" (II Cor. 9:8). Christ was full of grace, therefore perfectly loyal even to death. His grace can make us loyal.

The indigo of intensity and immensity. "Which long after you for the exceeding grace of God in you. Thanks be unto God for His unspeakable gift" (II Cor. 9:14-15). Piling benefit upon benefit, mercy upon mercy, gift upon gift, denotes the *legacy* of His great love. This exceeds all our conceptions (I Cor. 2:9), and surpasses comprehension (Eph. 3:19).

The violet of hope. "Hope to the end for the grace that is to be brought unto you at the revelation of Jesus Christ" (I Pet. 1:13). This attractive violet color is a delicate purple which is attached to lordship and kingship. Remember the prophecy, "Behold, thy King cometh unto thee . . . lowly, and riding upon an ass" (Zech. 9:9). Lowliness is not littleness, but loftiness condescending to bow and stoop to show mercy. The lowly one is the *lordly* one, righteous and royal in His regality, who will return to reign. He is the royal High Priest, exalted on the rainbow circled throne of grace, to whom we are bidden to come boldly. From Him we may secure justifying grace, enriching grace, saving grace, sufficing grace, abounding grace, exceeding grace, and inspiring grace, as represented in the rainbow colors. How attractively, appealingly, and winsomely this undefiled High Priest seeks to draw us to His loving heart and bestow from His liberal hands the abundant grace and abounding mercy from His infinite fullness!

THE UPBRAIDER

Then began He to upbraid the cities wherein most of His mighty works were done, because they repented not: Woe to thee, Chorazin! Woe to thee Bethsaida.... And thou, Capernaum ... if the mighty works, which have been done in thee, had been done in Sodom, it should have remained to this day.... It shall be more tolerable for the land of Sodom in the day of judgment, than for thee (Matt. 11:20-24).

To upbraid means to chide or accuse for that which is shameful. There are certain circumstances in which it is possible to show an attitude that is utterly inexcusable. Our Lord's ministry was of such a beneficent character, His words so winsome, His appeal so attractive, His message so meaningful, and His deeds so divinely great that to ignore Him and treat His mighty works with indifference warranted the sternest rebuke. Some folk argue that the word "destruction" causes that which is destroyed to become nonexistent.

The people of Sodom were destroyed, but the Lord told the inhabitants of the cities of Galilee that it would be more tolerable for the Sodomites in the day of judgment than for them. Therefore all the departed must again appear before His judgment throne. No one will be able to make the excuse of not having been present in His day to witness His mighty works. His eternal power and Godhead are manifest in His mighty work of creation which is clearly seen (Rom. 1:20). His eternal purpose of salvation is made known through the revelation of His Word. The infinite wisdom of His everlasting covenant has been confirmed by the manifestation of His Son, which is marked on our calendars of time as B.C. and A.D. The immutability of His will and counsel have been clarified by the ministration of His Spirit.

No person or group of people can place an embargo on God's wisdom and work. His work of creation appeals to the human reason, His Word of revelation appeals to the human conscience, His wisdom expressed in a manifestation appeals the human heart, and His manifold provision in administration appeals to the human will; he that willeth to do His will shall know if these things are of God (John 7:17). To reject such demonstrations of God's power, purpose, presence, and provision results in a hardened mind, a hardened conscience, a hardened heart, and a hardened will.

The Scriptures declare that the conscience may become seared as with a hot iron (I Tim. 4:2). Wherefore all are responsible in these matters and we are to be weighed in the balances, according to our privileges, opportunities, and attitudes, by one from whom nothing is hidden and who has a perfect understanding of all the circumstances and conditions of our environments.

Our Lord is totally immune from making any mistakes. There is no case He misunderstands, misconstrues, miscalculates, or misjudges. His knowledge is not second hand; He knew all men, and needed not that any should testify of man, for He knew what was in man (John 2:25). This is true as covering the whole concourse of humanity from beginning to end, for He Himself is the First and the Last (Isa. 41:4).

He it is that observed Naaman as being an honorable man, a great man with his master, the king of Syria, and a mighty man of valor, but also, who was a leper (II Kings 5:1). The Lord always commends where credit is due, but condemns when the deeds done are corrupt. He upholds those that seek help, "I will uphold thee with the right hand of My righteousness" (Isa. 41:10; Ps. 37:17). He also upbraids all that pay no heed to the many daily demonstrations of His love and mercy (Matt. 11:20), or that fail to believe that He is faithful in fulfilling His Word (John 11:40; Mark 16:14).

The Prophet Daniel refers to this one who upbraids as the Ancient of days, the hair of whose head is like pure wool (Dan. 7:9). The Apostle John describes His head and His hairs as white like wool, as white as snow (Rev. 1:14). This figure of speech signifies a mature mind, coupled with purity of wisdom and sincerity of motive. Therefore He never does or says anything that is unkind, unreal, unjust, or unwise.

THE UPHOLDER

> Who being the brightness of His glory, and the express image of His person, and upholding all things by the word of His power, when He had by Himself purged our sins, sat down on the right hand of the Majesty on high (Heb. 1:3).
>
> Uphold me according to Thy Word.... Hold Thou me and I shall be safe (Ps. 119:116-117).

The significance of this declaration as associated with the matchless range of Christ's upholding might and majesty lies beyond the capacity of our minds to grasp. The magnitude of Messiah's power to maintain all that He has made is most magnificent. It is necessary, in order to uphold all things continuously, that the Upholder must be a timeless being, of endless personality, in exercise of tireless energy, and in ceaseless control.

Christ upholds, by the Word of His power, the laws He has legislated, the life He has generated, the light He has initiated, the love He has demonstrated, the truth He has originated, the grace He has perfected, and the purpose He has determined. None of these spiritual values can be overthrown.

One of man's greatest problems lies in the difficulty he encounters in maintaining the structures he erects, the machines he invents, the enterprises he starts, and the institutions he founds. Wear and tear, decay and deterioration, moth and rust, canker and corrosion mar and mutilate his finest works. Howbeit with Christ it is far otherwise. Concerning His creation it is written, "He spake, and it was done; He commanded, and it stood fast" (Ps. 33:9). By that same word the universe is upheld, for the Scriptures declare, "The heavens and the earth, which are now, by the same word are kept in store" (II Pet. 3:7). Any thought of incapacity or incompetence finds no place in the mind of this Upholder. His matchless might, His sovereign strength, His preeminent power, His infinite wisdom, and His immutable will assure absolute ability to sustain and maintain His eternal purpose.

The perfect balance of His many wonderfully blended attributes and divine virtues should not only captivate our rapt attention and real affection, but draw out our hearts in continual adoration and worship. The Christ of God is forever abidingly consistent, administratively competent, and altogether complacent in every office He fills. His ability to uphold is unquestionable and His authority to maintain undeniable, for He has done so for thousands of years, and continues so to do.

Amid the strenuous experiences of life, David in his kingship realized that, in his resolve to follow the Lord, he was upheld (Ps. 63:8). He definitely understood that the one in whom he placed his trust was resolute in purpose, resourceful in power, and altogether reliable in His faithfulness to maintain His people. Some men of noble rank and high position have great responsibilities devolving upon them. Yet not one among them is competent enough to uphold any one section of this amazing universe, even for one day, let alone the entire system of things for centuries.

The placing of the planets in their orbits, the directing of the stars in their courses, and the controlling of the winds in their circuits are evidences of the vastness of the Lord's ability to make and maintain.

The question is twice asked in Isaiah's prophecy, "To whom will ye liken Me?" (Isa. 40:18,25) These are followed by two more questions, "Hast thou not known? Hast thou not heard, that the everlasting God, the LORD, the Creator of the ends of the earth, faintest not neither is weary?" (Isa. 40:28) The chapter twice over mentions the three factors that assure His ability to uphold; they consist of His might, strength, and power (Isa. 40:26,29). Eighty references will be found to these three words in the prophecy. No sign of decrepitude ever weakens His might. No palsying influence of old age saps away His strength. No withering frailty can ever deplete the majesty of His power. We may take notice also that mention is made of "creator, create, and created" twenty-one times in Isaiah's prophecy. This is the very one who pledges, "I will uphold thee with the right hand of My righteousness" (Isa. 41:10). Do we need to be reminded that our Saviour is Creator, as well as Upholder? He is Maker as well as Maintainer. He is the Originator as well as Overseer. He is Counselor as well as Caretaker. He is Sovereign as well as Shepherd. He is Lord as well as Leader. He is the Sun of Righteousness as well as Sustainer, upholding all things by the Word of His power. What a radiant prospect looms ahead when we dwell upon this fact! What ceaseless confidence is begotten by this assurance, in anticipation of endless joy! What measureless delight wells up in the mind at the thought of having one in supreme authority, who is changeless in His gracious sympathy and governing sufficiency!

Our blessed Lord certainly merits every rank of renown, every position of preeminence, every station of highest honor, every trophy of triumph, every regalia of royalty, every regency of righteousness, and every crown of conquest. Christ is perfectly titled as Upholder, for He upholds all that is pure and precious, all that is good and gracious, all that is fair and lustrous, all that is true and virtuous, all that is real and righteous, and all that is grand and glorious. Yea, if we may be permitted to state the matter more briefly, Christ upholds in every realm all that is morally, officially, spiritually, and judicially perfect, and therefore none of these qualities can perish.

From a paragraph in the book of Proverbs we may observe that this authoritative ruler is spoken of as "a King

against whom there is no uprising." Four of His qualifying
capacities are illustrated by the use of four suggestive figures.
A lion, which indicates He is strongest; a gazelle, which intimates He is swiftest; a he-goat, which implies He is sturdiest
(for this animal has never been known to slip); finally, a king
in complete control, informing us that He is stateliest (Prov.
30:29-31). In this pictorial way He is set forth in the mastery of
His power, in the ministry of His purpose, in the mystery of His
passion, and in the majesty of His prevailing. If we would state
these four features in another way, let us suggest that they
depict Christ in His capable ability, His constant activity, His
consistent advocacy, and His continual authority.

Many are the formidable capacities of the one who is the
Upholder of all things. The Scriptures present Him as being
adequately able to sustain the entire universe. The function
Christ fills in this select office is one of the grandest presentations of His Almightiness. The book of Job is aflame with the
use of this title, "the Almighty," which occurs thirty-one
times, and the person referred to harnesses His might to
minister to man's needs. "Behold God is mighty and despiseth
not any, He is mighty in strength and wisdom" (Job 36:5).
King David stated this same truth in a very impressive
declaration, "Thy kingdom is an everlasting kingdom, and
Thy dominion endureth throughout all generations. The
LORD upholdeth all that fall and raiseth up all ... that be
bowed down" (Ps. 145:13-14). He is heir of all things ...
upholding all things by the Word of His power (Heb. 1:2-3).
His Word supplies, supports, and sustains all spiritual
requirements. Wherefore let us remember that the words of
our Lord are unparalleled, His sayings are unequaled, and His
teachings are unexcelled by any one, anywhere.

The Upholder

The Maker of this wide wide world,
　　Designer of the spheres;
Upholder of the universe
　　And all that now appears.

Sustainer of the sun and moon,
  The seasons, and the tides;
Revealer of the Father's love
  And all of truth besides.

Upholding by His Word of power,
  The works His hands have made;
In righteousness and joy and peace
  His kingdom cannot fade.

Besides this ponderous universe,
  Upheld by His strong hand;
He ministers to human needs
  In every peopled land.

He molds the empires that arise,
  He overthrows their pride;
He wields the scepter of the skies,
  His rule and reign abide.

THE UNVEILED

The Revelation of Jesus Christ which God gave to Him (Rev. 1:1).

Two Greek words draw our attention as we approach our subject, "apocrypha" and "apocalypse." The first means to veil, the latter to unveil, which is the word rendered "revelation" in our English versions, hence our title, The Unveiled.

Amid the abounding array of marble monuments erected in honor of great personalities, or throughout the massive volume of national records describing renowned victories, or among all the memorial tablets commemorating deeds of valor and sacrificial service that have been made throughout the centuries, none is comparable to the magnificence of this unveiling of Jesus Christ and the magnitude of His triumph. The purpose of setting forth the splendors of the Son of Man, and to reveal the grandeur of His glorious person, constitutes the predominant aim of the revelation here given. We are gripped with an overwhelming sense of awe, as we open the first portion and gaze with adoring wonder on the stately form of the majestic person portrayed. He is disclosed in the exercise of irresistible power, with inescapable, all-perceiving, and penetrating eyes, and in exercise of His manifold prerogatives. This is the Almighty (Rev. 1:8), the altogether lovely Son of Man, our Revealer, Redeemer, Reconciler, and Regenerator.

What displays we meet with here of our Lord's spiritual vigor and virtue, of His governmental might and majesty, of His mediatorial mercy and ministry, and of His judicial authority and ability, as disclosed in the four visions of this book!

What varieties of fascinating features, such as the scintillating stars, the shining sun, the majesty of mountains, the luster of light, the symphonies of sound, the cosmos of color, the melodies of music, the glint of gems, the purity of pearls, and glistening gold — all are combined in setting forth the beauties and glories of the Son of Man!

What outbursts of praise and worship, admiration and adoration, ascription and acclamation, celebration and commemoration are expressed in the seven grand doxologies contained in this unique unveiling!

What inexpressible pleasure God the Father enjoyed when disclosing His Son's true character and real credentials, for the purpose of showing to His bond servants the regal nature of His Well Beloved! To do this, three hundred and thirty references to the figures, shadows, symbols, types, patterns, persons, and buildings of the Old Testament are made.

Messiah's Monumental Masterpiece

> What cenotaphs and scrolls of fame,
> The nations of the earth can claim!
> Bedecking cities, hills, and coasts,
> To lionize their honored hosts.
>
> But here we turn to nobler heights,
> That e'en surpass the eagle's flights,
> And view in penmanship unpriced,
> The unveiled glories of the Christ.

He bears the wounds in cause of right,
 By virtue of redeeming might,
His battle marks forever tell
 The conflicts fought with sin and hell.

The keys of death and hades bring
 Immortal honors to the King,
As trophies of the vanquished foe,
 Who ne'er can rally from the blow.

The conquests of His love outvie
 The matchless splendors of the sky,
While scintillating glories trace
 The victories of His sovereign grace.

Emblazoned on His thigh, a name,
 The King of Kings, in living flame,
In righteousness He wages war
 To end all strife forevermore.

No other scroll in all the world,
 Besides this one, has been unfurled,
That magnifies a Victor's fame,
 Who glorified the Father's Name.

The grandest triumph yet remains,
 When He o'er this earth's kingdom reigns,
All other powers He will subdue,
 And in His right, make all things new.

When God granted these four matchless visions of the Son of Man to the Apostle John, on the Isle of Patmos, for the Church, He did in nowise ignore the facts and features of the previous manifestation, as recorded in the four Gospels. But in this case we are given a clear, comprehensive view of the supernal splendors of the Son of Man as they are known in the heavenly realm beyond. Each vision in turn carries through to completion one aspect in particular of the fourfold ministry of Christ, which He exercised when on earth. His Kinship was expressed in Matthew, His Heirship in Mark, His Mediatorship in Luke, and His Judgeship in John. Within these four messages of the gospel, the Saviour's title, "The Son of Man," appears eighty-four times. Under this designation He is displayed as being relatively, legally, morally, and judicially qualified to uphold and maintain the will, the Word, the wisdom, and the work of God. These four supreme obligations He discharges righteously, honorably, faithfully, and perfectly.

When God made this fourfold commitment to man, Adam disregarded the will, he disobeyed the Word, he distrusted the wisdom, and he dishonored the work of God.

Of Christ, the last Adam, the prophet predicted, "The pleasure of the LORD shall prosper in His hand" (Isa. 53:10).

This is precisely what Christ claimed when He said, "The Father loveth the Son, and hath given all things into His hand" (John 3:35). The Father verifies this fact in each of the visions of the unveiling.

The seven stars are in His right hand (Rev. 1:20).

The seven-sealed book is in His hand (Rev. 5:7).

The sacred censer is in His hand (Rev. 8:3-4).

The sharp sickle is in His hand (Rev. 14:14).

Everything committed to the Son of Man He keeps unimpaired (John 6:39). No merit or credit is given to mankind in the plan of salvation; in this sphere Christ alone is altogether worthy.

The divine unveiling is given with an appropriate array of splendor, which forever contributes the assurance that the person of Christ, who loved the Church and gave Himself for it, is greater than His love. That as Creator and Redeemer of the universe He is mightier, in strength of character, than all His wondrous works. That as the perfect Mediator, He is personally of greater value than the entire range of His mediative ministry. That as Maker of all things new, He Himself is of richer worth than anything He remakes.

Never before has there arisen, among the celebrities of earth, an Administrator capable of adequately undertaking for humanity in every sphere of jurisdiction. There has never been an Executor who could fully discharge every obligation of maintenance and completely fulfill all the requirements of both God and man. There has never emerged from any race of people a mediator capable enough in character and competence of satisfying Heaven's righteous claims of justice and of saving and justifying man from guilt and condemnation. There has never appeared in this world another Adjudicator with power to kill and make alive, who had a perfect knowledge of all men and events, with capability of dispensing unerring justice, because of being characterized by inherent comprehension and infinite knowledge.

The unveiling makes visible the manifold fullness that is in Christ Jesus, so that we may identify and interpret Him in a wide variety of ways. For instance, in the ecclesiastical sphere, the Son of Man is Revealer (Rev. 1—3), Redeemer (Rev. 4—7), Reconciler, (Rev. 8—13), and Regenerator (Rev. 14—22).

In the legal realm, the Son of Man is Kinsman (Rev. 1—3), Avenger (Rev. 4—7), Ransomer (Rev. 8—13), and Bridegroom (Rev. 14—22).

In the official realm, He is Administrator, Executor, Mediator, and Adjudicator.

In the vocational sphere, He is expressed in the lampstand, the brazen altar, the incense altar, and the laver. In relation to these vessels He appears walking, sitting, standing, and reaping.

In the typical sphere, He is identified in His Headship with seven stars, in His Heirship with seven seals, in His Mediatorship with seven trumpets, and in His Judgeship with seven vials.

In the historical sphere, He may be interpreted in relation to the Church, the creation, the commonwealth, and the cities.

We might add to these descriptive features of the unveiling the symbolical, ceremonial, and numerical, all of which are harnessed to contribute a richer portraiture of the indescribable, indispensable, and incomprehensible Christ. The enormous range of His personal greatness is so extensive in magnitude we must confine our remarks to a skeleton outline. Let us take but some of the features that are described, from each vision.

Firstly, the administrative authority of the empowered Son of Man in His proprietorship and counselorship (Rev. 1—3).

His lustrous preeminence: the Prince of kings (vs. 5).
His vicarious sacrifice: loosed by His own blood (vs. 5).
His precious love: to Him that loveth us (vs. 5).

His famous title: I am Alpha and Omega (vs. 8).

His gracious condescension: the Son of Man (vs. 13).

His gorgeous characteristics: His head to His feet described in figurative form (vss. 14-16).

His victorious prevailing: alive forevermore (vs. 18).

His tremendous power: seven stars in His hand (2:1).

His vigorous constancy: the First and Last (vs. 8).

His judicious supervision: hath the sharp sword (vs. 12).

His prodigious credentials: the Son of God, eyes as a flame of fire (vs. 18).

His stupendous potentials: seven stars, seven spirits (3:1).

His spacious prerogatives: holy, true, hath key of David (vs. 7).

His ponderous range of renown: Amen, the beginning (vs. 14).

His glorious exaltation: sat down with My Father (vs. 21).

This brief outline describes His personal distinctions and is both massive and marvelous. We may say, in the light of it, that He is the basic substance of all revealed truth; the prophetic seal of all prophecy; the graphic focus of all types and shadows; the specific key to all Scripture; the dynamic power of all administration; the realistic expression of all the fullness of Deity; the intrinsic wealth of all spiritual riches; and the climactic goal of God's eternal purpose.

Secondly, the executive activity of the enthroned Son of Man in His Heirship and Governorship (Rev. 4–7).

In vision two, Christ is unveiled in His official capacity as the Executor, Redeemer, and Governor. His governmental administration is described in all the faithfulness of His Shepherdhood, having laid down His life for the sheep, He maintains His glorified flock. "The Lamb which is in the midst of the throne shall shepherd them and shall lead them unto living fountains of waters and God shall wipe away all tears from their eyes" (Rev. 7:17 Newberry).

His imperial dignity: seated on the throne (Rev. 4:2).

His celestial beauty: like a jasper and sardine stone (vs. 3).

His official capacity: rainbow circled, covenant token (vs. 3).

His creatorial authority: Thou hast created (vs. 11).

His sensational ability: prevailed to take the book (Rev. 5:5).

His supernatural sovereignty: Lion of tribe of Judah (vs. 5).

His crucial identity: a Lamb as it had been slain (vs. 6).

His universal victory: Thou art worthy (vs. 9).

His presidential propriety: opener of the seals (Rev. 6:1).

His governmental suzerainty: lion, ox, man, and eagle (vss.

1–8; Rev. 4:6–8); the genera of creation; these living ones are referred to eight times in vision two.

His magesterial scrutiny: how long O Lord: judge and avenge (Rev. 6:10).

His judicial regality: hide from face on throne and wrath of the Lamb (vs. 16).

His supernal finality: Lamb in midst of throne leads and wipes away all tears (Rev. 7:17).

The manifold expressions of His majestic power and wisdom as Creator are countless. While the magnitude of His merit as Redeemer is measureless, these two inestimable features form the substance of the second vision. We may sum up the section by saying He ever abides the same; the honor of His Heirship never declines; the vigor of His vitality never varies; the savor of His sacrifice never subsides; the fervor of His faithfulness never falters; the ardor of His advocacy never alters; the splendor of His strength never spoils; the valor of His victory never vanishes; and the favor of His friendship never falters. Christ alone is altogether worthy, absolutely worthy, and age-abidingly worthy.

Thirdly, the reconciliative advocacy of the exalted Son of Man in His Mediatorship and Suretyship (Rev. 8–13).

Let us scan the majesty of His Messiahship and Mediatorship which should command our attention and admiration in vision three.

His stately integrity: the Great High Priest in angelic form with the golden censor, before the throne (Rev. 8:3).

His sublime purity: "much incense was given to Him." The pure incense, a perfume, a perfection, pure and holy, signifies the personal attributes of Christ the High Priest (Exod. 30:34–35).

His superlative sanctity: with perfect mediative ability to present the prayers of all saints upon the golden altar (Rev. 8:3).

His stipulated royalty: the golden incense altar had its crown of gold (Exod. 30:3). In Christ, Kinghood and Priesthood combine (Heb. 7:1–3).

His supreme suitability: the Lord's moral merit assures representative consultation and continual intercession (Rev. 8:4; Heb. 7:25).

His significant activity: censor filled with fire from the altar and cast to the earth (Rev. 8:5). Only Luke records He came to do this (Luke 12:49). Result (Acts 7:30).

His sacerdotal capacity: the blowing of trumpets was a priestly vocation (Num. 10:8). The High Priest controls this, and administers it from the heavenly sanctuary (Rev. 8:6).

His sensational advocacy: a voice from the four horns of the golden altar (Rev. 9:13). Advocating the release of destructive forces to slay. See Amos 9:1,4: "I will set Mine eyes upon them for evil and not for good." The Prophet Daniel declares the same: "As written in the law of Moses, all this evil is come upon us" (Daniel 9:13). "I form the light, and create darkness: I make peace and create evil" (Isa. 45:7). That is, in the sense of calamity. "Shall there be evil in a city, and the Lord hath not done?" (Amos 3:6)

His steadfast fidelity: the cloud and the rainbow identify Him as the Angel of the covenant (Rev. 10:1; Gen. 9:12–13; 48: 16; Isa. 60:16).

His startling universality: "Set His right foot upon the sea and left upon the earth" (Rev. 10:2). There is but one Mediator between God and men (I Tim. 2:5). The devil has a parody on this as if to imitate (Rev. 13:1,11).

His strenuous authority: the mighty one, with foot on sea and land, uplifts His hand in harmony with heaven, to avow the end would not be further delayed (Rev. 10:5–6).

His stablished testimony: the twofold witness borne to the two anointed offices of Christ's Kinghood and Priesthood is age-old (Zech. 6:13); (compare Gen. 14:18–22; Heb. 7:1–3).

His supernatural victory: the kingdoms of the world become... of our Lord and of His Christ; and He shall reign for ever and ever" (Rev. 11:15).

His superior regality: We give Thee thanks, O Lord God Almighty. . . because Thou hast taken Thy great power and hast reigned (Rev. 11:17).

His scriptural identity: the seed of the woman that bruised the serpent's head. "A man child who was to rule the nations with a rod of iron" (Rev. 12:5).

His subjugating ability: overcoming the great enemy, the u-surper, deceiver, and subtle imitator in the realm of mediation (Rev. 13:1, 11–14).

The suitability, efficiency, and adequacy of Messiah in mediation is perfect and complete. We are here permitted a glimpse of the splendor of His angelic form; the honor of His availing Priesthood; the savor of His fragrant perfume; for He is the sponsor of His people's prayers. Notice also the grandeur of His covenant rainbow; the valor of His glorious triumph; the favor of His eternal blessing; for He is the victor who defeats the fourfold subtle strategy of the diabolical enemy. Christ in the sovereignty of His Lordship overthrows the great dragon, who is the destroyer. In the sufficiency of His Heirship He overcomes the old serpent who is the deluder. In the supremacy of His Mediatorship He overpowers the devil who is the devourer. Furthermore, in the superiority of His Judgeship He overrules Satan who is the deceiver.

Fourthly, the regenerative ability of the entitled Son of Man in His creatorship and judgeship (Rev. 14–22).

His changeless resemblance in the character of sacrificial suretyship: the victor, "A lamb stood on Mount Zion" (Rev. 14:1).

His flawless guidance in shepherd leadership: "These. . . follow the Lamb whithersoever He goeth" (Rev. 14:4).

His ceaseless governance in official commissionership: "To preach the gospel. . . to every nation, and kindred. . . and people" (Rev. 14:6).

His boundless preponderance in workmanship: "Worship Him that made heaven, and earth, and the sea, and the fountains of waters" (Rev. 14:7).

His measureless influence in universal kinship: "Son of man. . . on His head a golden crown. . . in His hand a sharp sickle" (Rev. 14:14).

His dauntless insistence in judicial executorship: "Reap: for the time is come for Thee to reap; for the harvest of the earth is ripe" (Rev. 14:15).

His endless elegance in celestial worthship: "Great and marvelous are Thy works. . . for all nations shall come and worship before Thee" (Rev. 15:3–4).

His peerless excellence in matrimonial companionship: "Let us be glad and rejoice, and give honour to Him: for the marriage of the Lamb is come" (Rev. 19:7).

His resistless justice in magisterial proprietorship: "A white horse. . . He that sat upon him was called Faithful and True. . . in righteousness He doth judge. . . make war" (Rev. 19:11).

His dateless precedence in immortal authorship: "He was clothed with a vesture dipped in blood: and His name is called The Word of God" (Rev. 19:13).

His matchless prominence in monumental kingship: "He hath on His vesture and on His thigh. . . KING OF KINGS, AND

LORD OF LORDS" (Rev. 19:16).

His flawless competence in essential judgeship: "I saw a great white throne. . . I saw the dead. . . stand. . . the dead were judged" (Rev. 20:11–15).

His ageless omnipotence in eternal creatorship: "He that sat upon the throne said, Behold, I make all things new" (Rev. 2:5).

His tombless inheritance in communal heirship: "I will show thee the bride, the Lamb's wife. . . that great city, the holy Jerusalem" (Rev. 21:9–27).

His fadeless effulgence in social relationship: "The city had no need of the sun. . . the glory of God did lighten it, and the Lamb is the light thereof" (Rev. 21:23).

His exhaustless sustenance in personal maintainership: "The tree of life, which bare twelve fruits: and yielded her fruit every month" (Rev. 22:2).

His reckonless preeminence in collateral authorship, creatorship, and mediatorship: "Alpha and Omega, the beginning and the end, the first and the last" (Rev. 22:13).

His trackless superintendence in supernatural statesmanship: "I am the root and the offspring of David, the bright the morning star" (Rev. 22:16).

These last two claims of Christ defy exposition. As Alpha and Omega, He is the Author and Revealer of truth. As the Beginning and End, He is the Creator and Upholder, and as First and Last, He is the Mediator and Maintainer. The final claim reveals that He preceded King David as the Root from which he sprang. He succeeded Him as the Offspring, and by far exceeded him as the Morning Star.

In summary of the section we may state that the merit of Christ's sacrificial character as the Lamb never perishes. The circuit of His judicial authority never recedes. The verdict and sentence of His judgment is never revoked. The Spirit of life, light, and love in His society abides forever unblemished. The prolific yield from the tree of life, the twelve manner of fruits is maintained eternally. The profit derived from the tribute of praise paid to His worthiness never ceases. The orbit of His creative power encompassing Heaven and earth never diminishes.

The complete and final portraiture of the person unveiled transcends all the estimates, calculations, and valuations of which the human mind is capable. We may now view the Son of Man in His regal might, His legal right, His moral merit, and His total power, fully identified and clearly interpreted by the Father.

V

In every sphere Christ stands highest in honor and holiest in renown. His preeminence in service, sacrifice, and superintendence is incomparable and His authority unsurpassed.

The VISIBLE IMAGE OF THE INVISIBLE GOD (Col. 1:15; Heb. 1:3; John 1:9)
> The perfect expression of Deity in mind, will, and heart.

The VOICE OF GOD (Ps. 29:4; Job 37:5; Rev. 1:12)
> Absolutely authoritative in every realm eternally.

The VISITOR (Gen. 50:24; Ruth 1:6; Ps.106:4; Luke 1:68)
> The most distinguished and dignified that ever came.

The VEIL (Exod. 36:31-35; Heb. 10:19-20)
> The personal preciousness and moral perfection of the Son of Man.

The VERITY (Matt. 5:18; John 1:51; Rom. 15:8)
> The final authority on the will, Word, and work of God.

The VESSEL (Matt. 1:23; Heb. 10:5)
> A prepared body for the manifestation of the Godhead.

The VERY HIGH (Isa. 52:13; Ps. 61:2; Matt. 21:9)
> Chiefest and holiest in preeminent honor and glory.

The VANGUARD (Num. 10:33; Deut. 1:32-33)
> Undaunted and undiverted by an encounter.

The VALUER (Lev. 27:12; Luke 5:5; John 12:7)
> Incapable of making a mistake or misjudgment.

The VICTOR (Ps. 98:1; Isa. 25:8; I Cor. 15:54,57)
> Foremost as conqueror and forever victorious.

The VALIANT (Ps. 118:14-16)
> Supremely chivalrous when facing infernal powers.

The VANQUISHER (Heb. 2:14).

The stupendous display of Christ's superior strength.

In addition to meditations adopted on the letter V, we had choice from numerous others, among which is the Vine (John 15:1), the Victualler (Luke 9:12,16-17), the Volitive Cleanser — "I will: be thou clean" (Luke 5:13), the Vindicator (Rev. 6:9-11), the Vicarious Substitute (John 10:11), the Victim of reproach (Ps. 69:9,19-20), the Virtuous Healer (Luke 8:46-47), etc.

"Yea, He is Altogether Lovely"

Lovely and Lovable in His Regal Majesty
Lovely and Lovable in His Royal Dignity
Lovely and Lovable in His Moral Beauty
Lovely and Lovable in His Essential Purity
Lovely and Lovable in His Personal Constancy
Lovely and Lovable in His Judicial Authority
Lovely and Lovable in His Supernal Glory

"Accepted in the Beloved"

"Let my Beloved come into His garden"

A quiet place where we may find retreat,
    In sweet companionship our Lover meet;
The friendship of this faithful One is true,
    He fills the soul with favors ever new.

These sacred precincts of secluded rest
    Where love and loveliness are manifest;
A place unentered by defiled feet,
    Where ravished hearts their Well Beloved meet.

From choicest gardens fragrant virtues rise,
    The perfume of affection's closest ties;
We trace unrivaled beauty in His face,
    His lovely countenance reflects His grace.

Endearment and enlightenment combine
    To set this Lover forth in light sublime,
His royal bearing and His loyal heart
    Declare His constancy and peace impart.

Here richest colors, fadeless in their charm,
    Are blended perfectly with hymn and psalm,
His crystal purity and comely voice
    Cause angel hosts to ceaselessly rejoice.

The soul ascends to altitudes of bliss,
    Where righteousness and peace are known to kiss;
Here multitudes are linked in sweet accord,
    To praise the Altogether Lovely Lord.

The very purest, deepest joys abound.
    The Well Beloved in majesty is crowned,
All hearts pour forth their praise in glad acclaim,
    Ascribing honor to His worthy Name.

The glory of the Father shines more bright,
    Where Christ is seen in Heaven's perfect light;
The fullness of the Godhead now appears
    To satisfy throughout immortal years.

I am Alpha and Omega (Rev. 22:13)

In claiming to be the Alpha, Christ is proclaiming Himself as possessing the foremost right to voice divine decrees, and as occupying the topmost rank in the realm of revelation. His supreme station of majesty and select position of dignity surpass all other leaders and legislators, and every known lover and liberator. Titles we have already considered, such as forerunner (Heb. 6:20), firstborn (Col 1:18), firstfruits (I Cor. 15:20) and first begotten (Heb. 1:6), verify His virtuous superiority and victorious supremacy. As Alpha He is the everexisting One, wherefore, the death on the cross of the physical body that was prepared Him did not in any wise interfere with His self-existence in being, wisdom, and power. Christ is, He is eternally, or ever the stream of time began flowing, or ever the earth was formed. The multiplication or depletion of world population does not develop nor deplete the Godhead. Essential, eternal being is without bounds: Deity has no dimensions, no horizons, and no lines of demarcation: infinity cannot be improved or impoverished. The terms we use, such as higher or lower, inferior or superior, greater or smaller, stronger or weaker, older or younger, major or minor, senior or junior, are features that do not pertain in the Godhead.

One of the inmates of a deaf and dumb institution, in Paris over a century ago, was requested to write his estimate and understanding of the eternity of God. The illuminating lines he penned are remarkable: "Eternity is duration without beginning or end; existence, without bounds or dimensions; present, without past or future. God's eternity is youth without infancy or old age, life without birth or death, light without sunrise or sunset, today without yesterday or tomorrow." Our Lord's eternal sovereignty is without start or finish. The position of Alpha in the alphabet predicates the first and best, proclaims the choicest and highest, and postulates the greatest and noblest, even as Christ surely is, always and altogether. In personal being, which comprises mind, will, and heart, our Beloved is ageless, changeless, and ceaseless. He surpasses all others in the loveliness of His gracious kindliness and supersedes all others in the loftiness of His glorious kingliness. His attractiveness never alters, His friendliness never falters, His faithfulness never forgets, His devotedness never dwindles, His truthfulness never tarnishes, His steadfastness never subsides, His virtuousness never varies, His preciousness never perishes, and His worthiness never wanes.

The Lord Jesus Christ is much greater and more glorious than the best of writers can declare or describe. His name and nature are sweeter than the most eloquent of the poets can explain or express. The splendors of His sovereign supremacy are more sublime than the stateliest of the saints can depict or define. The bounties of His lustrous love are more precious than the greatest appraisers can estimate or evaluate. The words and wisdom of His statements are more marvelous and wondrous than the princeliest of the philosophers can conceive or comprehend. The attributes He personifies and the action He takes in dealing with man's defects and deficiencies, human sin, and shame are vaster and more virtuous than the mind of man can grasp. The treasures of the truth He taught are more tremendous in their spiritual values than human reckoning can dictate or determine. Yea, the graces and glories of His perfect Governorship are more massive and majestic than the cleverest artist can picture or portray.

His name remains highest in human history, the choicest in celestial courts, the sweetest in spiritual songs, the stateliest in sovereign ranks, the loveliest in lustrous love, the richest in regal resource, and the worthiest in genuine worship. Christ in His preeminence and precedence soars mightily above the highest boundaries of material magnificence, to the remotest realms of regality and the most spacious regions of authority, for He ascended up far above all heavens that He might fill all thrones and sway all scepters forevermore. Let us bow down in the presence of His glorious Lordship and pray the prayer of Israel's greatest king, "Lead me to the rock that is higher," remembering as we do so, that we are addressing the Highest Himself (Ps. 87:5). "For thus saith the High and Lofty One that inhabiteth eternity, whose name is holy, I dwell in the high and holy place, with him also that is of a contrite and humble spirit, to revive the spirit of the humble, and to revive the heart of the contrite ones" (Isa. 57:15).

THE VISIBLE IMAGE
OF THE INVISIBLE GOD

The image of the invisible god (Col. 1:15).
The exact image of His person (Heb. 1:3).

Christ is the exact expression of the invisible God, He is the visible exhibition of the incorruptible Godhead.

He stated plainly, "He that hath seen Me hath seen the Father" (John 14:9). "I and the Father are one" (John 10:30); this affirms they are one in essence essentially, entirely, and eternally.

Christ's claim, "We are one" (John 17:22), refers to the very constituents of being, the same characteristics of personality, and the very subsistence of the divine nature.

Christ is the perfect and highest manifestation of Deity. All that is the Son's is the Father's also, and all that is the

Father's is likewise the Son's. "In Him dwelleth all the fulness of . . . Godhead bodily" (Col. 2:9). His excellence exceeds the noblest in angelic ranks, His omnipotence transcends the greatest of potential powers, and His omniscience surpasses the totality of all philosophical knowledge. In Emmanuel, the Eternal has displayed Himself, demonstrating His love, declaring His will, dispensing His mercy, and disclosing His glory. The Lord possessed a radiant effulgence none could gaze upon and, from a solitude no eye could penetrate, He came to resemble and reveal the true God. We understand from the character He expressed that God is perfectly righteous, exceedingly generous, wonderfully gracious, intrinsically precious, absolutely judicious, and completely glorious. There is no limit to His legislation, jurisdiction, and administration.

Christ made plain God's immortality and incorruptibility; the thought of a commencement or cessation of being is alike inadmissible. A beginning and ending cannot be applied to Deity, the Bible expression, "From everlasting to everlasting, Thou art God," is the only suitable language we may adopt. God is not eternal by sanction but by state. The eternity of Christ is fundamental to the stability of His infinite constancy and capability, and to the security of His immutable covenant. By virtue of His manifestation He has disclosed the indefinable spiritual realities and resources of Deity. He has declared the undiscoverable features of the world to come. He has also displayed the undeniable characteristics of the Father of mercies. The service He rendered in setting forth the Father is characterized by the holiest impulses, the purest motive, and the noblest aspirations. The ministry He fulfilled is more attractive than a garden of spices, for it yielded a bountiful compassion and displayed a beautiful expression of graceful goodness and considerate care. The lifework of Christ illustrated the Father's sovereign command (John 1:43), the Father's sufficiency of resource (John 6:11), the Father's supreme power (John 6:19-20), and the Father's sacrificial love (John 12:24-28). Throughout His entire ministry, the Lord of life exhibited the loveliness of an unselfish mind, the limitlessness of a unified will, the lithesomeness of an un-shackled spirit, and the lowliness of an understanding heart.

Great is the mystery of godlikeness. All the celestial features of the Eternal God are apparent in the Son. Christ secures no addition to His knowledge and knows no reduction. His power cannot be improved or impoverished. His love cannot be increased or diminished. His grace cannot be multiplied or minimized. His government cannot be extended or amended. His holiness cannot be advanced or abridged. His glory cannot be developed or decreased. He knows no suc-cessor, but is godlike, the visible image of the invisible God, who being in the form of God, did not hold to this as a per-sonal advantage. He took upon Him the form of a servant, obeying to the very death, for the advantage of others, in a God-honoring sacrifice. None other but the Son of God could have used the words Christ used in His amazing prayer, "O Father, glorify Thou Me with Thine own self with the glory which I had with Thee before the world was" (John 17:5). The fullest, clearest, greatest revelation of the Father has been given to mankind in the person of the Son, who said, "Believe Me that I am in the Father, and the Father in Me" (John 14:11). He was manifested relatively in kinship and no other kinsman is able to assure intimate relationship with the Father, together with immortal fellowship, imperishable friendship, and incorruptible partnership, all so radiant with hope and bright with certitude.

THE VOICE OF GOD

The voice of the LORD is powerful; the voice of the LORD is full of majesty (Ps. 29:4).

God thundereth marvellously with His voice (Job 37:5).

Then came there a voice from heaven.... The people therefore, that stood by, and heard it, said that it thundered (John 12:28-29).

The hour is coming, in the which all that are in the graves shall hear His voice (John 5:28).

I turned to see the voice that spake with me (Rev. 1:12).

Christ is a Voice and has a voice, He is definitely the Voice of God. The Apostle John declared, "I turned to see the voice that spake with me" (Rev. 1:12), this was the great voice behind him of verse 10, the voice that sounded like many waters (v. 15), a figure which is twice connected with the Lord as the Voice of God in the Old Testament. We are informed in the Scriptures that the grace of God appeared; and that the kindness and love of God appeared (Titus 2:11; 3:4); in like manner the Voice of God appeared. Christ in His own resplendent personality exhibits all of these divine virtues in manifold fullness. How incomparable is this Voice which may be heard walking (Gen. 3:8), which may be known calling (John 10:3,4,27), also which may be seen speaking (Rev. 1:12). The Voice of the Lord is referred to seven times in Psalm 29, where the effects recorded are far greater in magnitude than anything wrought by mighty angels. In virtue, this Voice is full of majesty, because of the speaker's sovereign Lordship; in volume likened to thunder, and in vitality described as breaking cedars and shaking the wilderness (Ps. 29:3-7). "He thundereth with the voice of His excellency.... God thundereth marvelously with His voice" (Job 37:4-5 RV). "Hark! A voice resounds! The glorious voice wherewith His thunders peal! We cannot track them when that voice is heard. Yes, with His voice God thunders marvelously. Great things He doeth. We comprehend Him not!" (Job 37:4-5 H.R. Minn's trans.)

In Psalm 29 superior majesty is exemplified in the person of Christ in that He supersedes the mightiest of angels and surpasses the strongest forces that operate in the entire universe. Both of these features are confirmed in Hebrews 1, which opens by affirming that God has spoken in His Son. What wonderful expressions of majestic beauty, dignity, and glory are seen in Him who is the brightness of God's glory and the express image of His Person! (Heb. 1:3) What amazing demonstrations of dynamic power, might, and strength His Voice has already given! What astounding declarations of His intrinsic affinity, ability, and authority are made of Him in the Scriptures.

Following one of His exclusive claims He said, "Marvel not at this: for the hour is coming, in the which all that are in the graves shall hear His voice, And shall come forth; they that have done good, unto the resurrection of life; and they that have done evil, to the resurrection of judgment" (John 5:28). Five hundred references to the word "voice" occur in the Scriptures, besides nineteen occasions where it appears in the plural. The first two of these are of deep interest, the words rendered "mighty thunderings" in the AV (Exod. 9:28), are actually, "Voices of God, Koloth Elohim," again in verse 29.

The Scriptures state that there are many kinds of voices in the world (I Cor. 14:10), so we may note a few of these. The voice of Abel's blood (Gen. 4:10) and the voice of the signs (Exod. 4:8). The heavens and day and night have a voice (Ps. 19:1-3), and the silent stars declare His greatness universally. We might add to these the voice of supplications, of words, of gladness, of the reverberating peals of thunder (Ps. 77:18; Rev. 10:3), but above all, "The voice of His word" (Ps. 103:20), which is "The voice of the Son of God" (John 5:25), who is, Himself, the Voice expressed in person. He never voiced a single word that was beneath His dignity as the Son of God.

The sevenfold portrayal of the Voice of the Lord which is presented in Psalm 29 describes personal attributes of character. The first expression is associated with many waters (v. 3), a figure which is used a thousand years later when the deity of Christ is unveiled. "His voice as the voice of many waters" (Rev. 1:15 JND), including the great deep, oceans, seas, rivers, lakes, springs, and fountains, a figurative suggestion of the multiplicity of matters about which the voice speaks. A wide variety of subjects is dealt with for enlightenment and for the enlargement of our understanding of invisible realities. His Voice is in power with authority to create and maintain, to uphold or overthrow. The reference to the word, *mabbul*, flood, in Ps. 29:10 is of deep significance; it occurs eleven times in Genesis 7—10 and once here. So the Voice of God caused and controlled that mighty cataclysm that destroyed the world that then was (II Pet. 3:6). This same

Voice will bring about the final consummation (Heb. 12:26-28). The portrayal given in Psalm 29 denotes that this Voice can displace the firmest trees, throw into turbulence the calmest waters, shatter the strongest rocks, subdue the strongest nations, and shake the entire universe. Yet withal the same assures the blessing of peace to His people (v.11).

THE VISITOR

> Joseph said ... God will surely visit you (Gen. 50:24).
> Naomi ... had heard in the country of Moab how that the LORD had visited His people in giving them bread (Ruth 1:6).
> Remember me, O LORD, with the favour that Thou bearest unto Thy people: O visit me with Thy salvation (Ps. 106:4).
> Blessed be the Lord God of Israel; for He hath visited and redeemed His people (Luke 1:68).
> Through the tender mercy of our God; whereby the dayspring from on high hath visited us, To give light to them that sit in darkness (Luke 1:78).
> God hath visited His people (Luke 7:16).

Have we not all had the experience of meeting a welcome visitor? Who is more worthy of receiving a wholehearted welcome than our gracious Redeemer? As ye have therefore received Christ Jesus the Lord, so walk ye in Him, rooted and built up in Him, and established in the faith (Col. 2:6-7). The word "visited" is first used, in the Bible, when the Lord visited Sarah and gave her strength to conceive seed when she was past age (Gen. 21:1; Heb. 11:11). Centuries later the Lord paid a visit to Israel in Egypt which resulted in emancipation from bondage, provision through the wilderness, and entrance to the promised land (Exod. 3:16-17). When the writer of Psalm 106 had surveyed the history of Israel's waywardness and willfulness, in the light of the Lord's gracious dealings and the remembrance of His convenant (vss. 44-45), he exclaimed as a preface, "Remember me, O LORD, with the favour that Thou bearest unto Thy people: O visit me with Thy salvation" (Ps. 106:4).

Christ is the most distinguished Visitor that ever came

into the world. He brought the greatest benefits and blessings that were ever bestowed on humanity. These included the knowledge of the Father of mercies (Matt. 11:27), His celestial house, His memorable Name (John 14:2; 17:6), and His munificent purposes, which comprise the supreme objective in His revealing of the invisible and eternal realities.

This Visitor imparted a comprehensive conception of the nature of the Holy Spirit and His manifold ministry. He made plain the gift of eternal life, immortal love, and everlasting light. During the manifestation He demonstrated the divine mastery of all subversive power in His exercise of sovereign authority. His personal presence fulfilled the types and shadows expressed in the Tabernacle, Temple, and throne of Israel. In Him the three highest offices of Prophet, Priest, and King were finally realized in one person. He showed forth the virtues of meekness and majesty, submission and sovereignty, gentleness and greatness, lowliness and loftiness, together with all that was amiable, desirable, and suitable to human welfare.

This Visitor came to be an example, but with a purpose, as our Emancipator. He appeared as the man Christ Jesus, but was also our Maker and Creator. He was approved as a welcome Teacher, but at the same time was the whole Truth. He came as Shepherd to lead His sheep, but He is also Sovereign Lord. He came as a mighty worker but is the most worthy of all celebrities as the Wonderful Counselor. The kindliness, the friendliness, and loveliness of this celestial visitor are amaranthine and age-abiding. He combines in His majestic character the sovereignties of the infinite as the Lord of lords. He comprises in His masterful capabilities the sufficiencies of the incarnate as Leader of leaders. He confirms by His matchless conduct the sympathies of the intimate as the loftiest of Liberators who loved us and died, the just for the unjust, to bring us to God. As Visitor from the heavenly realm, Christ ranks highest in renown, stands greatest in resource, and proves kindest in His regard for all whom He visits.

THE VEIL

Thou shalt make a veil of blue, and of purple, and of scarlet, and fine twined linen of cunning work: with cherubims shall it be made.... And the veil shall divide unto you between the holy and the holy of holies (Exod. 26:31-33 Newberry).

In His temple every whit of it uttereth glory (Ps. 29:9 marg.).

Jesus, when He had cried again with a loud voice, yielded up the spirit, And, behold, the veil of the temple was rent in twain from top to bottom (Matt. 27:50-51).

Having ... freedom to enter into the holiest by the blood of Jesus ... through the veil, that is His flesh (Heb. 10:19-20).

The magnificent veil with its combination of bright, fascinating colors and beautiful figures of cherubim intricately interwoven, signifies yet another feature of our Lord's personal character and ministry in manifold display.

The colors in themselves are very significant. The blue was particularly associated with the priestly garments. The Lord said to Moses, "Thou shalt make the robe of the ephod all, or wholly of blue" (Exod. 28:31). Purple was preeminently linked with the royal dignity and majesty of kingship. "Purple raiment that was on the kings of Midian" (Judg. 8:26). Mordecai went out from the presence of the king in royal apparel ... with a garment of fine linen and purple (Esther 8:15). See also John 19:2, where they put on Christ a purple robe and said, "Hail, King of the Jews."

Scarlet was primarily the color of distinction and was so used on various occasions; Daniel the prophet is an example, "Then commanded Belshazzar, and they clothed Daniel with scarlet" (Dan. 5:29).

Christ was a prophet mighty in deed and word before God and all the people (Luke 24:19). Luke mentions that they put on Him a gorgeous robe (Luke 23:11). Matthew tells us that the soldiers put on Him a scarlet robe (Matt. 27:28). Doubtless the robe He wore daily, for which the soldiers cast lots, was of blue, for He came to fulfill all righteousness. Matthew, Mark, and Luke record that Christ quoted from

Psalm 110, which avows His Lordship and Priesthood. He affirmed His Kingship before the governor (John 18:37). As to His being a prophet, this is repeatedly affirmed. This is Jesus the Prophet (Matt 21:11; Mark 6:4,14; Luke 24:19; John 9:17).

Wherefore the three bright colors of the veil—blue, purple, and scarlet—witness to the three great vocations of priest, king, and prophet. The fine linen represents His nature of purity and righteousness. Christ in manifestation displayed priestly mercy, kingly majesty, and the prophetic ministry. "The veil which is His flesh."

For further identification let us note that on the veil were the figures of the cherubim, wrought in skillful work. These are described by the Prophet Ezekiel as having the face of a lion, ox, man, and eagle, the genera of creation (Ezek. 10:14-15; 1:10).

In the final unveiling of Christ in the book of Revelation, these four are referred to ten times. Their connection with the veil expresses grace in manifestation. The Word became flesh and tabernacled among us and we beheld His glory, the glory as of the only begotten of the Father, full of grace and truth ... Grace and truth came by Jesus Christ (John 1:14,17). The lion represents the sovereignty of grace, "the grace of God which carries with it salvation for all men has appeared" (Titus 2:11 JND). The ox suggests the sufficiency of grace (it was the largest offering). Where sin abounded grace did much more than superabound (Rom. 5:20). The man speaks of sympathy manifest. The grace of God was exceeding abundant with faith and love which is in Christ Jesus (I Tim. 1:14). The eagle, which soars above all material obstacles, signifies the superiority of grace, which is unobstructed by any of the barriers of nation, race, caste, or color. As sin reigned unto death, even so might grace reign through righteousness unto eternal life, through Jesus Christ our Lord (Rom. 5:21).

The veil which in the cherubim reflected the manifold grace of God, hung on four pillars of the incorruptible wood of the shittah tree, each of which was overlaid with pure gold.

Likewise the four Gospels set forth the perfections of grace in our Saviour's precious life as Revealer, Reconciler, Redeemer, and Regenerator.

In the light of these matters relating to the veil, the three colors stand for the offices He fills, which depict universal government. The four figures of the cherubim reflect the fullness of His unmeasurable grace, while the gold bespeaks His unrivaled glory. The fine twined linen constituted a delightful picture of the beauty of His unstained virtue, the purity of His unmarred character, and of His untarnished heart. He is Jesus Christ the righteous.

Therefore in this gorgeous veil of blue, purple, and scarlet we may trace the index to four great realities: the supernal functions of His signal offices as Priest, King, and Prophet; the supernatural fullness of His spiritual grace in the four cherubim figures of lion, ox, man, and eagle; the superlative features of His moral beauty in the fine twined linen; and the sublime fashion of His celestial glory indicated in the pure gold of the four supporting pillars.

This exquisite veil was rent from top to bottom, an event not perpetrated by man. "It pleased the LORD to bruise Him," "Awake, O sword, against My shepherd" (Isa. 53:10; Zech. 13:7). Only by the rending of the veil of His flesh is a way of entrance to God established. He Himself said, "No one cometh to the Father but through Me" (John 14:6). The veil was rent but not removed. Christ is still the living way of access. We come to God, *dia,* through Him (Heb. 7:25). The amount it took to open a way through Panama cost America hundreds of millions of dollars, but the cost of opening a way to the Father of glory was infinite. When Christ commenced His ministry He affirmed, "Ye shall see heaven open" (John 1:51); He Himself is the door of entrance (John 10:9). Man has nothing in himself that merits access to the Father.

The rending of the Veil of His flesh in sacrifice, His sovereign Shepherdhood to lead, His supreme strength in Priesthood to sustain and safeguard, constitute our sole sufficiency for entry to the presence of God.

Gold, which represented divine glory, did not appear in

the veil; this aspect of Christ's deity was hidden from view during the manifestation, but immediately the veil was rent, the pure gold which covered the four pillars supporting it shone forth gloriously. Our Lord expressed the true significance of this on the occasion when Andrew and Philip brought to Him the Greek inquirers. He said, "The hour is come, that the Son of man should be glorified.... Except a corn of wheat fall into the ground and die, it abideth alone" (John 12:23-24). Again He said, after He had expounded to His disciples the prophetic Scriptures, "Ought not Christ' to have suffered these things, and to enter into His glory?" (Luke 24:26)

THE VERITY

Verily I say to you, Till heaven and earth pass, one jot or one tittle shall in no wise pass from the law, till all be fulfilled (Matt. 5:18).

Verily, verily I say to you, Hereafter ye shall see heaven open, and the angels of God ascending and descending on the Son of man (John 1:51).

I am ... the truth (John 14:6).

Jesus Christ became a minister of the circumcision for the truth of God, to confirm the promises made to the fathers (Rom. 15:8).

For accuracy of statement and genuine authority, Christ has no equal. In nobility of character He is the most reputable Counselor and in verity of claim He is absolutely truthful and reliable. Wherefore we should take the more earnest heed to the words He has spoken and the truth He has stated. In Matthew's record of the Lord's ministry he mentions the word "verily" being used as a preface to twenty-nine of His utterances. This is the amen of verification and Christ was the first to use it at the beginning of a sentence. The words following His use of "verily" in Matt. 5:18 signify His deity, for God alone knows the facts He stated of heaven and earth passing away. With greater emphasis He later reaffirmed this would take place, but that His words would abide forever (Matt. 24:35).

In John's Gospel, Christ claimed to be the truth in person (John 14:6) He used the words "true, truly, and truth" no fewer than forty-nine times. Christ declared to Pilate, the governor, that He came into the world to bear witness to the truth (John 18:37). He also gave warrant to the truth as being indestructible (John 10:35; 19:28,36-37). "How then shall the Scriptures be fulfilled, that thus it must be?" (Matt. 26:54) In no other portion of the Bible do we find the same profound degree of emphasis placed on the authenticity of Scripture, such as Christ here affirms. He also certifies and confirms the veracity of what He is about to speak by the double use of "verily, verily," on twenty-five occasions in the Gospel by John. His sublime declarations of truth are imperishable and irrefutable. His spiritual capacity and understanding were unlimited by any lack of knowledge, unmarred by any imperfect comprehension, and totally free from the slightest taint of uncertainty. The sublimity of His statements were conveyed in the simplest words and were accompanied by supernatural deeds such as had never before been done (John 15:24). With unequivocal confidence He verified the Genesis account of creation of man; let us remember He was there. He certified to the historicity of Noah and the flood, also of Lot and the overthrow of Sodom and Gomorrha.

When answering the rationalism of the Sadducees on the subject of resurrection from the dead and future life, Christ said to them, "Have ye not read that which was spoken to you by God, saying, I am the God of Abraham, and the God of Isaac, and the God of Jacob? God is not the God of the dead, but of the living" (Matt. 22:31-32). To examine thirty-five of the occasions where these three names are linked together in the Old Testament, places the imprimatur of verity on the twelve books in which they occur. Christ made repeated references to Moses and the law, David and the nation of Israel, Solomon and the Queen of Sheba, Daniel the prophet, Jonah and the Ninevites, Elijah and the famine, Elisha and Naaman the Syrian, and numerous others. By so doing He corroborates the historical, geographical, and national accuracy of Bible records. Thereby the Lord conclusively asserts the correctness and trustworthiness of the Scriptures. His credentials are infinitely greater than any possessed by the scholars, philosophers, scientists, or physicists of this world. Wherefore His complete knowledge of all truth, His capacity to discern to the uttermost, His colossal range of understanding, are qualities possessed by no other. No one but He knows the number of the stars and calls them all by name (Isa. 40:26). No one else is aware of the names of every family in Heaven and on earth (Eph. 3:15). Christ alone is entitled and qualified to verify all truth, this is certainly one of the supreme features of His sublime ministry during the manifestation. Not only so, but as the Amen, the faithful and true Witness, He has continued so to do ever since His glorification. This feature is even more fully revealed in the closing book of the Bible.

The state of inherent and intrinsic perfection which characterizes Christ expresses a disposition of wholesomeness and completeness that is beyond compare. He is immaculate in righteousness, inviolate in truthfulness, immortal in preciousness, and invariable in faithfulness. His faultless spiritual stature is devoid of all defects and impervious to deceptive influences. Wherefore His estimate is of greater worth than all other authorities combined. His witness to the verity of the Scriptures places them forever beyond even the shadow of doubt as to their divine origin and integrity.

THE VESSEL

They shall call His name Emmanuel, which being interpreted is, ·God with us (Matt. 1:23).
A body hast Thou prepared Me (Heb. 10:5).
God was in Christ (II Cor. 5:19).

The words "vessel and vessels" appear two hundred times in the Bible, and references are given to their being made of gold, silver, brass, iron, wood, stone, and earth. Their values and various uses are of real interest, especially those connected with the Temple and its services.

The statement is made of the Temple in the marginal rendering in our Bibles, "Every whit uttereth His glory" (Ps. 29:9). This statement would include the vessels.

When the Spirit of God reminds us through the Apostle Paul that "God ... hath shined in our hearts, to give the light of the knowledge of the glory of God in the face of Jesus Christ," the statement immediately follows, "We have this treasure in earthen vessels" (II Cor. 4:6-7). A person also is referred to as a vessel, in the second message sent to Timothy, "He shall be a vessel unto honour, sanctified, and meet for the master's use" (II Tim. 2:21). The Lord said of the Apostle Paul, "He is a chosen vessel to Me, to bear My name before the nations and kings" (Acts 9:15).

People also are likened to vessels, some are spoken of as vessels of mercy, while others are called vessels of wrath (Rom. 9:22-23). Some vessels prove to be of very great value. On June 6, 1972, at Christie's auction mart in London, a large porcelain jar made in China about the middle of the fourteenth century was sold for the handsome price of $485,000.

What are we to say of the golden Vessel of the heavenly sanctuary, the Vessel expressing the glory of the Father? This Vessel is imperishable because of being holy and therefore incorruptible (Acts 2:27).

All other vessels are perishable, He is imperishable; all are destructible, He is indestructible; all are dispensable, He is indispensable.

He is the most notable and memorable, the most valuable and desirable of all vessels, for God was in Christ (II Cor. 5:19).

If we have the light of the knowledge of the glory of God in the face of Jesus Christ, as a treasure in our earthen vessels (II Cor. 4:6-7), He had infinite treasure in the body prepared Him. We are called to the acknowledgment of the mystery of God and of the Father and of Christ, in whom are hid all the treasures of wisdom and knowledge (Col. 2:2-3). Christ is beauty beautified, purity purified, dignity dignified, majesty magnified, and glory glorified (John 17:5).

What a strange anomaly, that the one who perfectly personified the most exquisite virtue, the exceeding riches of grace, and who was the very essence of pure kindness, should be disregarded, despised, and deserted! They saw in Him no beauty to desire Him (Isa. 53:2).

In Scripture He likened His loneliness to being like that of a disregarded sparrow, I am ... alone as a sparrow upon a house top (Ps. 102:6). He describes Himself as being treated like a worm: "I am a worm, and no man; a reproach of men, and despised of the people" (Ps. 22:6). In His hour of deepest grief and agony, He pictures Himself as one deserted by friends and lovers (Ps. 88:18). This is confirmed in the New Testament, then all the disciples forsook Him and fled (Matt. 26:56). The sensibilities of mankind had become so distorted and depraved by sin as to be capable of saying, "Not this man, but Barabbas. Now Barabbas was a robber" (John 18:40). Therefore the choicest, kindest, most precious personal vessel that ever appeared among men was despised and rejected. The entire life of Christ is an unblemished record of divine goodness and heavenly graciousness in action.

What considerate regard! What tender compassion! What patient care! What willing help! What friendly love! What wise counsel! What instructive teaching! What winsome appeals! What attractive sayings! What authoritative commands! What miraculous signs! What clear predictions characterized His life's ministry!

Furthermore, most of the vessels men make are designed for one particular use, whereas the most virtuous Vessel of enormous value, namely, the living Christ, has a wide range of vocations of the highest importance, which He fulfilled. He came into the world to bear witness to God's Shepherdhood, as it was expressed in Psalm 23 and Isaiah 40. Not only did He confirm this, but identified Himself therewith by saying, "I am the good shepherd: the good shepherd layeth down His life for the sheep" (John 10:11).

He brought to humanity, by His manifestation, the reality of holy priesthood and fulfilled its highest function in redemption, reconciliation, and mediation.

In like manner He corroborated divine Saviourhood as portrayed by the prophets, to whom God stated, "I the LORD am thy Saviour and Redeemer" (Isa. 49:26); and again, "There is no saviour beside Me" (Hos. 13:4). This feature was also verified by His birth. The angel said, "I bring you good tidings of great joy, for to you is born this day in the city of David a Saviour, which is Christ the Lord" (Luke 2:10-11). Further witness is given in Samaria, "This is indeed the Christ, the Saviour of the world" (John 4:42). He has now returned to the right hand of the majesty on high to maintain His Shepherdhood (Rev. 7:17), retain His Priesthood (Heb. 7:24), and sustain His Saviourhood (Acts 5:31).

Space forbids dealing with the station of Kinghood, the standard of Manhood, the status of Servanthood, and the many other functions for which this priceless Vessel was fitted, and which He so perfectly fulfilled.

Forasmuch as man first mutilated and then destroyed the most costly Temple that was ever built on earth, little wonder that they should first mar and then destroy the most perfect Body that was ever manifested to mankind (Isa. 52:14; John 2:19-21).

THE VERY HIGH

Behold, My servant shall deal prudently, He shall be exalted and extolled, and be very high (Isa. 52:13).

Lead me to the rock that is higher than I (Ps. 61:2).

The highest Himself shall establish her Hosanna to the Son of David: Blessed is He that cometh in the name of the Lord, Hosanna in the highest (Matt. 21:9).

He . . . ascended up far above all heavens (Eph. 4:10).

The words "high, higher, and highest" are used four hundred and fifty times in Scripture, each of the three is used in relation to Christ. Highness is a title of honor and is addressed to those of princely or royal rank in the British Empire. No one is more worthy of the title than Christ, for He is Very High, yea, the Highest. God has highly exalted Him, and given Him a name which is above every name (Phil. 2:9). Most of us do our measuring by standards of value that have been set up by ourselves. God's standards are higher than ours by far, even higher than the heavens are above the earth (Isa. 55:9). King David in his last words declared, "The Rock of Israel spake to me." He addressed the Lord as "The Rock of Israel." This statement makes clear his earlier appeal, "Lead me to the rock that is higher than I."

The request confirms another Scripture, "I will make Him firstborn, higher than the kings of the earth" (Ps. 89:27). No matter what degree of high rank and noble status we may esteem Christ as having, He is higher in honor. Whatever estimate of Christ's strength and stability we may conclude He has, He is much greater. Wherever we may place Him in our conception relating to His prodigious power and ponderous might, He is far mightier. Whenever we arrive at a decision in our minds, when contemplating the high standards of His judicial authority, let us remember He is very much Higher. No matter what degree of high honor we may attribute to Him, He is Higher than we can imagine.

Christ exceeds the utmost capacity of the finite mind to determine the scope of His saving grace, or to define the range of His supernal glory. The spacious heavens and countless stars have a magnitude far beyond all human standards of reckoning. The mind of the Creator and the might of His upholding power, also the majesty of His greatness and the mystery of His goodness, elude the ability of the human mind to declare or describe. Man is surrounded by spaces too extensive, distances too enormous, powers too tremendous, and glories too lustrous to be able to comprehend them with the natural mind. Then what are we to say of the Maker and Maintainer of all these things?

We are captivated when we think of His suitability for headship as the Great High Priest robed in splendor, who has passed into the heavens, angels and authorities and powers being made subject to Him (I Pet. 3:22).

We rejoice over His reliability in Heirship as the only begotten of the Father (John 1:14), the Firstborn from the dead (Col. 1:18), and the Firstborn among many brethren (Rom. 8:29), who is appointed Heir of all things (Heb. 1:2).

We experience extreme delight when meditating on His

desirability in Kingship, as the King of kings and Prince of the kings of the earth (Rev. 1:5). Because of being almighty in regal power, He is able to subdue all things unto Himself (Phil. 3:21).

We are thrilled with the knowledge of His durability in Lordship as Lord of lords, whose administrative authority abides forevermore, whose kingdom is an everlasting kingdom (Dan. 7:27). The Lord shall be thine everlasting light (Isa. 60:19-20).

We are deeply grateful for the superiority of our Saviour in Leadership, for He leads to the waters of restfulness along the paths of righteousness (Ps. 23:2-3). Praise His Name, for He leads in the way everlasting and is the only Leader who knows that way (Ps. 139:24).

Thus saith the High and Lofty One that inhabiteth eternity whose name is holy, "I dwell in the high and holy place, with him also that is of a contrite and humble spirit" (Isa. 57:15). "If thou seest the oppression of the poor, and violent perverting of judgment and justice in a province, marvel not at the matter: for He that is higher than the highest regardeth" (Eccles. 5:8). Luke refers to the highest seven times, and records that the Highest has regard for everyone. The words "high, higher, highest, very high, and most high," are used of Christ in the exceeding excellence of His majestic glory. He is far above all principality and power and might and dominion and every name that is named, not only in this world, but also in that which is to come. He ascended up far above all heavens, that He might fill all things (Eph. 1:21; 4:10).

From this highest station of heavenly honor, Christ oversees, overrules, and overrides every domain (Ps. 68:4).

He is exalted, He is greatly praised, He is Very High, blessed be His glorious Name forever (Ps. 72:19).

THE VANGUARD

The ark of the covenant of the LORD went before them in the

three days' journey, to search out a resting place for them (Num. 10:33).

Ye did not believe in the LORD your God, who went in the way before you, to search you out a place to pitch your tents, in fire by night, to show you by what way ye should go, and in a cloud by day (Deut. 1:32-33).

When He putteth forth His own sheep, He goeth before them, the sheep follow Him (John 10:4).

He guided them in the wilderness like a flock, He led them on safely, so that they feared not (Ps. 78:53).

We are all aware that a vanguard goes on before, in advance of an advancing army. The Saviour of Israel fulfilled this function for the nation quite frequently. "The Lord your God which goeth before you, He shall fight for you" (Deut. 1:30). As in every other vocation, Christ in His Leadership is faultless, He is familiar with all the events of time and is fully aware of all the conflicts of life, as well as knowing the power of the enemy. He is most thoughtful and faithful to all who follow His counsel. As Leader, He is a divine gift to mankind, for thus saith the Lord, "Behold, I have given Him for a witness to the people, a leader and commander to the people" (Isa. 55:4). In this Leadership He is likened to the ark of the covenant.

At the close of the wilderness pilgrimage, the nation of Israel eventually arrived at the river Jordan. When three days had elapsed, they were commanded, when they saw the ark go forward, to go after it (Josh. 3:3). In like manner they were previously bidden to follow the cloud (Num. 9:17-20). The Messiah in His masterful Leadership, as declared in John's message, repeatedly used the words, "Follow Me," first to Philip at the beginning, through to Peter at the close (John 1:43; 21:19). The ark of the covenant is one of the most significant illustrations of Christ, as representing His authority and administration; in the midst when the nation was encamped and in the forefront when journeying. A picture of the reality of this is shown to John in the unveiling. The Lamb which is in the midst of the throne shall feed them and shall lead them unto living fountains of waters (Rev. 7:17). The ark governed the movements of the people, guided their marching circumstances, and guarded them in times of danger.

The crown of gold upon the ark signified the majesty of Christ's sovereign Lordship. The mercy seat symbolized the manifold mercy of His sacrificial loving-kindness, while the contents suggested the sufficiency of His ministry of maintenance in signal Leadership. The excellent requisites of power, pardon, provision, and protection are all included in this pictorial presentation of the Redeemer's personal Lordship and Leadership. The desirable realm to which He eventually leads His ransomed hosts is described in Scripture as being peaceful, restful, beautiful, and delightful, whither the forerunner has for us entered (Heb. 6:20), a kingdom which cannot be moved.

He Goeth Before Them (John 10:4)

He leads by living fountains
Mid restful, tranquil calm,
Secures from all defilements,
Safeguards from blighting harm.
He ratifies His promise,
Fulfills the purpose planned,
And leads where glory dwelleth
In Emmanuel's land.

The Vanguard of the ransomed,
Who guides to realms of peace.
He perfects their salvation,
And causes tears to cease.
None claims to share the merit,
Of Christ at God's right hand,
They all give Him the glory,
In Emmanuel's land.

Our everlasting portion,
The gift of Heaven above,
Immortal in His beauty,
The sustenance of love.
There is but one Redeemer;
In Him alone we stand,
The Lamb, He is the Glory,
Of Emmanuel's land.

THE VALUER

The priest shall value it, whether it be good or bad: as thou valuest it, who art the priest, so shall it be (Lev. 27:12).

And Simon answering said unto Him, "Master, we have toiled all night, and have taken nothing" (Luke 5:5).

Then said Jesus, "Let her alone: against the day of My burying hath she kept this" (John 12:7).

The Lord commanded Moses to place an estimate on the value of all things that were devoted to God by the people of Israel.

In Leviticus 27, the expression, "thy estimation," is used twenty times, when the priest is placing the value on the gifts that are brought to the sanctuary.

In relation to the Church, Christ wields the prerogative of estimating the value of all gifts and services that are rendered in His name, and He brooks no interference on the part of others. On the occasion when Peter was returning with his fishing boat and nets from a night of fruitless toil, Christ asked for the use of his boat so that He could conveniently address the multitude that had gathered on the bank of the Sea of Galilee. After Christ finished His message, He told Peter to launch out into the deep and let down his nets for a draught. Peter did not relish the request and said, *Epistates,* which is rendered "Master," "We have toiled all night, and have taken nothing," as much as to say, "Do you desire to increase our weariness to no purpose?"

The title he used is very significant, because *Epistates* means Valuer, Estimater, Appraiser, and is only used in Luke's record. Christ was exercising this very function, and so valued the use of Peter's boat, at a time when He was tired and on His way home, that He gave him two boatloads of fish to repay him for the loan of it. Christ is no man's debtor.

When Mary lavished the costly spikenard on her Lord as the disciples reclined at supper, some of those present felt it necessary to depreciate her loving act. Whereupon, Christ rebuked them and said, "Let her alone.... She hath done what she could, she is come aforehand to anoint My body to the burying. Verily I say to you, wheresoever this gospel is preached throughout the whole world, this also that she hath done shall be spoken of for a memorial of her" (Mark 14:6,8-9). How greatly He valued the ministry of Mary on this occasion, and His estimate of her devoted deed abides to this present day.

We should remember that the supreme Valuer is characterized by ineffable love, infinite tenderness, incomparable considerateness, and immortal wisdom. He never undervalues a kindly word spoken, or underestimates a loving deed done in His name. No one but He took notice of the poor widow who cast two mites, all that she had, into the Temple treasury. His estimate of her act has prompted and promoted more sacrificial giving throughout the centuries than any other example, save that of His giving Himself (II Cor. 8:9; Gal. 2:20). He fully understands what giving costs, therefore His valuation is perfectly accurate and unmistakably correct. By virtue of His being divinely sensitive, He takes notice of any neglect in returning thanks to Him for benefits received (Luke 17:17). Yea, in His compassion toward mankind, He is sensitive to a degree, and weighs the burden of a sigh, measures the pain of a heartache, senses the sorrow of severance from loved ones, perceives the motive of a desire, and discerns the aim of an aspiration. He fully knows, sincerely loves, and gently cares for every one of His redeemed people.

The value He places on a ransomed soul is not to be calculated on the basis of material wealth, but in the light of the infinite price He paid in redemption.

At the dawn of the present century, when the leading opal merchant of Queensland had been married for twenty-five years, he celebrated the anniversary by presenting to his wife the eight most precious stones that had been discovered on Lightning Ridge. Seven were mounted in gold on one side of a leather folder, while the one of supreme value was mounted in platinum on the opposite side, with a white satin background.

The merchant decided to visit America to seek fresh markets for his gems. Shortly before embarking on his venture, he asked his wife to permit him to take the folder on the trip.

"You are not going to sell my opals!" she exclaimed.

"No, my dear," he replied, "But I would like to be able to show the folk over West just what wonderful stones we have discovered in Australia."

With solemn injunction to return to her the treasures intact, his wife committed to him the precious gems. After his arrival in the United States one of the early contacts he made was with a well-known millionaire who seemed wholly disinterested in the wide variety of stones he had for display. As the disappointed merchant was about to leave the office, he took from his jewel case the leather folder and handed it to the millionaire to examine. Upon opening it, his eye alighted on one precious stone that captivated his whole attention. Pointing to it he said, "I will give you five thousand dollars for that one."

"No," said the visitor, "Those eight are not mine to sell."

Whereupon the millionaire said, "I will give you ten thousand dollars for that one."

"No," said the trader, "The entire selection belongs to my wife and I pledged to return it intact."

By now the millionaire really meant business, and offered more and yet more in order to secure his desired objective. Eventually, disregarding all previous refusals, he said, "This is my last offer, I will give you thirty-five thousand dollars if I may have that one."

After a brief pause the merchant said, "Very well, it's yours," and the deal was closed.

The actual market value of the stone in Australia at the time was two thousand dollars, but the millionaire had made his purchase at the prodigious price of thirty-five thousand dollars. Therefore, to him as the buyer, the price paid determined the value his treasure was worth to him, the estimate of its preciousness was decided by the amount it took to secure it.

So likewise, the ransom Christ paid to redeem the

Church, His Bride, from the bondage of sin and death, was an infinite one, and cannot be appraised by any of our human standards of reckoning. He loved the Church and gave Himself for it, and now considers His people His own special treasure; the Church is referred to as "the riches of the glory of His inheritance in the saints" (Eph. 1:18), and the manifold glories and virtues will one day be displayed in an immortal kingdom, to the wonder and admiration of myriads of angels (Eph. 3:10).

In the personal aspect of this great truth, the Apostle Paul could say, "The Son of God, who loved me, and gave Himself for me" (Gal. 2:20). What a realization!

THE VICTOR

> O sing unto the LORD a new song; for He hath done marvellous things: His right hand, and His holy arm, hath gotten Him the victory (Ps. 98:1).
> He will swallow up death in victory (Isa. 25:8).
> Death is swallowed up in victory (I Cor. 15:54).
> Thanks be to God, which giveth us the victory through our Lord Jesus Christ (I Cor. 15:57).

Christ has secured the supreme victory over the greatest foe. He has decisively triumphed in the age-long battle of good and evil, truth and error, light and darkness, life and death. He has definitively conquered in the age-old conflict between righteousness and lawlessness, authority and anarchy, obedience and defiance, submission and rebellion.

Wherefore, He is able to make His people victorious (Rev. 15:2). He leads His followers in triumph. Thanks be unto God, which always causeth us to triumph in Christ (II Cor. 2:14). He most surely makes His servants conquerors. The Apostle Paul, after naming the seven most severe calamities that can overtake mankind, confidently declares, "In all these things we are more than conquerors through Him that loved us" (Rom. 8:37).

We may glean an illustration of this from the record of David, king of Israel, who had many victories in his colorful career. Three of these were spectacular and very heroic. When a lad, he slew a lion that threatened his father's flock and later a bear suffered the same fate. During his teens, when his own people were challenged to furnish a man for single combat with Goliath the giant, David stepped forward courageously in the name of the Lord, and gained a renowned victory. These three events, taken figuratively, savor of overcoming the devil, the world, and the flesh. Beniah, one of David's mighty men followed the example which was set by his master. He slew a lion in a pit on a snowy day (I Chron. 11:22). This was a daring act, in a dangerous arena, amid a difficult atmosphere. He also slew an Egyptian of great stature, whose spear was as large as a weaver's beam. Egypt reflects the world in its material resources. Futhermore, Beniah slew two lionlike men of Moab, and Moab, from the origin of the Moabites, signifies the flesh (Gen. 19:37).

The Saviour Himself demonstrated victory in these three realms. He repelled the subtle temptations of the devil, "The prince of this world cometh, and hath nothing in Me" (John 14:30). Likewise, the carnal allurements of the flesh were resisted, "Which of you convinceth Me of sin?" (John 8:46), and again He stated, "Be of good cheer; I have overcome the world" (John 16:33).

An impressive grandeur and imposing splendor surround this Victor. He triumphed where all others had met defeat. He conquered where all other combatants had capitulated. He captured the headquarters of the strongest foe, and led captivity captive. The hosts of those confined by the bars of death in the kingdom of darkness were transformed, and transferred, in order to inherit the kingdom of the Son of His love, in light and liberty (Col. 1:12-13).

This prevailing Victor has never suffered defeat; at Golgotha He gained a mighty triumph, an unprecedented conquest, and an incomparable victory.

He is worthy to receive the greatest expression of gratitude, worthy of the weightiest volume of worship, worthy of the perpetual ascriptions of true praise, and worthy of the highest rank of real honor. Little wonder that He receives the homage of countless millions, as revealed in the book of Revelation. Therein, seven grand doxologies are rendered by the glorified, to the One who established the inheritance of the saints in light. For He is the founder of the holy, heavenly kingdom where righteousness reigns, where joy remains unceasingly, in unbroken peace. Within this dominion of everlasting glory in which love pervades, He perfects His redeemed forevermore. For this corruptible must put on incorruption, and this mortal must put on immortality ... then shall be brought to pass the saying that is written, Death is swallowed up in victory.

"Thanks be unto God, which giveth us the victory through our Lord Jesus Christ" (I Cor. 15:53-54,57). Christ is forever the Victor, sanctified in perfectness, beautified in loveliness, magnified in righteousness, and glorified in holiness, the altogether triumphant and transcendent Saviour.

THE VALIANT

The LORD is my strength and song, and is become my salvation.... The right hand of the LORD doeth valiantly. The right hand of the LORD is exalted: the right hand of the LORD doeth valiantly (Ps. 118:14-16).

Seventy-four occurrences of "valiant" appear in Scripture. The word refers to those who are strong and vigorous, brave and courageous, heroic and valorous, and who are worthy and chivalrous. The message to the Hebrews tells of those who through faith were valiant in fight (Heb. 11:33-34). Jesus, we are told, is the author and perfecter of faith (Heb. 12:2), wherefore He must needs be the valiant one preeminently, because all of these prevailers and overcomers derived their fortitude from Him. The word "valiantest" occurs in the book of Judges (21:10), and this may be rightfully used of Christ, who is more excellent in name and fame than all the mighty.

Let us recall just five of the great things our Lord has wrought by His right hand. He framed His work of creation without the aid of parliament or premier, without the assistance of congress or president, and without any chamber of deputies. He formed man of the dust of the ground by virtue of His own inherent wisdom. He provided the legislation for mankind and the laws of the universe without consulting a single counselor (Isa. 40:13-14). He planned redemption and salvation for humanity without the advice of angels, principalities, or authorities (Eph. 3:10). He purposed the world to come, the kingdom to come, and the ages to come without consulting scientists, physicists, or intellectuals. The only account we possess of these three features is the record given in His infallible Word. In relation to these stupendous activities, His right hand has wrought valiantly. Only one who is valiant can do valiantly.

We should remember that in the magnificent distinction of His personal greatness He is far superior to all His wondrous works. He is Lord of leaders, who frustrated the terrific onslaught of the powers of darkness (Col. 2:15). He is the Prince of kings, who outflanked the forces of the infernal foe and divested him of his armor (Luke 11:21-22). He is the Commander of the crusade against all the evil designs, of the mystery of iniquity (II Thess. 2:7). He is the captain of salvation who subdues all that is destructive of righteousness, peace, and joy (Heb. 2:10,15-16). The most famous of artists have failed in their attempts to portray the features of such a celebrity. His face expresses the mingling of majesty and meekness, of a sublime strength and sympathy, of a combined sovereignty and simplicity, of an attractive loveliness and lowliness, of true faithfulness and friendliness, yes, and a merging of valiance and patience, of glory and of grace. Who is qualified to paint such a combination of virtues in a portrait?

The inner light of His inherent dignity and regal nature shone out radiantly in the luster of His love and the light of His countenance. His greatness of soul is reflected in the decrees He uttered, the decision He made, the deeds He wrought, and the disposition He expressed. His beauty of spirit, comely personality, high courtesy, charming manner, and lavish generosity, combined with a captivating eloquence, surpassed the qualities of all other noble characters in history.

Yet of Him Isaiah wrote the prediction, "I gave My back to the smiters, and My cheeks to them that plucked off the hair: I hid not My face from shame and spitting" (Isa. 50:6). Seven hundred and fifty years after the prophet wrote these words they were fulfilled (John 19:1-3; Matt. 26:67). Although Christ knew well the terrible onslaught He would encounter at Jerusalem, He set His face as a flint to go (Isa. 50:7). He directed His steps toward the city so resolutely that He went on ahead of His disciples (Luke 19:28).

We speak at times of the heroic gallantry of some distinguished soldier on the battlefield, but all such pale in the presence of the Christ of Calvary. He was unaccompanied by a retinue of servants and unprotected by a personal body guard, when He faced superhuman assailants, altogether unswayed and unafraid. During His ministry He made no truce or treaty with unrighteousness in any form. His condemnation of hypocrisy, falsity, and tyranny was most pronounced. Gethsemane and Golgotha were now to become the battle-grounds for the fiercest of conflicts ever fought. There was never an encounter of such magnitude, involving good and evil, truth and error, righteousness and lawlessness, freedom and bondage, life and death, the issues of which were eternal. The prince of the regency of darkness, with his mind of malignity, his heart of hate, and his will of revenge, had conceived the most despicable and diabolical action against the Son of Man. Satanic power could not have invented a darker calumny or instigated a deeper insult than was inflicted on the Christ of God. Who else but the valiant Saviour would have continued to pursue his course of securing salvation for mankind, amid every possible disadvantage, devised by the most subtle of foes? Malicious cruelty and vicious hate were rampant. A motley crowd had been assembled and bribed to demand the death of the greatest Lover of all time.

The courageous demeanor and chivalrous deportment Christ exhibited under such dire circumstances by far exceeded the most valiant of all history.

No tribunal of justice and justification so magnificent is

in existence; no throne and regency of mercy and grace so majestic has ever been established anywhere; and no triumph and victory so manifold in range and renown is ever recorded as that of the cross of Christ (John 12:31).

The greatness of our Deliverer is thereby elevated to the highest degree, death is subdued, and the dominion of the devil disrupted. His cross and death astonished a nation, astounded a universe, and aroused all Heaven to great admiration and adoration in rendering deathless honor to such a conqueror (Rev. 5:11-12).

THE VANQUISHER

Having spoiled principalities and powers and made a show of them openly, triumphing over them (Col. 2:15).

That through death He might destroy him that had the power of death, that is, the devil (Heb. 2:14).

We derive our word "vanquish" from the Latin *vinco*, "to conquer." A vanquisher is one who secures deliverance and establishes defense for a people, by overcoming an enemy. This is another of those famous features, in relation to the character of Christ, that is worthy of our wrapt attention and admiration.

Insofar as this world is concerned, the conflict began at the commencement of Bible history. The enemy left his satanic nature's imprint upon the man God had created, by first capturing his mind. When this was accomplished he indulged his malicious spite against God. The human mind, which is the finest expression of God's creative wisdom, became corrupted and a recruit was gained on the side of evil, to promote disobedience toward God and propagate transgression. This moral tragedy would gratify the whole realm of fallen spirits in the kingdom of darkness, where God's holy name is profanely blasphemed. Wherefore God intervenes to uphold His honor and, even before He passes sentence on guilty man, He addresses the deceiver. Firstly, as Sovereign Lord of the universe, He imposes a humiliating penalty on Satan, and then proceeds to declare that a champion would arise and smite evil in its most vital part (Gen. 3:14-15). The conflict, the Conqueror, and His conquest are cited within the compass of one verse (Gen. 3:15).

When the fullness of time was come God sent forth His Son, born of a woman (Gal. 4:4). This great historic event made clear to the human mind the age-old conflict that was being waged through the centuries, between good and evil, truth and error, right and wrong, light and darkness, love and hate, life and death, yea, between Deity and devilry. As the years passed, the enemy gained as confederates the pharaohs of Egypt; the kings of Syria, Assyria, Babylon, Medo-Persia, Greece; and the emperors of Rome. History records that for the most part, Gentile rulers have been agencies of the prince of this world. "The kings of the earth stood up, and the rulers were gathered together against the Lord, and against His anointed [Christ]" (Acts 5:26).

The attitude of evil has not changed; the Church which Christ established has been in conflict for twenty centuries with the principalities, powers, and world rulers of the darkness of this age (Eph. 6:12 Newberry). Into the midst of this arena Christ came to meet the prince of this world in personal combat. During His ministry, the Lord referred thrice to the head of these infernal powers. Said He: "Now is the judgment of this world: now shall the prince of this world be cast out." "The prince of this world cometh, and hath nothing in Me." Also the Spirit's witness: "Of judgment, because the prince of this world is judged" (John 12:31; 14:30; 16:11).

In contrast, Christ is supremely greater, for He is the Prince of life (Acts 3:15), the Prince of peace (Isa. 9:6), the Prince of princes (Dan. 8:25), and the Prince of kings (Rev. 1:5). Never before nor since has the world witnessed a conflict of such magnitude, which involved God's honor and the destiny of countless millions. The encounter constituted the battle of the ages.

A dramatic illustration of the tremendous issues at stake is depicted in microcosm, during the reign of King Saul. Two national armies were set in battle array, those of Israel and the Philistines. Both were encamped on high ground, with the valley of Elah between them (I Sam. 17: 2). A champion in the Philistine army, a warrior of great stature, came to the forefront on the mount. He was known as Goliath of Gath, and was clad in a coat of heavy mail. He wore a helmet of brass to protect his head and was fully equipped with a great sword, spear, and shield. In scornful pride he shouted disdainfully, demanding that a man of Israel should come and fight him. Said he, "I am a Philistine, and ye servants to Saul? Choose you a man for you, and let him come down to me. If he be able to fight with me, and to kill me, then will we be your servants: but if I prevail . . . and kill him, then shall ye be our servants, and serve us. . . . I defy the armies of Israel this day; give me a man, that we may fight together" (I Sam. 17:8-10). King Saul and his officers were in a dilemma; distress and dismay dominated Israel's whole army.

At this critical juncture a young shepherd arrived from Bethlehem. How very significant! When he heard Goliath's repeated challenge he accepted it. Was it mere presumption? The two armies riveted their attention on the combatants in breathless suspense. The courageous calmness of David as he picked up five smooth stones from the brook, as he crossed it at the bottom of the valley, added to the tenseness of the hour. The destiny of two peoples hung in the balance. In a few moments the skill of David's well-directed aim felled the enemy, and with the use of Goliath's own weapon David completed the victory.

The greater David looked down from Heaven to hear the groaning of the prisoner, and to loose those that are appointed to death (Ps. 102:20). He descended and was found in fashion as a man and thereby qualified Himself to meet the foe, whose decree of death was over all men. The final victory was gained at Golgotha, a name derived from Goliath*, whose head may have been buried there, for David took it to Jerusalem when he transferred his throne from Hebron, where he had reigned for seven years (II Sam. 5:5; I Sam. 17:54; 21:9).

_____

* Stated by Harold St. John, from an old volume he read in the British Museum.

The results of the victory Christ gained are not confined to two nations, nor are they limited in their range to the scope of this present world. His transcendent triumph affected the moral and spiritual universes both terrestrially and celestially to a dimension of endless duration. The Bible expresses the period as the ages of the ages.

Our blessed Lord in a few pregnant words described figuratively this formidable battle by stating: "When a strong man armed keepeth his palace, his goods are in peace: But when a stronger than he shall come upon him, and overcome him, he taketh from him all his armour wherein he trusted, and divideth his spoils" (Luke 11:21-22).

We are apt to overlook this descriptive portrayal, which is one of the supreme reasons for the manifestation. "For this purpose the Son of God was manifested, that He might destroy [undo] the works of the devil" (I John 3:8). Although many details are concealed, sufficient is revealed to make clear the magnitude of the conflict of these mighty powers. Heaven and earth, Deity and humanity, righteousness and lawlessness, the reign of life and the reign of death were all involved. On the blighted soil of this earth the Son of God encountered the most bitter assault from the prince of darkness. Marvel of marvels that Messiah, the Prince of princes, the Messenger and Mediator of the everlasting covenant, the very embodiment in all perfection of beauty, purity, and glory, should deign, as Son of Man, to join battle with an infernal foe whose mind is malignity and whose will is revenge. The Vanquisher has vanquished the great dragon, the old serpent called the devil and Satan, who is the destroyer, the dread deceiver, and has frustrated his diabolical designs. The Vanquisher has also vindicated God's honor by His obedience unto death, and has verified His divine faithfulness as the great Avenger (Num. 35:19; John 8:44).

In a prophetic chapter, which contains seventy personal pronouns referring to Christ, take notice of the first two of ten questions that are asked: "Who is this that cometh from Edom, with dyed garments from Bozrah? [Botarah—fortress] This that is glorious in His apparel, marching in the greatness of His strength? I that speak in righteousness, mighty to save" (Isa. 63:1). This marvelous Vanquisher of the enemy was fully equipped with the armor of righteousness and the sword of the Spirit. His resources of exceptional energy to endure, sovereign strength to subjugate, majestic might to master, and princely power to prevail, comprised some of the virtues required to undo the works of the devil. These works were in direct opposition to God's purpose of light, life, love, and law. The magnificence of the Deliverer's victory over the evil one, the far-reaching dimensions of the dominion secured, and the utmost distinction and duration of the honors gained, are matters too vast for our minds to grasp.

Forty days after His conquest of death, the Vindicator ascended to the realm from whence He came, and had a triumphal entry and rapturous welcome into the Jerusalem above, the city of God. The stirring question, "Who is this?" (Matt. 21:10) that was asked at the time of His triumphal entry into earthly Jerusalem, is asked again as He approaches the portals of the eternal city, "Who is this?" and the answer is given, "The LORD mighty in battle" (Ps. 24:8). Hallelujah! What a Vanquisher! What a Vindicator! What a Victor!

> The greatest battle ever fought
>   The most famous victory won
> Involved the strongest princes known
>   And the Victor was God's own Son.
>
> Life and death were the odds at stake
>   With issues too great to conceive
> For Heaven with hell was engaged in strife
>   The honor of God to retrieve.
>
> The Prince who is the Light of Life
>   Addressed the foe that darkest night
> In words of pow'r, "This is your hour"
>   To win or lose time's greatest fight.
>
> The combat of the ages raged
>   For Good and evil were embroiled.
> God's Son in human form prevailed
>   And by Him Satan's pow'r was spoiled.

W

The WRITER (Exod. 24:12; 31:18; John 8:6,8; Heb. 8:10; Jer. 31:33; Rev. 14:1)

He writes what He is, God is love, so He requires love, "Thou shalt love."

The WELL BELOVED (Song of Sol. 1:13; Mark 12:6)

He is both attractive and affectionate in faithful constancy.

The WONDERFUL COUNSELOR (Isa. 9:6)

His divine counsel is perfectly faultless and flawless.

The WISDOM OF GOD (I Cor. 1:24)

Christ is the full and final expression of God's eternal purpose.

The WITNESS (John 18:36-37)

His statements were clear and courageous at all times.

The WAY (John 14:6)

He made the way to the Father plain and permanent in Himself.

The WAFER (Lev. 2:5-6; Exod. 29:33)

An expression of the evenness of His excellent virtues.

The WORM (Ps. 22:6)

The worthiest of celebrities considered worthless by man.

The WORKER (John 4:34; 5:17,36; 17:4; 9:4)

No work of His can be improved, none is imperfect.

The WORD OF GOD (Rev. 19:13)

Christ is the personal exhibition of God's will and wisdom.

The WATCHER (Gen. 31:49; Dan. 4:23; Ps. 102:7; Matt. 26:38)

Always alert and attentive in arranging affairs with a definite aim.

The WALL OF FIRE (Zech. 2:5)
His resources are available to safeguard and sustain.

"Jesus stooped down and with His finger
wrote on the pavement"

He substantiates His impeccability
He signifies His superiority
He justifies His sovereignty
He confirms His identity
He certifies His infinity
He affirms His authority
He vindicates His mercy
He verifies His deity

"The Lord delivered unto me two tables of stone
written with the finger of God"

The Wonderful Writer

He writes in characters too grand
For natural sight to understand;
His Father's likeness He imparts
By writing in His people's hearts.

No other scribe of flesh and bone
Can with His finger write on stone,
But Christ the Lord has done so thrice,
That He is God, let this suffice.

He pledges to transform the soul
And in God's image make us whole,
That we by grace might see His face
And all His loving-kindness trace.

He said He will make all things new,
That we His glory there may view;
Complete in holiness of love,
To serve Him in the realms above.

The foreheads of His people bear
Three written names in letters fair,
Which mark a nature all divine,
Where heart and home His joys enshrine.

His promises are really true,
   He has decreed a grand review;
He will His kingdom manifest,
   Pervaded by eternal rest.

How worthy is our Lord of trust,
   So rich in mercy yet most just;
His scepter and His crowns remain,
   The emblems of His endless reign.

I am Alpha and Omega (Rev. 22:13)

In this stupendous threefold claim, which Christ voiced from the excellent glory, He made use of three figurative expressions that we should most diligently investigate. The first of the three with which we are dealing, namely "I am Alpha and Omega," incorporates in one single stride the entire range and the replete renown of the revelation of His eternal Word, Himself the Revealer. This part of the claim stands first in order as the seal of His omniscience, and precedes His eventual work in creation which marks His omnipotence, Himself the Creator. This fact is stated in the second part of the claim, "the Beginning and End." He is so designated as the *archē* and *telos* in relation to creation in Col. 1:15-20. By virtue of His omniscience and omnipotence being expressed in revelation and creation, the stage is set for the manifestation. Through this means we are enlightened as to His omnipresence. A body was prepared Him and His delight was to do the Father's will. The secret of His sacerdotal service and sacrifice was designed and decreed in order to express His effectual will in mediation, Himself the Mediator. In this vocation He is the First and the Last, for there is but one mediator between God and men, the man Christ Jesus (I Tim. 2:5). Let us rehearse the wonderful words again, for they befit the lips of no one else but the Son of God.

"I am Alpha and Omega, the beginning and end, the first and the last" (Rev. 22:13). The order in this statement of claim is most significant, as we have endeavored to point out. *His eternal Word* as Revealer precedes *His eventual work* as Creator and prepares the way for expressing *His effectual will* as Mediator of the new covenant. The claim is irrefutable for it asserts that Christ not only fills the highest rank in official dignity but is enthroned at the paramount peak of power far above every name that is named, not only in this world but in that which is to come (Eph. 1:21). No created being can assume to aspire to any one of these celestial distinctions and colossal administrations which are supernatural and wholly divine.

Every realm of knowledge is involved in Him as Revealer, every resource and privilege is included in Christ as Creator, and every right and advantage is indicated in Him as Mediator.

When we assay to contemplate the attributes of Christ in all their plenitude and perfectness, when we attempt to calculate the activities of Christ in all their magnitude and magnificence, and when we aspire to concentrate on the assurances of Christ in all their certitude and consolation, we find ourselves facing the unalterable dimensions of immutability, the unattainable discernment of immensity, and the unanswerable determination of Emmanuel the Infinite One.

In all positions of dignity, majesty, and authority and in every rank of nobility, royalty, and competency, Christ stands preeminent. We are dealing with the greatest subject in the realm of knowledge, namely the person of Christ. In no virtuous capacity is He in anywise deficient; in no vigorous competency is He in the least decrepit, and in no victorious capability is He at all defective. Christ possesses, inherently, a perceptive understanding of all things, for He is omnipresent; He wields a protective power in all realms, for He is omnipotent; and He has a positive knowledge of all men, for He is omniscient.

THE WRITER

The LORD said to Moses, Come up to Me into the mountain, and be there: and I will give thee tables of stone, and a law, and commandments which I have written (Exod. 24:12).

He gave to Moses ... two tables of testimony, tables of stone, written with the finger of God (Exod. 31:18).

Jesus stooped down and with His finger wrote on the pavement (John 8:6,8).

I will put My laws into their mind, and write them upon their hearts (Heb. 8:10; Jer. 31:33).

I will write upon Him the name of my God (Rev. 3:12).

Having His Father's name written on their foreheads (Rev. 14:1).

The Bible speaks a great deal about this subject, the words "write, written, wrote, and writing" are used over four hundred thirty times in the Scriptures. When the Lord selected writing material on earth, for the purpose of writing His law, He chose tables of stone. Stone is durable and lasts a long time but it is breakable. The words thus written with the finger of God served as a lasting reminder of man's duty both toward Heaven and humanity. Yet the imperishable base on which the writing was done could not impart the power that was necessary to enable man to keep it. Therefore, the first covenant that was written on stone was deficient from man's viewpoint, as was purposely intended, for it did not make any provision to promote obedience; made no offer of power, pardon, or peace; and held out no gift of righteousness, redemption, or reconciliation.

So the Lord in His infinite wisdom selected an entirely different material on which to write the words of the new covenant. "I will put My laws into their mind, and write them in their hearts" (Heb. 8:10). This covenant is certified as being everlasting (Heb. 13:20), so this is one of the most gracious of the promises. Let us take notice of the eminent and efficient character of this Writer, who is the embodiment of infinite wisdom, knowledge, and understanding, and exercises perfect ability to express Himself by witnessing to mankind, in winsome words through the medium of revealed truth recorded in worthy writings, and more tangibly and plainly in wondrous works. His name stands highest in the ranks of the renowned and His divine nature is the very essence of righteousness, goodness, preciousness, and true holiness.

He is the Creator of the faculties for writing that man

exercises and also of the facilities that he has at his disposal for so doing. This divine Writer originated the alphabet and the capacity of speech which He bestowed upon man. More marvelous still, He created in man the faculty of memory which enables him to retain in mind a knowledge of the alphabetical signs and to utilize them when writing. In any or all of the vital capacities and virtuous abilities conferred upon mankind, He Himself is perfect in the same, wherefore He is the perfect Writer. He has essentially a full and complete knowledge of His subject matter and has never made an error or a single mistake in His writing. Scripture affirms that He is the author of faith, but also tells us that faith cometh by hearing, and hearing by the Word of God. Therefore He is the Author of the written Word that begets and promotes faith.

The Lord Himself is the Author of the insight and foresight that was granted to Moses the writer, whom God girded with such extraordinary capabilities. The five books he wrote supply the base for all revelation that was afterward given. The Lord repeatedly told Moses to write in a book.

When Joshua prevailed against Amalek because of intercession, the Lord said to Moses, "Write this for a memorial in a book, and rehearse it in the ears of Joshua" (Exod. 17:14). By the commandment of the Lord he wrote the record of Israel's journeys through the wilderness (Num. 33:2). On the occasion of his one hundred and twentieth birthday (Deut. 31:2), Moses was commanded to write a song and teach it to the sons of Israel, and he wrote this song the same day (Deut. 31:19,22). On the memorable occasion when Christ had claimed equality with Deity and verified it with a sevenfold witness, He said to the Jews, "Had ye believed Moses ye would have believed Me, for he wrote of Me. But if ye believe not his writings, how shall ye believe My words?" (John 5:46-47) At a time when the people of the whole countryside were present in Jerusalem for the celebrating of the feast of tabernacles, Jesus went to the Temple when the week of ceremonies was half way through and spoke boldly to the multitude. He said emphatically when addressing them, Did not Moses give you the law . . . none of you doeth the law? (John

7:19) This constituted a disallowance of the people's vow recorded in Exod. 19:7-8 (read Num. 30:14-15). Christ is the husband (Isa. 54:5), hence the bill of Israel's divorcement (Isa. 50:1). Because of the Lord's direct statement, None of you doeth the law, the Pharisees decided to test Him, to see if He kept the law. So they planned to be present as observers at an arranged act of adultery, and brought the woman involved before Him, and said, "Moses in the law commanded us, that such should be stoned: but what sayest Thou?" (The Romans twenty-eight years before had prohibited the Jews from administering the death penalty, so had He ordered the stoning, the Pharisees would have accused Him to the Romans.)

"Jesus stooped down, and with His finger wrote on the pavement" (John 8:6). There is no ground or earth in the Temple courts, all are paved in stone. Here is the one who with the finger of God first wrote the law. No one but God manifest could write with the finger on slabs of stone. His Deity unmistakably is verified and vindicated by His writing. By this act Christ elevated Himself immeasurably above the limitations of humanity. The words He spake to the Pharisees imply: he that is without this sin let him first cast a stone at her. King David could not carry out the penalty of the law against his son Ammon, because he himself had been guilty of the same sin. Christ was the only one present who was qualified to administer justice (John 8:46), but to prove He was the Saviour (John 4:42), He showed mercy. He not only protected her from the condemnation of the law, but also provided the power to enable resistance of wrongdoing.

The empowerment against disobedience is what is suggested in the figure of His writing the law in the heart.

> No other power but that which is divine,
>   Could write God's law upon this heart of mine;
> He uses not the inks and pens of time,
>   But His own spirit, in penmanship sublime.

This writing again affirms His Deity, for no one else is capable of using such material, as He did, to express the very stamp and hallmark of absolute right to the redeemed of the

Lord. Yet more amazing still is the divine skill He exhibits in writing the threefold name of God, of the Holy City, and His own new name, on the personality, so that each one bears the image, and the likeness of the eternal features that were forfeited at the beginning in Eden. Herein is signified our Lord's supreme triumph as a Writer, the representative group have His Father's name written on their foreheads (Rev. 14:1), and in the grand finale, the throne of God and the Lamb shall be in it, and His servants shall serve Him: And they shall see His face; and His name shall be on their foreheads (Rev. 22:3-4). "Behold, I make all things new." And He said to me, "Write: for these words are true and faithful" (Rev. 21:5).

THE WELL BELOVED

A bundle of myrrh is my wellbeloved unto me (Song of Sol. 1:13).

Now will I sing to my wellbeloved a song of my beloved touching his vineyard. My wellbeloved has a vineyard in a very fruitful hill (Isa. 5:1).

Having yet therefore one son, his wellbeloved, he sent him also last unto them, saying, "They will reverence my son" (Mark 12:6).

These three references occur in association with vineyards. They comprise a picturesque setting for friendly fellowship of the most intimate kind, combined with a life that is fragrant, and fruitful (Song of Sol. 1:2; 2:13). The symbolism of myrrh, in the first reference, indicates the companionship and communion of perfect love, a subject that is dealt with more fully in the first Epistle of John. In this Song of Songs, there is an entire absence of all such words as iniquity, transgression, and sin; no reference to the precepts of the law; and all doctrines of salvation, redemption, forgiveness, and the like are omitted. The very substance of the message relates to love and the beloved, two words which occur sixty-four times. The well beloved is pictured in every relationship of intimacy with a marked integrity. We have no difficulty in applying these characteristics to Christ, who is called the Beloved Son on eight occasions in the record of the first three Gospels. Notice also, that this witness to Christ is from no less a source than the throne in the heavens.

We are not dealing with what we may call a temporary title for the time being, for Christ is essentially and eternally the Well Beloved. Yea, He is the ever-blessed Beloved, beautified in holiness, magnified in preciousness, and glorified in perfectness. No substitute can ever replace Him in this capacity and no superior can ever surpass Him. He ever abides as the Well Beloved without either predecessor or successor, for in all stations of high rank He holds the preeminent place.

The more we delve into the depths of our beloved Lord's moral perfections, the more difficult it becomes to select figures of speech that adequately set forth His intrinsic worth. However, let us note somewhat of the appropriate factors that apply in the use made of this lovely metaphor, "A bundle of myrrh is my wellbeloved unto me." Myrrh is one of the most rare and costly of the aromatic gums; where used as a preservative, decay is retarded, and decomposition prevented. On this account the Egyptians used it when embalming the Pharaohs, and Nicodemus included this valuable and costly substance when embalming the body of Jesus (John 19:39). Myrrh was also the most precious item used in the processes of purification in the royal household (Esther 2:12), and was considered by the wise men as being most pertinent to be included in a gift for presentation to the one born king in Bethlehem (Matt. 2:11). The Patriarch Jacob esteemed this choice commodity worthy of a place in his gift to Pharaoh, king of Egypt (Gen. 43:11). We may find all these significant activities, in which myrrh was used, greatly enhanced by recalling the portrayal of Psalm 45. A majestic king is pictured emerging from ivory palaces in regal robes, all his garments diffusing the fragrance of myrrh (Ps. 45:8). So we are not surprised to be told that the perfecting of beauty in Esther's preparation for her debut before King Ahasuerus was amplified by the use of oil of myrrh (Esther 2:12).

These five features alone are sufficient to warrant the

use made of myrrh as representing the personal perfections of the Well-Beloved Son. When combined they assure a potent preservative, a pleasant perfume, a precious presentation, a proficient purifier, and a pronounced perfecter. We are aware that all of these benefits and blessings are centered for us in the Well-Beloved Son (Mark 12:6). Let us briefly review them without comment.

Christ is our Preserver. "Jude, the servant of Jesus Christ, and brother of James, to them that are sanctified by God the Father and preserved in Jesus Christ" (Jude 1). "The Lord shall deliver me from every evil work, and will preserve me unto His heavenly kingdom, to whom be glory for ever and ever" (II Tim. 4:18). "The Lord preserveth all them that love Him" (Ps. 145:20).

Christ is our Perfume. "Christ also hath loved us, and hath given Himself for us an offering and a sacrifice to God for a sweet-smelling savour" (Eph. 5:2). The anointing for priestly service was administered with a perfume (Exod. 30:35). The saints in Corinth were assured of this spiritual anointing (II Cor. 1:21), as a result it is written, "We are unto God a sweet savour of Christ" (II Cor. 2:15).

Christ is our Presentation. "Now unto Him that is able to keep you from stumbling, and to present you faultless before the presence of His glory with exceeding joy" (Jude 24). "Chosen in Him before the foundation of the world, that we should be holy and without blame before Him in love....He hath made us accepted in the Beloved" (Eph. 1:4,6). "That we may present every man perfect in Christ Jesus" (Col. 1:28).

Christ is our Purifier. "Who gave Himself for us, that He might redeem us from all iniquity, and purify unto Himself a peculiar people, zealous of good works" (Titus 2:14). "Put no difference between us and them, purifying their hearts by faith" (Acts 15:9). "If the blood of bulls and of goats ... sanctifieth to the purifying of the flesh ... how much more shall the blood of Christ ... purge your conscience" (Heb. 9:13-14).

Christ is our Perfecter. "After He had offered one sacrifice for sins for ever, sat down on the right hand of God.

... For by one offering He hath perfected for ever them that are sanctified" (Heb. 10:12-14). "Beloved, if God so loved us, we ought also to love one another. ... If we love one another, God dwelleth in us, and His love is perfected in us" (I John 4:11-12). "This also we wish, even your perfection" (II Cor. 13:9).

Let us remind ourselves again of these delightful words, "A bundle of myrrh is my wellbeloved unto me," a bag of myrrh, as some versions render it. The statement is like a fingerpost directing our attention and affection to the Well Beloved, in all the dignity of His desirability, in all the attractiveness of His affection, in all the winsomeness of His worthy character, and in all the riches of His unbounded resource. However many valuable features myrrh may furnish, the Well Beloved by far exceeds and excels them. For all those who love and trust Him, He it is who sanctifies, purifies, qualifies, beautifies, gratifies, justifies, and satisfies forevermore. He adds the perfume of incense to prayer, the pleasure of joy to praise, the positive guarantee in Himself to promise, and the pledge of certainty to the eternal purpose.

The Well-Beloved Son is the Father's love gift and He Himself is altogether lovely (Song of Sol. 5:16). This verdict never varies throughout the entire volume of revealed truth. He is lovely to memory in retrospect, He is lovely at present to faith in every aspect, and He is lovely to hope in prospect. This one predominant note peals forth perpetually from immortal lips, "He is altogether lovely." We cannot fail to notice, when reading the record of His life and ministry during the manifestation, that love and loveliness characterize the whole. Observe the loveliness in the nobility of His character, in beauty of form, in purity of heart, in maturity of mind, in constancy of care, in dignity of decrees, and in the ministry of peace. The Well Beloved is altogether lovely in His matchless mercy, staunchless sympathy, ageless ability, flawless fidelity, boundless beauty, changeless constancy, and fadeless glory.

In the light of *who* our Well Beloved is, *why* He is, *what* He is, and *where* He is, we believe that eternal salvation for all them that obey Him is most definitely assured (Heb. 5:9).

Let us gather our meditation in a few closing verses.

A bag of myrrh is my Beloved to me,
  The sweetest fragrance tells me it is He;
His winsome presence draws my soul apace,
  To contemplate the beauty of His face.

The sterling virtues of His purest mind
  Determine loving deeds of every kind,
For He *presents* me in the home above,
  With full acceptance to the Father's love.

My Well Beloved in whom I am *preserved,*
  Prepares in Heaven a place, He holds reserved,
And I shall see His glory by-and-by,
  His rainbow circled throne, beyond the sky.

The altogether lovely one is He,
  The Son of God, who gave Himself for me;
He *purified* me through the blood He shed,
  For on the cross He suffered in my stead.

The perfect Lover evermore to be,
  Has pledged His Word to *perfect* even me,
For when we see Him, like Him we shall be,
  A tribute to His triumph on the tree.

Oh lovely Lord, God's Well-Beloved Son,
  Who saw on earth the Father's will was done,
And now is glorified at God's right hand,
  With universal power at His command.

My Well Beloved, to me a bag of myrrh,
  Thy precious *perfume* makes me all astir;
Oh draw me to Thy loving breast once more,
  That I may truly worship and adore.

THE WONDERFUL COUNSELOR

His name shall be called Wonderful Counsellor (Isa. 9:6).

Thou hast done a wonderful thing; Thy counsels of old are faithfulness and truth (Isa. 25:1).

This also cometh forth from the LORD of hosts, which is wonderful in counsel, and excellent in working (Isa. 28:29).

According to the purpose of Him who worketh all things after
the counsel of His own will (Eph. 1:11).

The immutability of His counsel (Heb. 6:17).

This title is part of a fourfold description of the
predicted name of the coming Messiah, which indicates the
uttermost range of His official legislation and administration.
Today men with scientific knowledge and the use of a com-
putor are able to exercise control over a module two hundred
and thirty thousand miles away and carry on a conversation
with astronauts at that distance. They are able to control a
rocket after launching it for over a million miles, and
manipulate the mechanism attached thereto, so that
photographs of other planets are sent back to earth. This
amazing achievement enables us to contemplate the counsel of
this Wonderful Counselor's will, who determines that the
Pleiades, which is more than three thousand billion miles away,
controls our planetary system. The magnitude of Christ's
determinate counsel operates beyond the range of human
reckoning, for He has decreed that the influence of the
Pleiades draws all other constellations, at the rate of one
hundred and fifty million miles a year, in a vast orbit that
takes a thousand years to complete one circuit. "What is man
that Thou art mindful of him!" The Prophet Isaiah refers to
this Counselor as the Creator and frequently mentions the
many and mighty things created. He makes use of these words
in his message on twenty-one occasions, and speaks also of
"might and mighty" over thirty times, "mighty" being used in the
second of the four titles comprising the name. Never before in
any record were these four official designations linked together
in one personality.

A striking illustration of what is stated here was
signified in the pattern of the Tabernacle revealed to Moses on
the mount. The wonderful veil of the Tabernacle, which was
woven of blue, purple, and scarlet and fine twined linen, was
hung on four pillars of shittim wood, overlaid with gold (Exod.
26:31-33). We are plainly told in the New Testament that the
veil signifies Christ in personal manifestation (Heb. 10:20). The

four pillars overlaid with gold formed the background of support, to display the amazing beauty of the handsome veil. In like manner, behind the fourfold manifestation of the Son of Man recorded in the four Gospels, stand these massive realities of His divine character.

The four titles combined indicate His dignity as Legislator, His deity as Liberator, His desirability as Lover, and His durability as the Liquidator of all opposing powers, to become the Consolidator of everlasting peace. These intrinsic qualifications account for the mystery of His majestic mercy, His mighty works, His marvelous wisdom, and His miraculous ministry, portrayed during the manifestation. How true is the statement that Christ made, "No one knoweth who the Son is, but the Father" (Luke 10:22). We shall deal with the first of the four divine titles included in the Name, that is, Wonderful Counselor.

Seeing the question mark is used well over three thousand times in the Bible, let us adopt a few at this point. Who was it that gave to the eagle eyes to see afar off ? (Job 39:29) Who gave counsel to the plowman to know how to plow and sow seed? "His God doth instruct him to discretion." This is also true even in threshing, which is wonderful in counsel (Isa. 28:23-29). How much more does this Wonderful Counselor express Himself in His work of creation. Who taught the Lord His wonderful knowledge in compounding the many elements? Who taught the Lord to put the earth in orbit and maintain it with its estimated weight of six trillion tons? Who taught the Lord mathematics to enable Him to regulate the equinoxes and eclipses with such admirable precision? Who taught the Lord to create man and to crown this aspect of His creative work by manifesting Himself in manhood as the man Christ Jesus? The Lord Himself proposes such questions, "Who hath directed the Spirit of the LORD, or being His counsellor hath taught Him?... With whom took He counsel?" (Isa. 40:13-14) Verse 26 refers to this one as the creator of the stars. Who taught Him how many millions, billions, and trillions there are and who taught Him a name for each one? (Isa. 40:26)

Moreover the Lord affirms that His counsel shall stand and that He will do all His pleasure (Isa. 46:10). As the Wonderful Counselor, our blessed Lord embodies perfect wisdom, infallible knowledge, complete comprehension, absolute power, and infinite discernment. The confines of His counsels and the wisdom of His decrees cannot be calculated. No hindrance can hamper the fulfillment of what the Scriptures describe as the counsel of His own will (Eph. 1:11). Dr. A. T. Pierson stated, in one of his missionary addresses many years ago, that the seven wonders of the ancient world were surpassed by the victorious work of the Son of Man in relation to His Church. A brief consideration of these wonders will confirm the significance of this statement. The seven wonders in general are those of the Pyramids of Egypt, the walls of Babylon, the Colossus at Rhodes, the Pharos at Alexandria, the mausoleum at Halicarnassus in Caria, the statue of Olympian Jove at Athens, and the temple of Diana at Ephesus.

The Pyramids of Egypt. The greatest of these structures was built by the well-known Pharaoh, "Khufu," or "Cheops the Glorious," as he was named by a later generation. The geometrical and astronomical features of this ponderous structure of over a million stones is a monumental witness to human greatness. The Bible speaks of the counsel of the wise counselors of Pharaoh, and in contrast refers to the counsel of the LORD of Hosts (Isa. 19:11,17). But the marvelous events that took place at Pentecost, when Christ demonstrated His ability to overcome the social and national dislocation of tongues, and to establish the foundations for the building of a Church which consists of hundreds of millions of living stones, is a far greater monument. Moreover the dimensions of the Great Pyramid can be measured and its weight approximately determined, but the degree and range of Christ's regenerative power is measureless and the living stones for the building are numberless. The work abides eternally and is wrought according to the counsel of His will. Each stone is engraced with spiritual virtues which He Himself imparts.

The Broad Walls of Babylon. No city walls were ever

built higher and broader than those surrounding the Babylonian metropolis. Nebuchadnezzar diverted the Euphrates from flowing through the city while he had the bed and banks of the river paved in brick, for the twenty miles within the walls. The barricade built on both banks had each twenty-five double gates which opened to the main thorough-fares of the city. King Cyrus received the assurance in later years that the Lord would open to him these two leaved gates (Isa. 45:1) and on the night of Belshazzar's drunken carousal, they were left open, although it had been the custom for years to close them at nightfall. The renown of this colossal con-struction melts as a morning mist when we consider the walls of eternal salvation and the gates of everlasting praise that Christ builds for the City of God (Isa. 26:1; 60:18-19; Rev. 21:10-13,21-23). The scores of thousands of workers employed by Nebuchadnezzar are as a drop in the bucket, in comparison with the myriads Christ has called and chosen as co-workers in His victorious compaigns and conquests. As the Master-Builder of the centuries, His plans and specifications were determined according to the counsel of His will, and are more ponderous. His copious resources are more prodigious, and the character of His building material more precious than that used in any previous construction. Gems and gold, treasures that men esteem to be of greatest worth, are given what, at first sight, appears to be a lesser prominence than spiritual virtues and graces. But these glistening jewels that form the foundations are symbolic of the divine attributes that support and sustain the eternal city.

The Colossus at Rhodes. This stupendous statue in brass seventy cubits high was designed to represent Helios the sun god. Chares the sculptor took twelve years to execute the work. In the year 224 B.C. it was thrown down by an earth-quake and lay in a broken condition for a thousand years ere it was sold as scrap metal. The deification of the sun is one of the oldest religious conceptions in the world, and began soon after satanic power dominated man's mind.

Deity rightly belongs to the Maker of the sun, which is one hundred times larger than the earth. Although hundreds of millions of tons of its mass are consumed every minute, it remains the same. The width of this great orb is eight hundred and fifty thousand miles in diameter and over two million in circumference. How puny the Colossus appears in comparison. But the Wonderful Counselor, who made the sun and planned its maintenance, is also the Light of the world in all moral and spiritual standards, and is greater and brighter as the Sun of Righteousness than anything He has created.

As File Leader, He has opened doors to heathenism, paganism, and cannibalism to diffuse the Light of the knowledge of the glory of God, and established mighty monuments to His saving power. The splendor of His immortal loveliness is the effulgent brightness of Heaven's celestial light, so there is no need of the sun in that realm (Rev. 21:23).

The Pharos of Alexandria. This famous lighthouse just south of Palestine was four hundred feet high, and the light of its fires could be seen for miles across the Mediterranean Sea. The structure, which cost about a million dollars, was commenced by Ptolemy Soter and completed by Ptolemy Philadelphus. This latter ruler instigated the translating of the Hebrew Scriptures into the Greek language, which became known as the Septuagint Version. The brilliance that shone from this enormous lighthouse was not even as the flicker of a taper in comparison with the universal sunlight, when we consider the magnitude of the light of truth, which the gospel had diffused through thousands of languages to hundreds of millions of people. Millions of mariners on the sea of life have been saved from the rocks and reefs of ruin, and guided into the haven of everlasting rest, by the counsel of His will.

The Magnificent Mausoleum at Halicarnassus in Caria. The edifice deservedly ranks among the seven wonders of human construction in the world. Mausolus, who began the structure shortly after 387 B.C., died before the great task was completed. His renowned widow Artemisia, well known for her military strategy and prowess, perfected the undertaking as a monument to her husband's memory. Because of this, the name mausoleum has since been attached to all great tombs.

As late as the tenth century A.D. the structure was still

standing and consisted of a lofty oblong basement one hundred fourteen by ninety-two feet. Thirty-six columns surrounding the masonry supported a pyramid of twenty-four steps, the apex of which was crowned by a chariot group in white marble. The select site and extraordinary design of the monument, together with the beauty of the coloring and select symmetry, combined to make it a masterpiece of art and artifice.

We may contemplate the wealth and workmanship expended in such an edifice, but how it all pales in the light of the counsel of His will, in bringing many sons unto glory. Our Lord's Workmanship (Eph. 2:10), in the transforming of the souls of men, imparting His divine nature, and in bestowing imperishable spiritual gifts, make His Name to be a memorial throughout all generations (Ps. 135:13), not of enshrined death, but of endowed life, of enduring life, of life eternal.

The Statue of Olympian Jove at Athens. The sculpture itself combined the highest religious conceptions of Greece and Rome that were represented in the characters of Jupiter and Zeus. The ponderous temple built to enshrine this divinity was commenced by the tyrant Pisistratus, but the gigantic task was not completed until 130 A.D. by the Emperor Hadrian. In the sphere of imposing magnificence, it was the greatest of heathen temples and was supported by one hundred twenty-four Corinthian columns. The laurels of distinguished conquests were brought by imperial victors and laid on the lap of this supposed lord, who was believed to be the protector of the higher features of society's well-being.

The message that speaks of the counsel of His will also refers to the measure of the stature of the fullness of Christ (Eph. 4:13). Much more, we are informed of the building of a Holy Temple...builded together for a habitation of God, in the Spirit (Eph. 2:21-22). Christ is the express image of the Father, and as the visible image of the invisible God has displayed the glory of His very countenance (John 1:14). Our divine Lord has proven Himself to be the invincible champion of humanity's cause and the Securer and Protector of all social, moral, and spiritual rights. He by far exceeds in ability, excels in achievement, and eclipses in authority all the highly distinguished and richly endowed personalities of the historic ages. No memorial exists in the whole realm of human knowledge that in any way compares with the fame of His wondrous Name. This accounts for the reason why Art has crowned Him in its three forms of poetry, music, and painting. In addition, His Name is printed millions of times more every year than that of any other person.

The Temple of Diana at Ephesus. This great granite temple became proverbial because of its octastyle design, which consisted of eight columns at each end, together with its diphycercal feature of two rows of enormous pillars exterior to the walls. Each pillar was the gift of a king, with a shaft sixty feet in length. The laborious undertaking took two hundred twenty years to complete, and the materials, consisting of cedar, cypress, Parian marble, and gold, were lavished upon it to a degree that savored of prodigality. This huge structure, with its bejeweled figures of the many-breasted goddess Diana, unified Asia Minor. The corrupt system of its ritual stood in proud defiance of all that was pure. In contrast, the manifold spiritual graces, that garnish the holy society of the Lord's redeemed hosts, made Diana's shrine as insipid to sanctified love, as the gross sensuality of Sodom seemed sordid to Abraham, whose eyes had beheld the purity and glory of the city of God. When once the affections have been entranced with a vision of the Saviour's purity and comeliness, the soul has no eyes for the haunts of pollution and corruption.

The Apostle Paul was familiar with each of these famous wonders and during his missionary career experienced an uproar in this very temple at Ephesus (Acts 19:35). Paul was persuaded that the works of the ascended Lord far surpassed and outvied, in degree, design, and durability, the greatest works of mankind. The counsel of this Wonderful Counselor survives when that of all others ceases to exist. The duration of His dominion by virtue of His almighty authority subdues all sinister powers, for He has a prestige that is preeminent, permanent, and perfect.

In view of what this Wonderful Counselor has already

planned and performed, let us come to Him continually for counsel, and trust Him with the utmost confidence. Let us not leave room for the question to be asked, "Is thy counsellor perished?" (Mic. 4:9) What an advantage we have in the right of access to one whose gracious advice is always available and absolutely accurate. He never misjudges a human need. He never misguides a seeker. He never misdirects an inquirer. "To whom then will ye liken Me?" (Isa. 40:25) No other Counselor has the kindness, the kinship, and the knowledge of this one. The Spirit of God, in the prophecy of Isaiah, designates Him the Counselor, the Creator, the All-Wise, the Almighty.

THE WISDOM OF GOD

Christ the power of God, and the wisdom of God (I Cor. 1:24).
But of Him are ye in Christ Jesus, who from God is made to us wisdom (I Cor. 1:30).
The wisdom that is from above is first indeed pure, then peaceable, gentle, easy to be intreated, full of mercy and good fruits, without partiality, and without hypocrisy (Jas. 3:17).

The Son of Man brought into visibility new imponderable dimensions. He widened the horizons of many things and broadened our comprehension both of visible and invisible realities. He opened the doors of investigation to much that had been obscure and gave us convincing demonstrations to verify the amazing authority invested in His hands. One of the astounding disclosures He made related to the immensity and immeasurability of divine wisdom. The Son of Man greatly enlarged our conception of this attribute of Deity and is Himself the personification of the same. Prudence, understanding, instruction, and discretion are some of the constituents of this celestial wisdom. "I wisdom dwell with prudence" (Prov. 8:12). "When wisdom entereth into thine heart... discretion shall preserve thee, understanding shall keep thee" (Prov. 2:10-11). "To know wisdom and instruction ... to receive the instruction of wisdom" (Prov. 1:2-3,7). The Scriptures use the word "wise" also of those who are skilled in technical, professional, and ornamental arts. The supreme expression of wisdom is personified in Christ, whom God hath set forth as being the power of God and wisdom of God (I Cor. 1:24). Wisdom alone is unarmed without power to act, and power alone is useless without wisdom to direct. Christ is the source, the spring, and stream of both these qualities. The Apostle John tells of being carried away in Spirit to a great and high mountain, where he was shown the holy city. We have the privilege of being conducted to the lofty heights of the heavenly Himalayas, to get a glimpse of the seven sun-kissed peaks of wisdom's mountainous range (Jas. 3:17). These stainless glories glisten in the fadeless light above. The peaks are purer than the snow and as perfect as the great white throne of the Eternal God. The grandeur of the description given is purposely designed to draw out the aspiration of our hearts in admiring adoration and praise. The loftiness of wisdom's glorious majesty and the loveliness of her gracious motives speak to us of the self-revelation of God the Father, in the person of His beloved Son.

Because wisdom is an attribute inherent in Deity, the natural mind cannot grasp her great qualities apart from revelation. The wisdom that is from above is first indeed pure (Jas. 3:17 Newberry).

Purity is foremost and fixed in wisdom's divine character, free from all defects and defilements, untainted, untarnished, and unstained in any form whatsoever. People in general appreciate pure air, pure water, and pure food; why not place a greater premium on pure wisdom, which is available and accessible in Christ? No lovely blossom that may be seen bursting in virgin beauty from its tender bud, no radiant day dawn diffusing its clear light across the horizon, and no freshly fallen snowflakes on mountain top are as pure as the wisdom from above. If we are to have a reasonable comprehension of the manifold qualities and meticulous verities that are centered in God's great gift of perfect wisdom, we need to remember that spiritual sight is necessary. "The eyes of your understanding being enlightened; that ye may know" (Eph. 1:18). If we are to behold the beauty and purity of Him who personifies the fullness of heavenly wisdom, we must be strengthened with might by His Spirit in the inner man ... in order to comprehend (Eph. 3:16). The pure in heart shall see God (Matt. 5:8).

Peaceable. The only other occurrence of the word "peaceable" in the New Testament is in Hebrews, where it is classified as being the fruit of righteousness (Heb. 12:11). Righteousness likewise is personified in the Scriptures (Jer. 23:6). Peace is a virtuous quality that conquers, by gaining confidence through sacrificial service, not by contention and conflict. Of Christ it is written, "He is our peace" (Eph. 2:14). Therefore in this wisdom from above there is an entire absence of all forms of arrogance, variance, and turbulence. Even turbulent waters can be quieted by a breathless stillness, or by His subduing word, "Peace, be still" (Mark 4:39). Peaceableness quells confusion by an irresistible calm. The disposition of divine wisdom is fervent but not feverish, serene but not sullen, composed but not captious. Her demeanor is not irksome but winsome, not troublesome but gladsome, not tiresome but awesome; so is He of whom this speaks. The very nature of peace is one of harmony, agreement, and concord, like the congenial aroma from a cluster of fragrant roses pervading the whole atmosphere of a beautiful conservatory. When the spirit of wisdom harmonizes the volitional, intellectual, and emotional capacities, peace prevails. Also the cardinal virtues of faith, hope, and love become deftly blended and balanced in the regenerate life. This peaceable characteristic implanted by wisdom may be silent but never sulky, still but never stagnant, quiet but never querulous, and is proof against malice, envy, and slander.

Patient. The word translated "gentle" in the AV is rendered "patient" in I Tim. 3:3, and "moderation" in Phil. 4:5. The underlying idea is that of forbearance, a deportment that expresses courtesy and shows considerate regard for others. Testings and trials vindicate this virtue but never vanquish it. Patience safeguards her reputation against annoyances, irritabilities, agitations, provocations, and the like, and avoids inflicting or imposing these undesirables on others.

Patience has been allotted a perfect work to perform (Jas. 1:4). Christ never marred His perfect character by impatience. Even when nailed to a brutal cross beside a public highway, drenched with excruciating agony, and the butt of the jibes and curses of a ribald crowd for three long hours, there was not the slightest sign of impatience. It is written of Him, "I waited patiently for the LORD" (Ps. 40:1). This is the psalm which tells of the perfect body that was prepared Him, a body that became more mutilated than any other (Isa. 52:14). His patience proved that He was perfect and entire (Jas. 1:4).

Persuasive, easy to be entreated. Wisdom is sympathetic and attentive to the pleadings of the needy. How very true this is of Christ. The Son of Man readily responded to every entreaty for mercy and help (Matt. 8:2,5,16; 9:2,18,22,27; 15:22). How approachable and accessible He was and is today. Wisdom invites and appeals (Prov. 8:1-4), but never imposes herself where she is not desired. How clearly this feature is seen in the blessed Saviour. He frequently uttered invitations such as, "Come unto Me, all ye that labour and are heavy laden, and I will give you rest" (Matt. 11:28). "If any man thirst, let him come unto Me, and drink" (John 7:37). "Him that cometh to Me I will in no wise cast out" (John 6:37).

The people of Gadara entreated Him to depart from their coast, and He immediately withdrew.

> He had wrought for them a sign
> Of love and hope, of tenderness divine
> They wanted swine.
> Today He stands without your door and gently knocks
> But if your gold, or swine the entrance blocks
> He forces no man's hold, He will depart
> And leave you to the treasures of your heart.
>
> John Oxenham

Again He said "If thou knewest the gift of God, and who it is that saith to thee, Give Me ... Thou wouldest have asked of Him, and He would have given thee" (John 4:10). Easy to be entreated, very easily induced to bestow spiritual virtues and graces. Messiah is infinite in resource as the Son of

God, intimate in relationship as Son of Man, inveterate in His resolute promises as the Good Shepherd, and invariable in His regard for His people as the Great High Priest.

Productive, full of mercy and good fruits. This statement assures us that the wisdom from above is bountifully prolific in goodness, kindness, righteousness, and holiness, yea, all that is virtuous, precious, joyous, and glorious. The inner values of the earlier qualities now become visible in manifold expression. These spiritual supplies furnish the instruction, provision, and direction that qualify for special service, that is honoring to the Lord of Heaven and earth. The mercies of the Lord are demonstrated throughout the entire creation, for all of which we are indebted to the excellency of His transcendent nature of wisdom. We may mention some of these: the fragrance of flowers, the beauty of birds, the foliage of forests, the majesty of mountains, the fruits of the field, the flavors of food, the shining of sunlight, the splendor of sunsets, the scintillation of stars, the succession of seasons, the refreshment of rains. the distilling of dews, the melodies of music, and a thousand more, express the amazing riches of wisdom's mercies. In addition and in greater volume are the blessings of wisdom which are too numerous to mention, all of which emanate from Christ Jesus the Lord. We are blessed with all spiritual blessings in the heavenlies in Christ (Eph. 1:3), in whom are hid all the treasures of wisdom and knowledge (Col. 2:3), not by growth or mature experience, but in eternal essence. How refining the influence, how revealing the instruction, and how rewarding the insight wisdom imparts, all of which surmount human reasoning. The Christ of whom this speaks can no more be unwise than He can be untrue or unkind or unreal.

Prudent without Partiality. The two completing features of wisdom's perfect character are stated negatively, to throw into clearer light the preciousness of her virtue, which is described as better than choice gold and rubies (Prov. 8:10-11). In the following verse it is written, "I wisdom dwell with prudence," therefore partiality has no place in wisdom's nature. Her nature knows no variance, and although discreet she is not disagreeable; although cautious she is not crafty; although impartial she is not indifferent to entreaty for help or mercy. There is no wavering or hesitancy in wisdom's decisions, her stately deportment and keen discernment always direct to that which glorifies God, even as Christ affirmed, "I do always those things that please Him" (John 8:29).

Prejudice and bias are wholly excluded from wisdom's character. Although Christ did not respect the person of any, He had regard for every one. He regarded the prayer of the destitute (Ps. 102:17); the blind beggar of Jericho exemplifies this fact (Luke 18:40), also Mary in her low estate is regarded and highly favored (Luke 1:48).

To be prudent is to have a complete foresight of all conditions that will arise, and ability to plan perfectly and righteously the course to be taken to reach the desired aim. Christ, who is the First and the Last, is able to plan the end from the beginning (Isa. 46:10). Prudence administers sound judgment with discretion, all matters are decided accurately and with a correct estimate in the light of eternity. Yea, prudence has an open countenance in expressing liberality, hospitality, and mercy as directed by wisdom, for the glory of God.

Proper without Hypocrisy. The wisdom from above is real without a trace of deceit or pretense. Her sincere disposition is entirely free from all duplicity and disloyalty. She is never caught feigning and would rather forego her deserved credit than do anything dishonest to obtain distinction. Wisdom would rather imperil her reputation than impair her deservedness. None of her tastes are perverted nor her desires depraved. There is no fraudulence in her plans and no spuriousness in her purposes. Her ways are ways of pleasantness and all her paths are peace (Prov. 3:17). Every last detail bespeaks the Son of Man, who from God is made unto us wisdom (I Cor. 1:30).

This versatile description of wisdom's variegated fullness, as displayed in her vast range and venerable character, is most clearly manifest in the perfect life of God's beloved Son. Yea, and every other attribute of the Godhead is demonstrated and verified in Him who is the visible image of the invisible God, and in whom are hid all the treasures of wisdom and knowledge. His purity abides untarnished, His peaceableness continues undiminished, His patience endures unblemished, His persuasiveness remains unaltered, His productiveness flows unrestricted, His prudence persists undismayed, and His propriety stands undefaced. "Who is wise, and he shall understand these things? prudent, and he shall know them?" (Hos. 14:9)

Christ is wisdom personified and as Head of the Church which He builds of living stones a spiritual house, and for which the seven pillars have been hewn (Prov. 9:1), He demonstrates His infinite wisdom, for the instruction of the heavenly hierarchies (Eph. 3:10). The great and precious purpose of God, expressed through the Church, becomes an object lesson for the principalities and authorities in the heavens. Let us remember that their faculties are keener and more elevated than ours and their perception more comprehensive. They had witnessed the wisdom of God in the many marvels attached to the creating of the heavens and the earth. However, when they saw God's solution to the gigantic problems of Satan's subtlety and of man's guilt, in his disregarding the supreme counsel of the Lord's immutable will, and his disbelieving and disobeying the sovereign command of His indestructible Word, they wondered with awesome admiration. The incredible plan of substitutionary sacrifice, the sinless Son being made sin for us and dying as the just for the unjust, to bring about the possibility of regeneration and reconciliation for mankind in order to establish the Church, displayed to the whole heavenly hierarchy the *manifold wisdom* of God. None but God Himself could have designed and determined such an amazing plan, wherein divine justice was honorably maintained, while those guilty were fully exonerated and justified. Here we meet the supreme expression and exhibition of the wisdom of God which is portrayed in the person of Jesus Christ, the chief cornerstone of the entire structure. He Himself is the Mediator of the new covenant, the majestic Head of the body, the magnificent Foundation of the building, the matchless First-born of the family, and the mighty Defender, the Chief Shepherd of the flock. He not only established the Church, but has sustained and supported its fellowship, missionary enterprise, and Bible translations for twenty centuries against all opposition, oppression, and persecution. "To the intent that *now* unto the principalities and authorities in the heavenlies might be known through the Church the *manifold wisdom of God*" (Eph. 3:10). The Wisdom of the Lord causes even angels to wonder and worship.

THE WITNESS

Jesus answered, "My kingdom is not of this world...." Pilate therefore said to Him, "Art Thou a king then?" Jesus answered, "Thou sayest, that I am a king. To this end was I born, and for this cause came I into the world, that I should bear witness to the truth" (John 18:36-37).

The renowned nobility and dignity of our divine Lord's personal character continues to increase magnificently the further we proceed with our investigation of His names, titles, and vocations. In this capacity He by far exceeds all other witnesses, because of the manifoldness of the witness He bears. Let us mention a few of these ere we deal with the witness of His good confession before Pontius Pilate the governor, which is recorded in all four of the Gospels and stated also by the Apostle Paul in I Tim. 6:13.

His memorable witness to the Father and His love. On seven occasions in the Gospel by John, Christ affirms this. He stated, "The Father loveth the Son, and hath given all things into His hand" (John 3:35). So the degree of the Father's love is demonstrated by His cheerful generosity in bestowing His great gifts. The first man, Adam, had all things entrusted to him and he lost everything. When all things were committed to the second man (I Cor. 15:47), the last Adam (I Cor. 15:45,47), He said, "This is the Father's will that hath sent Me, that of all that He hath given Me I should lose nothing" (John 6:39).

The Father's love is the choicest and wealthiest of all treasured virtue, and is as dateless as the abiding ages, as boundless as the azure skies, and as changeless as the eternal Godhead. The whole volume of love's fullness and faithfulness flows forth from the Father ceaselessly, and rests in unabating immensity and complacency on the Well-Beloved Son.

The Father loveth the Son and showeth Him all things that He Himself doeth (John 5:20). Love fully confides and wholly entrusts all secrets. The mutual cooperation is perfect and without variableness. The Father regards the Son in the highest fervor of love and endows Him with the holiest favor of love conceivable. The declaration Christ here makes, betokens the absolute agreement and inviolable harmony that exists in divine relationships. This steadfast harmony is inestimably precious and expresses the fact of the Father's love, which the Son reciprocates and which is fathomless, yea, and measureless.

In further witness He affirmed, "Therefore doth My Father love Me, because I lay down My life, that I might take it again" (John 10:17). In this case the Father's love is the outcome of the Son's obedience unto death. By so doing the Son honored the Father, magnified His mercy, and glorified His name forevermore. In continuing His witness He said, "As the Father hath loved Me, so have I loved you: continue ye in My love" (John 15:9). The "as ... so" used here is one of the twelve correlatives Christ mentioned in His teaching as recorded by John.

There is no example in human history, throughout the entire course of natural relationships, that Christ was able to use as an illustration of His love to His people. Not even the fragrant love of Jacob for Rachel, or the fervent love of Boaz for Ruth, or the fascinating love of Jonathan for David, could in any wise furnish the requirement. He had to go altogether outside the realm of mankind to find a love similar in character to His own. In the whole range of knowledge there is but one whose love is equal in integrity and intensity to His own love. Wherefore He went far back to the very source of the spring of infinite love, to the everliving, everlasting Father, when stating, "*As* the Father hath loved Me, *so* have I loved you."

Furthermore He said, "The glory which Thou gavest Me I have given them; that they may be one, even as We are one . . . that the world may know that Thou hast sent Me, and hast loved them, as Thou hast loved Me" (John 17:22-23).

Here are words that deal with matters that are too profound and too mysterious for mortal minds to grasp. Could love do more than Christ has done for those who receive Him? In view of the value of His mediatorial merit as an intercessor, He secures for us participation in the enjoyment of the Father's infinite love. The assurance He gave to His disciples, of His love for them, was not merely a note of superficial sentiment, for He proved to them the intensity of His affection by offering Himself in sacrifice and in passing through the sepulcher to secure for them the Father's love, such as He himself enjoyed. Could we today but partially estimate the crucial suffering, self-denial, and self-sacrifice He encountered to emancipate the enslaved, we also would have convincing evidence of His superlative love for us.

The quality of this is certainly that of a special love, a dynamic love, a majestic love, yea, of an intrinsic love, belonging solely to the infinite Father and His incomparable Son.

In the final witness He gave to this wonderful love He said, "O righteous Father, the world hath not known Thee, but I have known Thee. . . . I declared to them Thy name, and will declare it: that the love wherewith Thou hast loved Me may be in them, and I in them" (John 17:25-26). What an unveiling this really is of celestial secrets that are homed in the eternal counsels of the Most High! What an affiliation, to be associated with God's beloved Son! What a glorious relationship we are brought into by virtue of His gracious regard! The Son affirms that He is speaking of matters that are known to Him, and no one else could have told us what He did, of that love which is the special glory of the Father. He said, "We speak that we do know, and testify that we have seen; and ye receive not our witness" (John 3:11).

His reliable witness to the former personalities in early Jewish history. We chose the word reliable with care, to express this phase of His witness, because He knew each one of the patriarchs and spoke to them personally. He knew each of the prophets from Samuel to John and gave to them the messages they delivered to the nation. He was fully acquainted with all of the priests and kings of Israel and established their official positions. Yea, He knew all men and did not require witnesses to inform Him concerning anyone (John 2:25). By Him every family in Heaven and earth is named (Eph. 3:14). He determined names for Jacob's twelve sons, which had meanings suitable for inscription on the twelve gates of the city of God.

His infallible witness to the fixity and finality of the Scriptures. On the occasion when He declared Himself to be the Son of God, and referred five times to the witness of the works He did in His Father's name, to substantiate His claim, He emphatically stated, "The scripture cannot be broken" (John 10:35). When referring to His betrayer He said, "I know whom I have chosen: but that the scripture may be fulfilled, He that eateth bread with Me hath lifted up his heel against Me. Now I tell you before it come that, when it is come to pass, ye may believe that I am He" (John 13:18-19). This was further confirmed when He addressed the Father, "Those that Thou gavest Me I kept, and none of them is lost, but the son of perdition; that the scripture might be fulfilled" (John 17:12). On twelve occasions in John's message reference is made to the Scriptures. Our Lord's chief witness to the divine inviolability of the Scriptures was spoken in Gethsemane, when His disciples sought to safeguard Him from arrest. "Put up ... thy sword.... Thinkest thou that I cannot now call upon My Father, and He shall presently give Me more than twelve legions of angels? How then shall the scriptures be fulfilled, that thus it must be?" (Matt. 26:52-54 Newberry)

Even though it meant to Him trial, affliction, scourging, and crucifixion, Scripture must be honored. Twelve legions was the number of David's army at the zenith of his power, 288,000 men (I Chron. 27:1). Christ could have requested more than that number of angels at a time of abject weakness. No stronger verification of His statements could be given than when He declared, "Heaven and earth *shall* pass away, but My words *shall not* pass away" (Matt. 24:35).

His remarkable witness to features and factors of the far remote past, also to future events. He referred to male and female having been made at the beginning, and told the Apostle John that He was the beginning of the creation of God (Matt. 19:4-6; Rev. 3:14). In this capacity He knew all about origins, for all things were made by Him and for Him (Rev. 4:11). He had the living models of wild animal life, domestic animal life, human life, and bird life in Heaven before He made them on earth. He also had the models of the Tabernacle, Temple, throne, and city of God, with twelve gates in Heaven, before He revealed the patterns on earth. The Tabernacle was for dwelling, the throne for ruling, the Temple for blessing. All are featured in the city of God in Rev. 21, God's presence, power, and pleasure in blessing His people, in a perfected society. "Known to God are all His works from the beginning of the world" (Acts 15:18).

He established the official functions of priest, king. and prophet for mediation, administration, and instruction. These had to do with the heart, the will, and the mind. Christ fulfills all three of these vocations and in all His dealings with individuals He calls into exercise heart, will, and mind. Those who speak of the Christian faith as merely a sentimental idea, have not investigated its character, for it makes its demand on the human reason and will as well as on the heart.

Our Lord's witness to future events covers a great variety of forecasts over a very wide field. When there were no printing machines, telegraphic communications, or telecasts, He said the gospel would be preached in all the world for a witness to all nations. He said His words would not pass away and today what He said is being printed in millions of copies annually, in three thousand languages and dialects. He told us that the moral corruption and violence that existed in Noah's day would characterize the close of the present age. Sixteen times in His final message in Matthew, He spoke of coming again, and gave a detailed account of the conditions that would exist in the period when He returned. No power exists in any sphere that can refute His witness or resist the fulfillment of the things He stated would come to pass.

We must forego writing about His undeniable witness, featuring invisible realities in the life to come, the world to come, and the kingdom to come. Or His irrefutable witness, foretelling the resurrection of all that are in the graves and demonstrating it in miniature at Bethany, He Himself being the resurrection and the life, and the greatest verification of His witness. We require also to pass by many other aspects of His authoritative and authentic witness, and conclude the section with His well-known confession.

His admirable witness to the fact of His kingship and kingdom of truth before Pontius Pilate the governor. The Apostle Paul speaks of this witness as a good confession because it was clear, correct, and courageous. Christ boldly claimed to be king when there was not the slightest evidence of regal status or sovereign regency. His outspoken claim was not to gain an advantage or to arouse pity for Himself; His confession tendered to increase derisive sneers from His accusers. He was outwardly divested to the utmost degree of everything that the world considered conducive to kingship. He had no bejeweled crown or golden scepter; no palatial residence or royal possessions; no retinue of servants, or revenue from subjects; and no army ranks or attendant guards. What a sorry spectacle, disdained by rulers, derided by priests, despised by the people, and deserted by His disciples! While in this wretched set of circumstances, Pilate said to Him, "Art Thou a king then?" Jesus answered, "Thou sayest that I am a king. To this end was I born, and for this cause came I into the world, that I should bear witness to the truth" (John 18:37).

According to the divine counsels of kingship revealed to Moses, it was specified that the ruler was not to be alienated in nature from the people he governed. No stranger or foreigner was suitable for kingship (Deut. 17:14-15). To fulfill all righteousness Christ was therefore born. Christ is King, by virtue of the inherent power of truth, which is the very nature

of His royal might and majesty. Unmingled, unalloyed truth is
the predominant and vital factor of His kingdom, a Greek
word meaning regency, and to this fact He witnessed. He
confessed that He was King of this spiritual regency of truth
that governed the minds, wills, and hearts of men, of which He
Himself is the personification, as well as witness.

No one else in circumstances of abject humiliation ever
made so prodigious a claim while in such a sorrowful plight, on
the lowest level of dejection. Moreover, this confession of being
a King will yet receive universal acknowledgment, on the
loftiest plane of highest honor, by multitudinous hosts. Christ
is the King of a kingdom of spiritual truth. He came into this
world of mankind and ministered truth in His teaching. He
manifested truth in the life He lived. He mirrored truth in all
His activities. He maintained truth inwardly and outwardly in
all aspirations and attitudes. He is the truth in embodiment,
and truth embodied in a person is almighty power. In all
witness He is truthful, forceful, and faithful. The truthfulness
of His claim as being King, and of His bearing witness to being
the Truth, indicates that He is Truth transparent, Truth
trenchant, Truth triumphant, and Truth transcendent. As
king of the Jews He is a racial king. As king of Israel, He is a
national king. As king of saints He is an ecclesiastical king. As
king of righteousness and peace, He is a spiritual or moral
king. As king of Heaven, He is a celestial king. As king of
glory, He is a supernal king. Thrice in the New Testament He
is named "King of kings."

THE WAY

Jesus said unto him, I am the way (John 14:6).

How full of meaning is the message conveyed in these
four brief words, "I am the way." The Lord lends His
profound name and links with it His personal majesty in
becoming the way of access to the Father. This right of approach and acceptance to the Father's presence cannot be
obtained on the basis of any form of human merit, nor can

such a privilege be bought with money, or secured by any legal or material means whatsoever. The Son of Man has the sole prerogative to prepare and conduct anyone before the Father; He is the only Way.

The first use of the word is connected with the tragic circumstance of man being barred and blocked from the way of approach to the tree of life. "So He drove out the man; and placed at the east of the garden of Eden Cherubims, and a flaming sword which turned every way, to keep the way of the tree of life" (Gen. 3:24). The way had been open and the tree of life accessible, but man failed to take advantage of his privilege and chose the path of flagrant disobedience and disbelief. Wherefore the gateway was closed against him. Christ came to open the door of access, and on the first page of the Gospel from whence the title of the text is taken, Christ assured Nathaniel this would be so by affirming, "Verily, verily, I say unto you, Hereafter ye shall see heaven open" (John 1:51). This fact He made concrete when He declared, "I am the way.... No one cometh to the Father but by Me."

The Lord makes use of this mediative figure of speech to express the fact that He is the way of reconciliation for mankind, and that He is available for all men universally, irrespective of class or clan, caste or color. In fulfilling this function He can never be displaced, He is the Way right now, and will continue to be so forever. This is that of which David speaks, "The way everlasting" (Ps. 139:24).

In no other book ever written is the character of a single person so prominent and preeminent as that which is given to Christ in the Scriptures of truth. He Himself is the total embodiment of the truth He taught, the complete character of the covenant He came to confirm, and the entire expression of the eternal Godhead, for in Him dwelleth all the fullness of Godhead bodily. He is not only the revealer of God the Father, but is God the Father revealed. He is not merely the exponent of truth but is the truth in embodiment. He is not simply defining a provisional way to the Father, but is definitely the Way in person.

In the notable world changes that have taken place in

the past, whether it be in the social, cultural, national, or political realms, great personalities have influenced the molding of events. Yet in no case has the promoting character been the personification of the movement. As Canon Liddon has written, "Plato is not Platonism ... Mohammed is not Islam ... but Christ Himself is Christianity." Some years ago, the leading rabbi of Chicago wrote concerning Messiah, "The significant fact is, time has not faded the vividness of His image. Poetry still sings His praise. He is to this day the living comrade of countless millions. No Moslem ever sings, 'Mohammed, lover of my soul,' nor does any Jew chant of Moses the teacher, 'I need thee every hour.' This is not genius of doctrine, nor ability of organization, but the inherent power of personality, of Emmanuel—God with us."

Christ's exceptional and eloquent claims eulogize and express what He is in Himself, far more so than any statement man may make in regard to Him. Not a single one of all the leaders, teachers, or legislators of the past dared to say, "I am the way." Christ is "the way of peace" referred to in Isa. 59:8. The Apostle Paul corroborates this when referring to Christ, declaring, "He *is* our peace" (Eph. 2:14). He *is* "The Way of righteousness" (Prov. 8:20). Again it is written of Him, "Who of God is made unto us ... righteousness" (I Cor. 1:30). Wherefore He is named "THE LORD OUR RIGHTEOUSNESS" (Jer. 23:6). He is "the way of holiness," described by the prophet (Isa. 35:8). The redeemed are spoken of as chosen in Him ... to be holy and without blame (Eph. 1:4).

These and other features are all conjoined in one, "Having therefore, brethren, boldness to enter into the holiest by the blood of Jesus, By a new and living way, which He has consecrated for us, through the veil, that is to say, His flesh" (Heb. 10:19). This wonderful change in the way of access to the divine presence was not brought about by a gradual development, and not by a combined effort of human planning, but by the power and prowess of a living person. He is called the light of knowledge (II Cor. 4:6); He is the bread of God (John 6:33); He is the sacrifice for sins (Heb. 10:12);

He is the word of truth (Col. 1:5); He is the faithful witness (Rev. 1:5); He is the true vine (John 15:1); He is the way to the Father (John 14:6).

If the Scriptures of truth had not been revealed;

If the Shepherd of Israel had not been manifested;

If the Sacrifice of the cross had not eventuated;

If the Saviour of the world had not been disclosed;

If the Spirit of love had not been sent from Heaven;

If the Son of Man had not appeared as the enshrinement and embodiment of the whole, what a dismal disinteresting world this would have been!

Spacial distance in Scripture represents moral distance, therefore we are spoken of as far off (Eph. 2:13). Because Christ is the Way, we may be made nigh. He is the Way from death to life, from darkness to light, from distance to nearness, and from the distress of bondage into largest liberty.

He introduced a princely Way, for He is the Prince of princes; much more, He is a kingly Way, for He is the King of kings; and He is a lustrous Way, for He is Lord of lords. He invests in His own person, the whole way, the complete truth, and the replete life. He is the concentration of all that is real, spiritual, and vital, yea, He is the supreme wonder of all revelation.

In providing the way, He is the Way He provides.

In teaching the truth, He is the Truth He teaches.

In imparting the life, He is the Life He imparts.

These features are not true of anyone else; what He is in personal being fills the entire presentation of the substance of the New Testament. For instance in this one Gospel of John, His names and titles occur over three hundred and fifty times, while His first person pronouns — I, My, Mine, and Me — together with the second and third person — Thee, Thou, Thy, He, Him, and His — appear over fifteen hundred times. For a pleasurable exercise, mark the personal pronouns relative to Him in John 8, and you will find not less than one hundred and forty-nine. Christ in person is the one great source and center of all spiritual blessings (Eph. 1:3); the sole citadel of all the promises of God (II Cor. 1:20); the single repository of all the treasures of wisdom and knowledge (Col. 2:3); and the only reservoir of all gifts and graces (Rom. 8:32). And so we might continue until language becomes bankrupt for want of ways and means of describing Him.

Because Christ is the Way, He is the Leader and Forerunner to all that is everlasting (Heb. 6:20).

Inasmuch as He is the Truth, revealing the Father, He is the Lover and Firstborn of the household of God (Rom. 8:29). In view of His being the life-bestowing vitality as Life-giver, we are reminded that He is the Firstfruits of them that slept (I Cor. 15:20,23; Col. 3:4). Yea He is "all, and in all" (Col. 3:11).

Of all the ways known to us, and there are many, for we are familiar with the terms pathway, roadway, highway, throughway, railway, seaway, airway, and skyway, the most wonderful and costly of them all is the new and living way which conducts us to the Father of mercies, the Father of lights, the Father of spirits, and the Father of Glory. This beloved Son of Man, who, in His majestic manhood, stands loftily above all others, is the most winsome, handsome, and awesome person, not only in this world, but in that which is to come.

THE WAFER

> If thou bring an oblation of a gift offering (meat offering AV) baken in the oven, it shall be unleavened cakes of fine flour mingled with oil, or unleavened wafers anointed with oil (Lev. 2:4-6).
> One wafer out of the basket of the unleavened bread that is before the LORD (Exod. 29:23).

If this elaborate system of sacrificial offerings outlined in this book was not received through divine revelation, where is there the record of any person who had the genius to invent it all? Well over a thousand years after the ceremonial had been established, Messiah the prince was manifested, and fulfilled the spiritual import of the entire set of sacrifices.

The burnt offering was ordered for atonement and acceptance (Lev. 1:4). The purpose of the meal or gift offering was for apprehension and appreciation. We do not appreciate that which we fail to apprehend. The peace offering was for agreement and association. "Can two walk together, except they be agreed?" asked the Prophet Amos (3:3). The sin offering required an acknowledgment of guilt and the grant of absolution through grace. The trespass offering demanded that amends should be made for any breach of ownership, friendship, partnership, citizenship, and the like, together with the presentation of a ram. This led to an advancement in the understanding of a neighbor's rights, as well as that of the divine claims. So this offering included amendment and advancement. Christ dealt with this in the prayer He taught His disciples, and it is the only petition He stopped to explain. Each one of these offerings was accompanied with varying sets of rules and regulations, specially suited to the purpose for which the sacrifice was instituted.

Accompanying the oblation of the gift offering a wafer was required, which was made of fine flour mingled with oil and anointed with oil. The figure represents the perfection of the spiritual life of Christ, and of His being anointed for the fulfilling of special service.

The baking of the wafer could be carried out by three methods: in an oven, on the hearth, or in a frying pan. The heat would therefore come in three directions, from above, from beside, and from beneath. This signified that He was to be tested by Heaven's standards, by human standards, and by hell's methods. Christ used the figure when He spake of the rain descending, the wind blowing, and the floods rising (Matt. 7:25-27). We are all tested from these three sources.

The specified directions that are given in connection with this wafer, its preparation and presentation, pave the way for the enlightenment and the enlargement of our conceptions relative to the character of the Lord Jesus Christ our Saviour. Let us take notice of some of the details. Fine flour is stressed four times in the chapter; if we take a pinch and examine it carefully, we find there is no unevenness in the tiny particles. This feature is true in relation to Christ. Every detail of His life is perfectly balanced. No excessive characteristic stands out more prominently than another. The blended excellences of

His person are all in absolute harmony. Almightiness and meekness, loftiness and lowliness coincide.

Simply A Wafer

Fine flour was the texture, anointed with oil,
    Prepared at the homestead, by personal toil;
Then baked without ferment, no leaven or yeast,
    Part burnt on the altar, and part for the priest.

The fullness of Godhead disclosed here we see,
    Within a thin wafer, made by His decree;
The common ingredients are those of His choice,
    The very instructions bear sounds of His voice.

Over and above what is exhibited positively, we note on the negative side all that savors of defect and deficiency is entirely absent. There is no irregularity in His service, no inconsistency in His conduct, no indiscretion in His public life, no incompetence in His work, no impediment in His speech, no incompatibility in His temperament, and no imperfection in His spirit.

During the first year of World War I, conference engagements took the writer to Tasmania in midsummer. Hospitality was extended by the proprietor of three large lumber camps. The residence was adjacent to the largest of the sawmills. Before sunrise on Sunday morning, I strolled to the rear of the mill, where high mounds of sawdust had accumulated through the years. Sitting down on a huge log at the base of one of the miniature hills of sawdust, I read aloud the second chapter of Leviticus.

Putting my hand back I took a handful of the sawdust and noticed that every grain of it was of uniform size. Turning my attention to the fine flour of the wafer, the next hour was occupied in writing down features of Christ that seemed to recur to the mind from the psalms: His obedience, His patience, His endurance, His excellence, His diligence, His deliverance, His justice, His confidence, His permanence, His countenance, His observance, His reliance, His assurance, His perseverence, His influence, His omnipresence, His omniscience, His omnipotence, His resemblance, His prudence, and His preeminence. These constitute twenty-one of the forty-two features recorded. Continuing the meditation in the light of all Scripture, let us mention half the number of the attributes of Christ that are revealed for us: His goodness, His righteousness, His graciousness, His kindness, His meekness, His faithfulness, His pureness, His tenderness, His preciousness, His mercifulness, His gentleness, His changelessness, His perfectness, His Holiness, His steadfastness, His truthfulness, His friendliness, His joyfulness, His peaceableness, His blamelessness, and His loveliness.

We shall now also state twenty-one out of the forty-two official titles that express His manifold merit: His Messiahship, His Governorship, His Judgeship, His Mediatorship, His Headship, His Kingship, His Lordship, His Sonship, His Heirship, His Leadership, His Partnership, His Ownership, His Executorship, His Suretyship, His Workmanship, His Authorship, His Companionship, His Progenitorship, His Guardianship, His Proprietorship, and His Testatorship. Each of these is of equal importance, forasmuch as a whole Christ constitutes each one. The whole of Christ is Governor, Mediator, Proprietor, and so on.

These official capacities are not measured by any system of degrees. The variations of higher and lower, larger and smaller, longer and shorter, wider and narrower, or the comparatives of bigger, brighter, and better, do not have any part or place in capacities and capabilities that are immutable.

Let us introduce another set of particles incorporated in this wafer and make reference to His incarnation, His ministration, His humiliation, His submission, His subjection, His transfiguration, His temptation, His intercession, His devotion, His dominion, His dedication, His instruction, His meditation, His compassion, His jurisdiction, His affliction, His substitution, His crucifixion, His resurrection, His ascension, and His glorification. This leaves room for the reader to add another twenty-one aspects to the list. Space forbids referring to more than one other set of personal characteristics. This time we may recall His deity, His humanity, His sympathy, His pity, His integrity, His purity,

His dignity, His constancy, His royalty, His regality, His ability, His majesty, His amity, His infallibility, His sovereignty, His liberality, His superiority, His stability, His sanctity, His loyalty, and His victory. We might have made reference to His Manhood, Shepherdhood, Priesthood, Saviourhood, etc., or in another category to His knowledge, His privilege, His heritage, His peerage, and such like.

There are thousands of particles in the fine flour contained in a single wafer; we have but made suggestions for about three hundred of the characteristics centered in the person of Christ who is typified therein, not one of which is out of balance or harmony with His infinite character. In Him are all the treasures of wisdom and knowledge (Col. 2:3).

The Lord is Himself the reservoir and repository of all qualities, virtues, beauties, excellences, perfections, and attributes. In a wafer there is no crust and crumb, the heat penetrates through and through. Christ was tested internally and externally, in motive and ministry, in aspiration and activity, and was proved to be without spot and without blemish. The divine statement governing the whole Levitical system of sacrificial offerings is expressed in a sentence, "It shall be perfect to be accepted" (Lev. 22:21). Our New Testament assurance is clearly stated, "According as He hath chosen us in Him before the foundation of the world, that we should be holy and without blame before Him in love ... To the praise of the glory of His grace, wherein He hath made us accepted in the beloved" (Eph. 1:4-6).

Wherefore in the person of Christ we discover intrinsic worth, immortal wealth, and infinite wisdom, perfectly combined, for in Him the rarest beauty and richest bounty are equally blended.

In the figurative use that is made of a common wafer, we are permitted a glimpse of the magnificent range of Christ's multiform graces, which are measureless; we are allowed a glance (however dimly) of the scope of His matchless virtues, which are countless; in order that we may learn a little of the magnitude of His manifold glories, which are fadeless. To whom and to what are we to liken our precious Saviour and

Substitute, who is without equal and without rival? Maybe some will attempt to gauge the extent of Christ's resources by linking together the myriad marvels of radiant sunsets, stellar multitudes, alpine glories, mountain gorges, ocean wonders, forest splendors, scenic grandeurs, and floral odors. But all of these are perishable things, whereas He is incorruptible and ineffable, everlastingly precious and eternally glorious.

The Wafer

A Microcosm of the Manifold Merits of Messiah

All precious is Jesus, our Lord and our King,
  The heavens adore Him and constantly sing;
Acclaiming Him worthy, in anthems of praise,
  The sweet rose of Sharon, the Ancient of days.

Of all figures, a wafer is used to reflect
  His untold perfections, all free of defect;
His multiform virtues assure endless fame,
  His manifold graces endear His great name.

Of ten thousand the chief, yet lowly in heart,
  Transcendent in beauty that ne'er will depart;
Lovely of countenance, the purest in mind,
  So winsome in meekness, so wondrously kind.

Most precious is Jesus, our Leader and Guide,
  The fairest and choicest of all else beside;
So faithful, so constant, without spot or stain,
  His kingdom endureth, He ever will reign.

THE WORM

But I am a worm, and no man; a reproach of men, and despised of the people. All they that see Me laugh Me to scorn (Ps. 22:6).

This psalm opens with the sorely afflicted victim of sullen scorn and awful agony asking two pertinent questions, and immediately answering them. Why should the obedient Son be forsaken by God? and why, when in urgent need, should His plea for deliverance go unheeded? He was the only one who could legitimately ask these two questions. In answering the first He vindicates the character of God by saying, "But Thou art Holy." He does not accuse God of indifference to His plight, or inattention to His plea as Job, David, and Jeremiah did, when being sorely tried.

In answer to His second question, He refers to Israel enthroning the Lord on their praises at the Red Sea, because they were not forsaken, nor did their cry for deliverance go unanswered.

But the Son was made sin for us, detestable, undesirable, a fact which caused that perfect body that was prepared for Him to become more marred and mutilated than that of any other man (Isa. 52:14), so much so that His facial appearance was so disfigured and His bodily form so emaciated that the very semblance of His manhood was obliterated. Wherefore He cries, "I am a worm, and no man." There is no semblance of manhood in a worm. The statement was looked upon by the early Church as a miracle of language, but it is more truly a miracle of love, that He should deign to be made sin in all its hatefulness to the holiness of God.

The terrible infliction imposed on Him by wicked hands made Him become a ghastly object of disfigurement. Whereupon the malignant minds of the perpetrators of the vicious cruelty meted out to Him considered Him as being so abnormally wicked that God had grievously smitten Him. They said, "We did esteem Him stricken, smitten of God, and afflicted" (Isa. 53:4). A century ago someone wrote the lines:

> Shame tears My soul, My body many a wound,
> 　Sharp nails pierce these, but sharper that confound,
> Reproaches that are free, while I am bound.
> 　Was ever grief like Mine?

Our minds are incapable of keeping in view at one and the same time the vast chasm between a being, of perfect beauty who is altogether lovely, transfigured and made to be absolutely obnoxious and revoltingly repulsive, the object of malicious scorn and contemptible satire. "As a worm and no man, a reproach of men, and despised of the people," He was denied the respect and common courtesy of ordinary manhood. Even the disciples withdrew from His company, not wishing to be identified with one in such a sorry plight. He was likewise deserted by all those He had befriended and healed. But the sorest trial was experienced when He was forsaken of God. How sadly those tragic words of the psalms befit His lips. "I looked on My right hand, and behold, there was no man that would know Me; refuge failed Me; no man cared for My soul" (Ps. 69:20; 142:4). He was disowned and denied.

He it was who had withdrawn from the sphere of almighty power to a state of abject weakness, as a babe upon a mother's breast (Ps. 22:9). He descended from the zenith of celestial honor to the zero of cruel humiliation. He left the loftiest pinnacle in glory for the lowest pit in gloom (Ps. 88:6), and from the ministry He received from one hundred million angels down to isolation from all companionship. "Lover and friend hast Thou put far from Me, and Mine acquaintance into darkness" (Ps. 88:18). Although Maker and Maintainer, Originator of all things, He is deprived of everything, without even a foothold, "I sink in deep mire, where there is no standing" (Ps. 69:2); the Upholder of all things engulfed in a quagmire and none to uphold. Of Him they said, "This is the heir; come, let us kill Him, and the inheritance shall be ours" (Mark 12:7). The Maker who decreed that it was not good for man to be alone (Gen. 2:18), and who pledged to man He would never leave nor forsake him (Deut. 31:6,8), is Himself totally deserted, and is described as a sparrow alone upon the housetop (Ps. 102:7). This loneliness is not merely isolation by a distance of space, but isolation of Spirit. No one on earth shared with Christ the finer sensibilities of His compassionate nature. No one entered into an understanding of the real purpose for which He came. He had nowhere to lay His head (Luke 9:58). This did not merely refer to being without a pillow, for He had such (Mark 4:38); also at Bethany. His meaning is far more profound, for He was intimating the solitariness of the life He lived.

The world has no sympathy with His divine goodness, pureness, and holiness, all such virtues were considered as disagreeable. Formal religionists detested the selfless meekness of true might, they looked upon it as weakness, and advocated self-assertiveness; said His brethren to Him, "Show Thyself to the world" (John 7:4). When one of lofty character displays the lowliness of a sincere humility, religionists call it littleness and speak of the person as spineless, insipid, or decrepit. Nobody in the whole realm shared with the Son of Man the true purpose of His mission and manifestation. Respectability despised Him; obduracy defied Him; hypocrisy denounced Him; bigotry disdained Him; instability denied Him; timidity deserted Him; treachery betrayed Him; while reproach broke His heart (Ps. 69:20).

In our human relationships, the strength of true dignity is exhibited when a man is thrown upon His own resources and left alone. Therefore in the life of the Son of Man this matter is clearly demonstrated. He prevailed in conflict with the devil and temptation in an unsympathetic wilderness, alone.

He conquered in the solitary all-night vigil of prayer on the mount, alone.

He faced the scrutiny of trial before Pilate the governor in the judgment hall, alone.

He answered the challenge of Caiaphas the high priest, and bore witness to the truth of His Messiahship firmly and fearlessly, alone.

He accepted the cup of anguish and agony, submitting to His Father's will, amid the gloomy darkness of Gethsemane, alone.

In each of these and on several other occasions, although He stood alone so far as human relations were concerned, He was not alone in spirit, for He said when passing judgment, "I am not alone," and when witnessing He affirmed, "The Father hath not left Me alone" (John 8:16,29).

But when made sin He encountered complete isolation: "My God, My God, why hast Thou forsaken Me?" (Matt. 27:46) He endured the cross, embraced its shame, dying in sublime solitariness, alone. He was sore stricken by the enemy but not subdued; deserted but not defeated.

Do not insult Him with your pity or compassion but bow in adoring worship for the Godlike fortitude He exhibited in loneliness..

To stand for the truth when you have an audience before you that is wholly in agreement is no test of fidelity. But when confronted with frowns and sullen suspicion, with the chilly atmosphere of cold criticism and disdain. to stand alone under such circumstances and bear unequivocal witness is what Christ did. No social institution or religious organization claimed Him. as belonging to their order. No one in His day shared His claims or relished His teaching. The magnitude of His claim, "I am the Light of the world," was unappreciated. The magnificence of the words He uttered fell on deaf ears when He said, "I am the living bread which came down from heaven: if any man eat of this bread, He shall live for ever: and the bread that I will give is My flesh, which I will give for the life of the world" (John 6:51). For the light of the world and the life of the world to emanate from a single soul comprised thoughts too vast for mortal minds to grasp or accept. The Roman authorities would consider such statements preposterous, and the religious audiences would esteem them presumptuous, and more than once spoke of stoning Him.

The very sanctity of His purity and the sincerity of His fidelity was a rebuke to their hypocrisy. As written in the previous volume:

> He never trimmed the truth at any time,
> Nor pandered to the rich of any clime.
> He sought not from the leaders of His day,
> One spark of fame, of light one single ray.
> His pure and holy life disturbed their creeds,
> His selfless love exposed their selfish deeds.

As Son of Man Christ claimed to be the repository of potential forces of such magnitude that they affected the entire universe. "All power in heaven and on earth," "The Light of the world, " "the Life of the world," and such like. Would not the national leaders who listened to His statements, and rejected them, have expressed the same stark unbelief if He had told them of the potentialities He had placed in a tiny atom? Of which, a single one of a certain type, which is far too small to be seen by the naked eye, contains sufficient energy to dissolve the whole earth back into gasses. This, the Lord has pledged to do (Isa. 24:19).

We possess no other record B.C. or A.D. describing one so strong and mighty becoming so weak and helpless. Nowhere in the realm of history do we find an account of an upholder and sustainer being left without a fraction of support. No other writing exists wherein a lustrous lover and faithful friend like the Son of Man is severed of all relationships, without even an acquaintance (Ps. 88:18). Never before had one who established all companionships been left companionless. In no other book in the whole world of literature do we discover any account of a person of regal renown experiencing such utter weakness (Ps. 22:9), helplessness (Ps. 69:2), friendlessness (Ps. 88:18), and loneliness (Ps. 102:7)) as disclosed in the four great sorrow psalms. A worm and no man, a reproach of men and despised of the people. He was dishonored, disdained, deserted, and disregarded.

One of the deeper lessons associated with this similitude is the fact that, from woodworms of the country, Moses obtained the crimson color to dye the ram-skin covering of the entire Tabernacle. According to the length and width of the covering, and the measurement of the skin from one ram, it took one hundred and forty-four skins to cover the whole area.

During the encampments, the Tabernacle was pitched in the midst (Num. 2:17). The four families of the priests were camped on the north, east, west, and south sides of the Tabernacle: the families of Merari were on the north: Moses, Aaron, and his sons, eastward; Gershon and families, westward; Kohath and families, southward. Extending out on the north were the three camps of Dan, Asher, and Naphtali; on the east, Judah, Issachar, and Zebulun; on the west, Ephraim, Manasseh, and Benjamin; on the south, Reuben, Simeon, and Gad. The standards were on the northern, eastern, western, and southern points of the compass, forming a cross at least twelve miles long and ten miles wide. When Balak took Balaam to a mountain, he showed to him, from behind a rock, but one arm of the cross—a fourth part of Israel (Num. 23:10). In the midst of this tremendous cross, when the outer badger skin covering was removed, the crimson sign appeared.

This would constitute a more wonderful illustration of

redemption than the blood sprinkled on the sideposts of the doors in Egypt. The initial letters of north, east, west, and south spell "news," the good news of redemption by the cross illustrously illustrated.

We need to remember that the Son of Man, who descended to the deepest depths of ignominy, is now enthroned in the highest heights of supremacy (Eph. 4:9-10). The Maker of all things "made Himself of no reputation" (Phil. 2:7). Yet He is the one who guilds all forms of the celestial and terrestrial in both their vastness and minuteness. He gave center to the whirling planets, orbit to the flaming comets, circuit to the whirring winds, dynamic to the thunderous storms, limit to the waves and tides, summit to the mountain peaks, aroma to the spicy herbs, nectar to the lovely flowers, luster to the insect wings, and most wonderful of all, an optic nerve to the eye to see and focus the symmetry and beauty of all things in both proportion and color.

Wonderful as all such demonstrations of His handiwork may be, they refer only to transient benefits and temporal mercies. The spiritual blessings He bestows are eternal and consist of manifold virtues, multiform graces, multitudinous treasures of wisdom and knowledge, magnificent perfections of moral beauty, purity, and glory, yea, spiritual adornments with colors and perfumes that never fade or perish, which are assured in an inheritance incorruptible, undefiled, and un-withering (I Pet. 1:4).

The more we contemplate who He is—Creator, Upholder, Sustainer, and Perfecter—the more amazing it becomes for us to grasp that He deigned to assume a human form, and taste death for every man (Heb. 2:9). The people of His day considered Him uncomely, and lacking in desirable beauty; they turned from Him and gave Him no esteem (Isa. 53:3).

When our Lord adopted this startling figure of humiliation, "a worm," He gave us the most astounding portrayal possible of His condescending grace and love. So low did He go, that He became the song of the drunkards (Ps. 69:12), and vile men used His name as a curse word, when uttering an imprecation on their enemies.

Although He made Himself of no reputation, He did not lose His reputation, for He has been given a Name that is above every name (Phil. 2:9). No expenditure of His grace lowers the high tide of His abiding fullness, and no amount of distribution of His riches to millions of souls has diminished His abounding wealth. The administration of His power throughout the ages has in nowise weakened His strength nor lessened His might. The effluence of His effulgent light, that has shone brightly for centuries, has not dimmed His radiant glory. He is all that is desirable, admirable, reliable, and durable. In view of what He became on our behalf, it behooves us to believe Him, trust Him, worship Him, and testify to His worthiness.

Similitudes of the Saviour

The lowly Worm, the Root, the Rod,
   The Way that leads our souls to God;
The Branch, the Plant, the Vine, the Tree,
   Are figures, Lord, which speak of Thee.

The Light of Life, the morning Star,
   A glowing Sun, that shines afar;
The Son of Man, the faithful Friend,
   The one on whom our hopes depend.

The lovely Rose, the Prince of Kings,
   Whose worthy praise all Heaven sings;
The Lamb of God, the Living Bread,
   The Builder, and the Church's Head.

The precious Stone, the stable Rock,
   Our Peace, our Rest that interlock;
The Word of God, the entrance Door,
   Our Shepherd King, forevermore.

THE WORKER

My meat is to do the will of Him that sent Me, and to finish His work (John 4:34).

My Father worketh hitherto, and I work (John 5:17).

The works which the Father hath given Me to finish, the same works that I do, bear witness of Me, that the Father hath sent Me (John 5:36).

I have glorified Thee on the earth: I have finished the work ... Thou gavest Me to do (John 17:4).

I must work the works of Him that sent Me, while it is day: the night cometh, when no man can work (John 9:4).

The Apostle John was chosen to present the works which Christ wrought during His manifestation, more fully than any other writer. He makes reference to work and works twenty-eight times, more frequently than do the other three records combined. On six occasions Matthew stresses Christ's mighty works; Mark uses the term thrice; and Luke twice; but John omits the word "mighty" entirely. When addressing Nathaniel, the Lord told him that he would see greater things than he had already witnessed (John 1:50), and in His teaching that followed, He used the word "greater" twelve times. In this connection He referred to "greater works." The anticipation implied in the term predicates the inscription which the Spanish government adopted for their coinage, after Columbus had discovered America, "Plus Ultra," evermore beyond. Greater, greater, greater is still relevant in Christian expectation to this day, for God's latest acts that have been determined, such as Christ's return, the resurrection of the dead, and such like, are His greatest acts.

The physical creation of the universe constitutes the work of His hands. Scripture declares, "Of old hast Thou laid the foundation of the earth: and the heavens are the work of Thy hands" (Ps. 102:25). Inasmuch as John opens his record by stating that Christ as the Word is the Maker of all that is made, he sets forth the same Maker at work, amid the conditions existing during His manifestation. They are works of a character such as no one else had ever done, for He said, "If I had not done among them the works that none other ... did, they had not had sin" (John 15:24). Concerning Him the Scripture had stated centuries before, "There are no other works like Thy works" (Ps. 86:8). His works on earth were assigned by the Father; as the Son, He was appointed and sent to do them, and was fully adjusted to accomplish all perfectly, as working in complete harmony with the Father's will. By the use of a similitude, He declared that His very sustenance was to do the will of the Father who sent Him and to finish His work. In this employ He enjoyed a superior satisfaction to that which is secured from partaking of physical food. He did all the work without personal preference, and without pretense, so that He said without reserve. "I do always those things that please Him" (John 8:29).

In the Gospel by Mark, where Christ is portrayed as the one Son, the Well Beloved and sole Heir requesting His revenue, the main aspect of His work was that of contending with the usurper, and the casting out of unclean spirits, to which ten references are given. No mention is made of this phase in John, where as Regenerator His chief work is rebirth to newness of life, with authority to make those that received Him children of God. The seven signs He wrought demonstrate His power and ability to do this. The seven persons He dealt with, from Nicodemus to Lazarus, illustrate the fact, while mention of the seven renowned characters of Old Testament history, including Abraham, Moses, David, and Solomon, definitely corroborate His preeminent work, for He is far greater than they all. So important is each feature of the work expressed in these renowned characters that to take three of them—Jacob, Moses, and David—we note their names occur two thousand three hundred and forty times in Scripture.

As progenitor, Jacob imparted the twelve features that comprised his character to his twelve sons. The twelve combined portray Jacob. As Regenerator, Christ called twelve of Jacob's sons and implanted in them twelve features of His divine nature, and could say of them representatively, "Behold, I and the children which God hath given Me" (Isa. 8:18). This is a greater work, and answers the question of the Samaritan woman at the well (John 4:12).

Space forbids detailing these features, or dealing with all seven, but a sentence or two on one other, may prove helpful to any interested reader.

Our Lord declared that He is both the Root and Offspring of David. To this king He gave in a profound measure the twelve capacities and capabilities featured in the twelve tribes of Israel. Wherefore David was enabled to gather together the twelve tribes and consolidate the kingdom. He was the embodiment of the Spirit of Israel.

Christ as King of Israel (John 12:13) came to "gather together in one the children of God that were scattered abroad" (John 11:52). He announced there would be one flock and one shepherd (John 10:16 Newberry). The mystery of His will concerning this unification has been made known (Eph. 1:9). His kingdom is everlasting (II Pet. 1:11; Dan. 7:27). This constitutes a far greater work than King David achieved.

The magnitude of the work committed to the Son by the Father is pictured in miniature in John's message. At one stage Thomas concluded it would be cut short if Christ ventured to go again to Jerusalem. He answered the objection by saying, "Are there not twelve hours in the day?" (John 11:9) as much as to say, "I have sufficient time to do the work that has been appointed, and until that is finished, no power can antedate My end."

Christ used the word "finish" twice in the early stages of His ministry, and changed it to "finished" twice at the close. The expression "I (have) finished the work which Thou gavest Me to do" (John 17:4), was followed later from the cross with, "It is finished" (John 19:30). This latter use does not appear to refer to His public work, but to that of glorifying the Father. This feature was not completed without obedience unto death. This aspect is much more than finishing the work. John is the only writer that records these statements and key words of His message are "glory, glorify, and glorified," which occur over thirty times. "It is finished" definitely relates to this supreme objective which, as Son of Man, He maintained throughout His devoted ministry. Great profit results from meditating on the superior character of the Worker, as well as on His incomparable works.

He is the Maker—all things were made by Him, and also the world (John 1:3,10). In the AV "made" is used twenty-eight times. "He made the water into wine" (John 4:46). "He that made me whole" (John 5:11,14-15). "I have made a man every whit whole" (John 7:23). This is so to the end. He is the Mediator; the angels of God ascending and descending on the Son of Man. "No one cometh unto the Father, but by Me" (John 1:51; 14:6).

He is the Messiah; the woman saith to Him, "I know that Messias cometh, which is called Christ: when He is come, He will tell us all things." Jesus saith to her, "I that speak to thee am He" (John 4:25-26).

He is the Master; this title appears on ten occasions; we shall mention the first and last. "They said unto Him, Rabbi, (which is to say, being interpreted, Master,) where dwellest Thou?" (John 1:38) "Jesus saith to her, Mary. She turned herself, and saith to Him, Rabboni; which is to say, Master" (John 20:16).

He is the Manifester. "This beginning of signs did Jesus in Cana of Galilee, and manifested His glory" (John 2:11). "I have manifested Thy name to the men which Thou gavest Me out of the world" (John 17:6).

He is the Monarch; possessing preeminent power. "Father, the hour is come; glorify Thy Son, that Thy Son also may glorify Thee: As Thou hast given Him power over all flesh, that He should give eternal life to as many as Thou hast given Him" (John 17:1-2). The titles *King* and *Lord* occur sixty times in John.

He is the Maintainer. "As the living Father hath sent Me, and I live by the Father: so he that eateth Me, even he shall live by Me. This is the bread which came down from heaven ... He that eateth of this bread shall live for ever" (John 6:57-58). "For without Me ye can do nothing" (John 15:5).

He is the Minister. "Jesus knowing that the Father had given all things into His hands, and that He was come from God, and went to God; He riseth from supper, and laid aside His garments; and took a towel and girded Himself. If I then, Lord and Master, washed your feet; ye also ought to wash one another's feet" (John 13:3-4,14).

In taking on Himself the very nature of manhood and entering the ranks as a worker, Christ's purpose was not designed to work for world betterment. He told His disciples that the world hated Him, and that in the world they would have tribulation. Even in His prayer ministry, He did not pray for the world (John 17:9). All through His activities He was wholly absorbed in honoring the Father, fully and faithfully.

As the Son of Man, His effective and efficient endeavor enthrones Him above all others, in view of the nature of the works He wrought.

As the Son of God, His expressive and exclusive splendor as Maker, exalts Him to the highest pinnacle of honor, by virtue of His superior character. He is altogether lustrous and precious, famous and glorious.

THE WORD OF GOD

In the beginning was the Word, and the Word was with God, and the Word was God. The same was in the beginning with God (John 1:1-2).

The Word was made flesh, and dwelt among us, and we beheld His glory (John 1:14).

He was clothed with a vesture dipped in blood: and His name is called "The Word of God" (Rev. 19:13).

Behind the expression of sound, speech, and substance lies the fact of thought. The philosophy of Hebrew doctrine declares that behind thought is a thinker, whose mind is infinite in wisdom and knowledge. The Word of life in past centuries had been expressed in speech (Heb. 1:1). The evidence of the invisible Godhead was also demonstrated in a tangible creation. However it was not until the manifestation of Christ that humanity received a clear and full revelation of God's personal being. The emergence of Christ from the obscure to the obvious, fulfilled an age-old prophetic forecast, "Your God shall come" (Isa. 25:9; 35:4-6). This may account for the deputation John sent to Jesus to ask the question, "Art Thou He that should come, or do we look for another?" (Matt. 11:3)

The Apostle John describes the coming into visibility of the previously invisible Maker and declares Him to be the very prototype of God. He who is everlastingly the Word is made flesh, and manifests the Father in His grace and truth. He disclosed the Father perfectly in mind, will, and heart, distinguished His personality, and definitely displayed Deity to mankind. Notice in the apostolic testimony, the extensiveness of the range that is covered in this historic appearance. The Word, that ever was from the beginning, was seen from the time of the incarnation (John 1:14), was looked upon when the manifestation to Israel took place (I John 31:33), and was handled after the resurrection from the dead (Luke 24:39; I John 1:1). The Word became flesh in order that humanity might behold Deity in manifest human form. This meaningful designation, "The Word," denotes one who is the exhibition of the power and will of God, who is the exponent of the purpose and wisdom of God, and who is the expression of the Person and Work of God. Christ, as the Word of God, embodies the revelation of all Truth, He exhibits the resemblance of Deity in perfect likeness, and expresses representatively the divine glory in radiant demonstration. John's record states this wonderful truth in a single verse, "The Word was made flesh, and tabernacled among us, and we beheld His glory, the glory as of the only begotten of the Father, full of grace and truth" (John 1:14). In Him we meet the complete demonstration of the Will of God, the Word of God, the Wisdom of God, and the Work of God in living, personal form.

No one but the Lord God omniscient possesses the wisdom and ability to impart truth to mankind, through human channels, that is adaptable to all conditions of human life, in all countries, and among all classes of people universally. The spiritual truth of the Word of God surpasses the limits of time, and is therefore equally vital for each generation of mankind. There is no age nor clime, no race nor people to which the Word of God cannot be applied. Truth is applicable to all creatures for all time, irrespective of change. The Word of God is as appropriate to the conditions that exist today as it was to those pertaining in the first century A.D.

God's Word can never be outdated, outvied, or become obsolete. Christ, who displays the title and personifies the Word of God (Rev. 19:13), is likewise indestructible and indispensible. He is always available and accessible everywhere on earth, and remains the same, yesterday, and today, and forever (Heb. 13:8; with 4:12).

The Scriptures also furnish us with a record of the Spirit of God, whose character and ministry are interpreted through the medium of sixteen symbols, and of whom seven designations are recorded. Of these latter we shall select but one to serve our present purpose, namely, "The spirit of wisdom and revelation in the knowledge of Him" (Eph. 1:17). The Spirit of God is a supreme centralist and the most perfect synthesist in the whole realm of knowledge. The divine Spirit has centered all truth in God the Son, and made all lanes and lines converge and contribute to the setting forth, in perfect profile, the peerless portraiture of the preeminent personality of Christ.

The main course adopted in unfolding the subject material, which comprises the Old Testament, appears to be as follows. In the Mosaic section, Genesis to Deuteronomy, Christ is portrayed in prefiguration. A manifold variety of symbols, signs, and sacrifices foreshadow His character and conduct, His features and functions, also His virtues and vocations. Only a mind of infinite knowledge could foresee, centuries beforehand, what the types used were to typify, what the signs given were to signify, what the symbols submitted were to symbolize, and what the shadows furnished were to specify in shadowgraph, of the real substance. Christ, as the expressed Word, is the *basic substance* of all that the shadows forecast (Heb. 10:1). In verification of this Luke records, "And beginning at Moses and all the prophets, He expounded unto them in all the scriptures the things concerning Himself" (Luke 24:27).

Christ is the *historic center* of all recorded Bible history, "To Him give all the prophets witness" (Acts 10:43). He is the *prophetic seal* of authenticity to all prediction, "The testimony of Jesus is the spirit of prophecy" (Rev. 19:10).

He is the *dynamic power* of all authority, "By Me kings reign, and princes decree justice" (Prov. 8:15). "All power is given unto Me in heaven and on earth" (Matt. 28:18).

He is the *intrinsic wealth* of all spiritual values, "In whom are hid all the treasures of wisdom and knowledge" (Col. 2:3). "His riches in glory" (Phil. 4:19).

He is the *specific governor* of all nations, "The kingdom is the LORD'S, He is the governor among the nations" (Ps. 22:28).

He is the *realistic expression* of Deity, "He that hath seen Me hath seen the Father" (John 14:9). "The image of the invisible God" (Col. 1:15). "The express image of His person" (Heb. 1:3).

These are but a few of the many ruling lines of revealed truth concerning Messiah, yet if these seven features only were removed from Scripture, the Bible would be bereft of both plan and purpose. Yea, it would leave us without incentive or objective. We might even go further and say the structure of the volume would have no clearly defined commencement, no definite center, and no determined consummation. Christ, the Living Word, is indispensible to the entire record.

In the five books of Moses, Christ is foreshadowed as the Seed promised, the Son beloved of the Father, Shiloh the sent one, the sacrificial Lamb, the smitten Rock, the serpent uplifted, the sustaining manna, and such like, all of which figures are referred to in the New Testament in relation to Christ.

The historical section consists of the twelve books from Joshua to Esther, wherein Christ is seen in prevision. Joshua was by Jericho, when he lifted up his eyes and looked and behold, there stood a man over against him, with his sword drawn in his hand, and in answer to Joshua's question he declared, "Nay, but as Prince of the host of the LORD am I now come." This caused Joshua to fall to the earth and worship (Josh. 5:13-15). Gideon saw Him, as "the Angel of the Lord," He appeared to Solomon, and Isaiah the prophet saw Him when the throne of Judah was vacant, after King Uzziah died (II Chron. 26; with Isa. 6:1).

These theophanies, or appearings in angelic form, signify the dominion of Christ, in which capacity His authority and administration are foreseen.

The philosophic section, Job to the Song of Solomon, which deals with Hebrew wisdom, presents Christ in prescience, which simply means having a knowledge of things beforehand, ere they have been displayed. Wherefore Job declares, "For I know that my redeemer liveth, and that He shall stand in the latter day upon the earth" (Job 19:25). Psalm forty-nine states, "None ... can by any means redeem his brother" (v. 7). "But God will redeem my soul from the power of the grave [hades]: for He shall receive me" (v. 15). Christ is foreknown in redemption, mediation, and salvation, dispensing mercy and displaying loving-kindness. He is known to be the Saviour, the Shepherd, and the sovereign Lord.

In the prophetic section, from Isaiah to Malachi, Christ is proclaimed in prediction. We are informed of names He would be called, titles He would bear, garments He would wear, vocations He would fulfill, the majesty He would display, the ministry He would discharge, combined with His sacrificial death, resurrection, and elevation to the right hand of God. All of these matters are clearly foretold. Therefore the entire scope of the Old Testament is occupied with the foreshadowing, foreseeing, foreknowing, and foretelling of the Christ who would appear, and He came, as the Word made flesh, the very Son of Man.

In the Old Testament the Spirit of God presents Messiah as being the Maker (Ps. 95:6; Isa. 54:5), Mediator, and Maintainer (Ps. 9:4; 16:5). He is also made known to mankind as the Almighty, the Ancient of days, and the Ark of the covenant. He is designated the Builder of the spiritual temple (Zech. 6:12-13), the Breaker of bondage, and the Branch of the Lord. He is given without reserve the title of Creator, Cornerstone, and Chiefest among ten thousand. He is declared to be the Deliverer, the Daysman, and the Defender. He abides as the Everlasting One, who establishes the everlasting covenant of peace, and loves with an everlasting love. As Messiah, He fulfills the fascinating figure of Firstfruits; in

His preeminence He fills the function of Firstborn; and in prevailing He holds the foremost rank as Forerunner. Space forbids our inserting three hundred more of His titles, names, designations, offices, vocations, and functions, which go to make up the written Word under the old covenant. If these verities were deleted from the Scriptures of truth, we would have but a lifeless, meaningless framework.

In the wide range covered by the use of so many figures and symbols, types and shadows, throughout the whole of the Old Testament, we find that each and all of these contribute some aspect of the physical beauty, moral glory, spiritual majesty, and judicial finality of the Christ who is the Word of God.

In turning to the New Testament we discover that the central conspicuous figure of the person of Christ is even more pronounced. As an instance of this we notice that the name *Jesus* occurs no less than six hundred times in the four Gospels, while His use of the first personal pronoun, "I," far exceeds that number. The fourfold portraiture presents a complete view in miniature of His earthly manifestation and ministry. Matthew depicts Him as the kinsman-king based on Deut. 17. The claim made by Jewish leaders, "We have no king but Caesar," was a flagrant violation of the Mosaic law. In Matthew's record, Christ used the expression, "I say unto you," fifty-six times. The message constitutes the most strongly affirmed declaration of truth that was ever delivered to mankind. He advanced the title, "the Son of Man," on thirty-two occasions, to emphasize His universal relationship to all humanity. In this capacity He undertook in relative responsibility and reliability to answer for human guilt. Every realm is involved, for He has all authority in Heaven and on earth. The gospel message is not restricted to any one nation, race, or class. In stressing its universality, Christ used the word "whosoever" thirty-six times.

Mark declares His Heirship, He is the Son of God in the first verse. This is corroborated by three voices from three different sources. His Heirship entitles Him to the revenue from the crown lands and He came to collect it. The leaders said, "This is the Heir; come, let us kill Him, and the inheritance shall be ours" (Mark 12:7). In this relationship Christ expressed His representative right and requirement. Because of His being the one Son and sole Heir, every right is implied. His legal authority is referred to ten times. To His power of command and the casting out of demons over thirty references are given. The devil, Satan, and unclean spirits are mentioned thirty-five times. The Heir's mighty works counteract the power of the usurper, and the commission in Mark's message is to go into all the cosmos, that is, the material world that comprises the inheritance. This is the Gospel that records what Christ does. The words "do, did, does, and done" appear seventy-seven times, and it is the only record that states, "He hath done all things well" (Mark 7:37).

Luke's Gospel presents the Mediatorship of the Son of Man in His redemptive resolve and resoluteness. The words "redeemed and redemption" do not occur in Matthew or Mark, but appear in Luke for the first time in the New Testament. Christ had first to substantiate His right in relationship to mankind, which He does as the Son of Man. Secondly, he had to vindicate the law, which is done in Mark. Luke describes His universal regard; "all" is used one hundred and fifty-four times in the message. He had regard for everybody, even for the handmaiden of low degree (Luke 1:48). Yea, it was predicted of Him, "He will regard the prayer of the destitute, and not despise their prayer" (Ps. 102:17). He regarded the prayer of the lepers (Luke 17:13); He regarded the plea of the poor blind beggar of Jericho and of a dying thief (Luke 18:39-40; 23:42-43).

In His priestly mediation He is touched with the feelings of our infirmities (Heb. 4:15). To demonstrate that He is touched, He touches. He touched the man full of leprosy (Luke 5:13). He touched the bier of the dead young man (Luke 7:14). He touched the ear of the servant of the high priest (Luke 22:51). His touch cleansed the leper, raised the dead, and restored the ear Peter had severed. Fifty-six relationships are recorded in Luke's message, including father, mother, sister, brother, son, daughter, friend, neighbor, wife, widow, etc. The Son of Man has regard for all. He knows the grief of a wounded spirit; He comprehends the sorrow of a bereaved soul; He weighs the burden of a broken heart; He senses the tragedy of a disabled body, whether through lameness, deafness, blindness, or dumbness. He feels the solitude of the leper's loneliness, and He regards the distressing circumstances of the poor widows.

Luke presents a graphic picture of the Son of Man, which portrays His prolific pity, His gentle grace, His considerate care, His tender touch, His friendly favor, His sincere sympathy, His loving look, His winsome words, His peaceful purpose, His kingly kindness, His sacrificial service, His manifold mercy, His Christly compassion, and His real regard. Never before were so many virtuous features centered in one person. The Spirit of God through Luke, the beloved physician, depicts the Word manifest in His kingliness and kindliness, in His loftiness and lowliness, in His lordliness and loveliness, and in His faithfulness and friendliness, all of which characteristics are beautifully blended in perfect harmony.

The Apostle John pictures the Son of Man in His regenerative resource and repleteness, for every resource is included. As Maker, He is unbounded, unlimited, and unconfined. John declares His omnipotence in both power and purpose. The power is demonstrated in creation, "All things were made by Him; and without Him was not any thing made that was made" (John 1:3). The purpose was expressed in remaking lives. The Creator is the only one who can produce a new birth. In addition to His omnipotence, His omnipresence is disclosed, as pictured in the experience of Jacob, to which Christ makes reference (John 1:50-51), and as portrayed in His manifesting Himself in the midst of His disciples in the upper room (John 20:19). This incident confirms His statement, "For where two or three are gathered together in My name, there am I in the midst of them" (Matt. 18:20). His omniscience is also expressed, "He knew all men." The words "know, knew, and knowing" occur one hundred and twenty-eight times. He knew everybody (John 2:24); He knew and taught the possibilities and privileges of prayer (John 15:7); He was familiar with all that was in prospect, "For the Father loveth the Son, and showeth Him all things that He Himself doeth" (John 5:20). Herein is included His coming again, and the reception to the Father's house (John 14:3).

In the capacity of being the Word, He is the complete expression of the mind of God, and fully sets forth the divine purpose, "My Father worketh hitherto, and I work" (John 5:17). The work of creation is followed by His administration as Son, "The Father loveth the Son, and hath given all things into His hand" (John 3:35). The Son's jurisdiction as Judge is also affirmed, "The Father judgeth no one, but hath committed all judgment to the Son" (John 5:23). Christ certainly possessed a clear comprehension of the entire situation as it existed and would exist. He said, "All that the Father giveth Me shall come to Me; and him that cometh to Me I will in no wise cast out.... Of all which He hath given Me I should lose nothing" (John 6:37,39).

The Word was manifested in the sublimity of the divine Sonship, a Sonship which is expressed in a wide variety of ways, which include seven signs that are not possible of being wrought by anyone else. The Word is the embodiment of Deity, so that both eternal life and essential truth are personified in Him. His manifestation was not merely to declare the truth, for He affirmed, "I am the truth." He did not suggest a course of procedure for the securing of life but definitely declared, "I am the life." He did not deal with the diverse rays comprising light, but stated emphatically, "I am the light." He did not voice opinions and air suggestions as to possible paths of approach to God, but forcefully affirmed, "I am the way ... no one cometh unto the Father but by Me." He did not put forth premises as to the possibility of a resurrection from the dead, but boldly attested, "I am the resurrection." He did not enumerate, as some do, a variety of doorways for entering into salvation, but with singular directness declared, "I am the door: by Me if any man enter in, he shall be saved."

Christ did not teach that man possessed a spark of the

divine that could be developed by special culture or suitable environment. Judas was under the best possible culture for three years but it did not alter his character. As to environment, you may place a pig in a plush parlor, and not achieve the slightest change of its nature. You may surround a bad apple in a basket with fifty good ones without transmitting any benefit. Christ stressed the need of a new birth, which the Apostle Peter endorses by stating, "Being born again, not of corruptible seed, but of incorruptible, by the word of God, which liveth and abideth for ever" (I Pet. 1:23). We are not in the habit of offering bread to dead lips, but Christ tells us of the true bread from Heaven, which a man dead in sins may eat and live. He unhesitatingly avowed, "I am the living bread which came down from heaven: if any man eat of this bread, he shall live for ever" (John 6:51). Wherefore Christ, the Word made flesh, is expressed as the Lamb, the Light, the Life, the Truth, the Resurrection, the Way, the Bread, the Vine, and all else beside; Yea He "is all, and in all."

Let us take notice of the claim He made as being the real fulfillment of the significant vision the patriarch Jacob had, of a way opened up between earth and Heaven, for man to return to God (Gen. 28:12; John 1:51).

He also directed attention to the brazen serpent and said, "As Moses lifted up the serpent in the wilderness, even so must the Son of man be lifted up" (Num. 21:8-9; John 3:14). The song of the springing well that immediately followed (Num. 21:17), He applied to the gift of God, "If thou knewest the gift of God" (Himself—John 3:16) ... "The water that I shall give ... shall be in him a well of water springing up into everlasting life" (John 4:10,14). On the sabbath day He visited the pool of Bethesda inside the city, at the sheep gate, and demonstrated that He Himself was the providential provision sent from Heaven to emancipate from the paralyzing effects of sin (John 5:2,8). Did not all Israel, after the emancipation from Egypt, eat manna in the wilderness? He replaces this figure of sustentation by introducing Himself as the true and living bread which came down from Heaven (John 6:33,51). Did not the nation on their journeyings drink of the spiritual rock which followed them? Christ appended to this feature the gift of the Spirit, in the plenitude of His fullness (John 7:38).

Whatever may have been the surmisings of the Jewish leaders concerning the character of the lustrous light that filled the Tabernacle of old, or that flooded the holy of holies in the first Temple, as to whether it was derived from solar light, lunar light, sideral light, or supernatural light, Christ left no room for conjecture, for He emphatically declared, "I am the light" (John 8:12).

When the Jewish leaders boasted of the renown of Abraham, Christ stated that before Abraham had his existence, He Himself abode, the I Am of eternal renown. The residents of Jerusalem held the pool of Siloam in high regard, because of the place it held in their national history. The name means *sent,* which He taught was for a sign, pointing to Himself as one sent by the Father (John 9:7). The people gloried in the shepherdhood of the patriarch Jacob, and also of King David. He claimed to be the great Shepherd of Isa. 40:11, and the good Shepherd that would lay down His life for the sheep (John 10:11). Did not Moses pray that the beauty of immortality might be given to man? (Ps. 90:1,17) Did not David speak of the heart living forever? (Ps. 22:26) Did not Isaiah and Daniel declare this would be brought about by resurrection? (Isa. 26:19; Dan. 12:2) Then how can we mistake the meaning of Christ's words, "I am the resurrection, and the life: he that believeth in Me, though he were dead, yet shall he live" (John 11:25)? We might continue and rehearse the feasts, the priesthood, the ceremonial, and history of Israel, and point out the great transfer Christ made of all these features by directing their values to Himself, the personification of the Word, and the purpose of His ministry. Interwoven are the seven greatest characters of Jewish history, and each of the distinctive characteristics set forth in their lives He expresses fully and perfectly in His own person. All of this and much more verifies the veracity of the statement, "His name is called The Word of God."

Before world maps were printed, with clear foresight He declared that the gospel would be preached throughout the

whole world to all nations. He assured His disciples beforehand of the enduement of power from on high so that they
would become witnesses to Him in Jerusalem and in all Judaea,
and Samaria, and to the uttermost part of the earth (Acts
1:8). After His ascension, He demonstrated His power at
Pentecost, and definitely set forth the fact that, having divided
the language of families at Babel, He held the prerogative to
speak to each group in their own tongue. What a wonderful
witness to His inherent Deity! The display of the Word in the
Acts of the Apostles and the twenty-one letters from Romans to
Jude becomes increasingly fascinating. The unparalleled
historic sensation caused by the resurrection from the dead is
crowned with the unprecedented glory of the ascension, which
set an immortal seal upon the triumph which followed His
descent. The most fitting counterpart of His supernatural
birth is His superhuman ascent. These two historic features are
inseparable (Eph. 4:9-10). Christ Himself certified these facts
to explain the nature of His personality. "What and if ye shall
see the Son of man ascend up where He was before?" (John
6:62) Seven times, in the sixth chapter of John, He affirmed
that He came down from Heaven. The Word in person, that
was with God, became flesh and tabernacled among us. He
now occupies His superior place of highest authority far above
all heavens, angels, principalities, and powers being made
subject unto Him (Eph. 4:10; I Pet. 3:22).

There are forty references to the Word in the book of
Acts, fourteen of which are expressed as "the Word of God,"
and eight as "the Word of the Lord." The four names and
titles — *Lord, God, Jesus,* and *Christ* — appear three hundred
eighty-two times and the apostles in their preaching quote
forty-eight verses from ten of the Old Testament books, besides
numerous brief references to other features. These facts
contribute further evidence that the Saviour they were
proclaiming was the Word of God in personal manifestation.

Under the Lord's sovereign administration of the gospel
in the power of the Spirit, the Ethiopian eunuch, who
represents the race of Ham, receives salvation through
believing the Word (Acts 8:26-40). Saul of Tarsus, who

represents the race of Shem, is intercepted on the way to Damascus and submits obediently to the Lord (Acts 9:1-31). Cornelius the Roman centurion, who represents the race of Japheth, likewise responds to the message. From Shem, Ham, and Japheth the seventy nations arose that are recorded in Genesis 10. Wherefore when Cornelius responded, Peter, with spiritual insight declared, "He is Lord of all" (Acts 10:36), *He* is emphatic, implying, He Himself is Lord of all. Christ is Lord of all racially, redemptively, and regeneratively.

The Epistles from Romans to Jude, all of which give Christ the preeminence in all things, may be divided into three groups. As headings for these groups we shall adopt the threefold statement Christ made when He said, "In that day ye shall know that I am in My father, and ye in Me, and I in you" (John 14:20). *I am in My Father* signifies the sufficiency of Christ. Philip had said, "Lord, show us the Father, and it sufficeth us." In John 6:7 and II Cor. 12:9 this word is rendered "sufficient", and on four occasions "content". The sufficiency of Christ for salvation, sanctification, and justification is fully expressed in Romans, I and II Corinthians, and Galatians.

Romans is occupied with the gospel, which is referred to thirteen times, and described as being the power of God unto salvation to everyone that believeth (Rom. 1:16). The sufficiency of the power of God to save, as expressed in Christ, is made known to all nations (Rom. 1:5; 16:26), all Israel, all people, all men, all the world, all the earth, Jews, Greeks, Gentiles, Barbarians, wise, unwise, rich, poor, bond, free, any, every, all, and whosoever; most of these are used repeatedly, four of the most common total one hundred times. Righteousness and life in Christ are gifts to faith (Rom. 5:17; 6:23). The first eight chapters deal with His sovereign administration, every benefit is through Him. The second eight emphasize His supreme authority as Lord (see Rom. 13:6-9). The titles Lord, Jesus, Christ, and God, appear three hundred twelve times. Seventy-three verses are quoted from the Old Testament, from fifteen different books, which serve to verify that Christ is "the Son of God with power,

according to the spirit of holiness, by resurrection from the
dead" (Rom. 1:2-4). The basic teaching in Romans is
associated with the spiritual value of the brazen altar and its
sacrifice. The security featured in the four horns of the altar,
for those that are accused, is fully expressed in Rom. 8:34.
Christ tasted death as our substitute to remove our condemnation. He was raised from the dead for our justification,
received at God's right hand to assure our acceptance, and
continually intercedes for our maintenance. These are the four
great factors in salvation, deliverance from condemnation,
clearance from accusation, acceptance in the Beloved's
perfection, and maintenance through His continual intercession. Therefore the complete sufficiency of Christ is
portrayed in salvation, and the adequacy of His perfect work
begets the full assurance of faith, because He is able to save to
the uttermost all them that come unto God by Him, seeing He
ever liveth to make intercession for them (Heb. 7:25). Such
love on God's part in giving His Son guarantees all things (Rom
8:32). This incomparable, unseverable love leaps all barriers,
surmounts all obstacles, supersedes all charges, and safeguards
from all destructive forces. Divine love is incorporated in the
eternal purpose, therefore the temporal things of change,
power, time, and distance cannot sever from the bond of its
embrace.

The Saviour is superior to all time changes and every
tide of variableness. How can change affect the love of a
changeless Lover? How can power and might divide from a
Lover who is almighty? How can the events of time isolate from
a Lover who is eternal? How can space sever from the Beloved,
who is omnipresent? Law is powerless to part us from this
precious Lover. The entire plan and purpose is legal,
logical, and lasting. God's holy law has been vindicated, His
righteousness has been verified, the ruthless foe has been
vanquished, and reconciliation has been vouchsafed to those
once alienated from God through sin. Verily, verily, God has
been glorified through the Word, Christ Jesus the Lord.

The messages to the Corinthian church picture Christ
in His sufficiency for sanctification (I Cor. 1:2; 6:11). The

teaching interprets the spiritual significance of the laver. The cross of Christ, the choice of God, and the call of the Spirit constitute its entire substance. The fourfold choice of God is the index to the four presentations of Christ quoted from the writings of Moses: the cursed tree (Deut. 21:22-23; Gal. 3:13), the pascal lamb (Exod. 12:3; I Cor. 5:7), the smitten rock (Exod. 17:6; I Cor. 10:4), the firstfruits (Lev. 2:12-14; I Cor. 15:23). These four are summed up in a single verse, Of Him are ye in Christ Jesus, who of God is made unto us wisdom, righteousness, sanctification, and redemption.... He that glorieth let him glory in the Lord (I Cor. 1:30-31; see Jer. 9:23-24). The four titles — Lord, God, Jesus, and Christ — occur four hundred seventy times. The words "sufficient and sufficiency" are used six times in II Cor.; and we meet with the wonderful assurance, "Always having all sufficiency in all things" (II Cor. 9:8). This amazing sufficiency in Christ, the Word of God, is inexpressible. The word "abundance," which is used twenty-five times and is rendered variously "more abundantly and exceedingly abundant," is applied to comfort, grace, glory, power, wisdom, and a score of other verities that are available and accessible in the Saviour. Four of these features are referred to one hundred times in II Cor. Through the passion of His cross He purchases us; by the provision He makes as our Passover He purifies us; by His presence as the Rock He preserves us; and by His power as the Firstfruits He perfects us in resurrection. The gospel is referred to twenty-one times in the messages to the Corinthians.

The content of the letter to the churches of Galatia maintains the same lofty standard of sufficiency. No room whatsoever exists for any other supposed gospel to intrude. The sufficiency of the divine provision, making it possible for man to be justified in Christ, is absolute and final (Gal. 2:16-17; 3:11,24). The contents is based on the spiritual import of the lampstand, which implies revealed truth. Christ is the Revealer.

A Redeemer was necessary who could implant the nature of sons (Gal. 4:5), impart the title of heirs (3:29; 4:7), initiate relationships to the Father (4:6), and induct into real

liberty (5:1,13). Christ alone is all-sufficient, and the merits of
His crucifixion pervade the whole message. The titles Lord,
Christ, Jesus, and God occur ninety-six times in this brief book,
and the word "gospel" twelve.

"And ye in Me," our standing in Christ. These words
are verified in Ephesians to II Thessalonians, where the
preposition "in" occurs three hundred twenty-five times. All
spiritual blessings are in Christ, our acceptance is in the
Beloved, in whom we have redemption, forgiveness, an
inheritance, and "the eternal purpose is purposed in Christ
Jesus our Lord" (Eph. 3:11). This purpose was determined
before this visible creation, wherefore none of the worthies
such as Abraham, Moses, David, Solomon are mentioned.
"For ever, O LORD, Thy word is settled in heaven" (Ps.
119:89). This is a profound statement with two applications,
especially so in the light of, "In the beginning was the Word,
and the Word was with God, and the Word was God. The
same was in the beginning with God. All things were made by
Him" (John 1:1-3). "He hath chosen us in Him before the
foundation of the world" (Eph. 1:4). Our ascended Lord is far
above all heavens (Eph. 4:10). The magnitude of His love has
four dimensions which surpasses knowledge (Eph. 3:18). The
spiritual significance of the twelve loaves of the shewbread
table is taught in Ephesians. Christ is the Bread of Life full of
grace and truth, and the twelve references to grace in the
message represent the twelve loaves for growth, and increase of
the body (Eph. 4:15-16).

From the highest station of sovereignty, "the form of
God," He descended to the lowest state of submission, "the
form of a bond-servant," and although He had the loftiest
reputation in Deity, He made Himself of no reputation in His
humanity. He is now entitled to a name above every name
(Phil. 2:6-10). We may recall that in Psalm 87:5 He is called
the Highest, while in the following psalm He is in the lowest pit
(Ps. 88:6). This self-abnegating service is a sweet savor to God
and is represented in the incense altar (Phil. 4:18). This is the
one who has the preeminence in all things, in whom are hid all
the treasures of wisdom and knowledge, for in Him dwelleth

all the fullness of Godhead bodily, and because we are in Him, we are filled to completion. So then when Christ who is our life shall appear, we also shall appear with Him in glory (Col. 1:18; 2:3,9,10; 3:4). In the light of our Lord's wonderful character we can relish with hopeful expectancy His coming descent from Heaven, the word of the Lord affirms it (I Thess. 4:14-18). The ark of the covenant had its crown of gold, expressing sovereignty; a mercy seat signifying sympathy; and the rod that budded and pot of manna within, symbolizing the sufficiency of the priesthood of Christ in resurrection to sustain. The spiritual reality of this is portrayed in Colossians, and the veil—which is His flesh (Heb. 10:20), is the subject of Thessalonians, in which character we expect Him to be manifested. This completes the seven articles of the Tabernacle: the brazen altar, the laver, the lampstand, the shewbread, the incense altar, the ark, and the veil. Christ as the Word personified, is the antitype and substance of the whole set of figures.

"And I in You." Christ indwelling the life of a believer enables him to conform to the standards of Christian living. He is our strength and this teaching occupies the messages from I Timothy to Jude.

We might adopt as our key verse to this section the statement of the Apostle John, "I have written to you, young men, because ye are strong, and the word of God abideth in you" (I John 2:14).

None of the philosophers of Greece or Rome, India or China, had the ability to impart to their disciples the power to enable them to live up to the standards they were taught. The very character of Christ, who is the Word of God, supplies the strength to conform to His teaching through His indwelling presence. King David constantly rehearsed the fact that the Lord was his strength (Ps. 18:32,39; 19:14; 27:1). "Strong, strength, and strengthen" occur over one hundred times in the Psalms.

The letters to Timothy give instruction for personal behavior, godly living, and sanctified service; the secret of the ability is to be strong in the grace that is in Christ Jesus (I Tim.

3:15; II Tim. 2:1). The indweller is "the blessed and only Potentate, the King of kings, and Lord of lords" (I Tim. 6:15).

In Titus, Christ makes possible purity of life, honesty of heart, and integrity of purpose, so as to adorn the doctrine. All activity is stimulated by the radiant hope of His return. Philemon shows that the strength of His grace begets a spirit of tender compassion toward others.

Hebrews presents the majestic character of the indweller, unchanging and constant. The very effulgence of divine glory and creator is the same also who purged our sins, and makes perfect to do God's will. In James, as the Wisdom of God, He enables the discharge of all practical duty and promotes humility. In Peter's messages, He is depicted as the one who suffered in all the relationships of life and who fortifies us to follow His example and express His manifold virtues, having called us out of darkness into His marvelous light.

John dwells on the family features of the children of God, characteristics made possible through the manifestation of the Word. Our human capacities require visibilities; we cannot grasp the abstract, the absolute, the infinite relative to Deity. We require someone to look at, speak to, go to, hear tell of divine love. God the Father entrusted His Son to display and declare His love to mankind in person, and this He did most wonderfully.

Jude supplies a compendium of the sixty-four books that go before; this appears to be done to prepare us for the final unveiling of Jesus Christ, whose name is called "the Word of God." The Spirit of God uses ten of the characters, cities, and one country from the Pentateuch and incorporates over forty of the great truths, titles, and teachings of the New Testament for this purpose. These include, "the only Lord God and our Lord Jesus Christ"; "the apostles of our Lord Jesus Christ"; "the mercy of our Lord Jesus Christ"; "God the Father"; "The Holy Spirit"; save, saved, salvation, and Saviour; grace, mercy, peace, faith, love, and life eternal; power, majesty, dominion, and glory. In contrast to the saints, the word "ungodly" is used six times and they are described by over twenty different figures of speech and are destined for His judgment, condemnation, vengeance, and the blackness of darkness forever.

Science has discovered that there is sufficient power stored in a single atom of a certain kind to destroy the earth. In Jude the Spirit of God presents the core of sixty-four books on a single page. Christ reduced the six hundred and eleven precepts of the law down to two commandments. But far more amazing than all this is the fact that the Lord God has given to us the sum total of His eternal Word in a single Person. Let us take particular notice of the unveiling.

As we turn to the final portrayal in Scripture of Christ as the personal expression of the Word of God, we make bold to say that nowhere in the whole realm of monumental records, historical memorials, and masterpieces of commemoration, is there anything as magnificent in scope and covering such a wide range in the magnitude of worthy honor as the unveiling of Jesus Christ, which God gave to Him (Rev. 1:1).

In His prayer prior to His crucifixion He said, "Now, O Father, glorify Thou Me with Thine own self with the glory which I had with Thee before the world was" (John 17:5). This request has most certainly been answered, as witnessed in the four visions John was given on the Isle of Patmos.

The first vision is associated with the golden lampstand, a figure which suggests revelation. In this section the Son of Man is glorified as the Revealer of truth (Rev. 1—3).

The second vision is linked with the brazen altar, which signifies redemption. In this section the Lamb of God that was slain is glorified as the Redeemer of mankind, even from every kindred, and tongue, and people, and nation (4—7).

The third vision is connected with the golden altar, which speaks of reconciliation. In this section Christ as the Angel of the covenant is glorified as the Reconciler of things on earth and things in Heaven (8—13).

The fourth vision is featured in conjunction with the laver or brazen sea (I Chron. 18:8), which symbolizes regeneration (Titus 3:5 RV); called molten sea (I Kings 7:23-25). In this section the Maker is glorified as the Regenerator who declares, "Behold, I make all things new," including New Jerusalem. The entire display is preeminently the unveiling of Jesus Christ, whose name is called the Word of God.

At the beginning of the Bible, the book of Genesis traces everything to its primal source and moral commencement; at the end, in the book of the Revelation, everything is seen directing to final consummation and moral conclusion. In the four visions which present the complement and completion of the ministry of Christ as recorded in the four Gospels, there are no fewer than three hundred thirty references to the figures, symbols, types, shadows, persons, and places of the Old Testament. These include the Throne, the Priest, the Prophet, and the King. All are required to unveil Jesus Christ who is the Word of God.

Not only are features from the whole of creation called upon, but the entire edifice of truth is also requisitioned with one predominant objective, that of setting forth the personality, deity, and finality of Christ Jesus the Lord and Saviour. He demonstrates in the four visions the truth He declared when He said, "The Father loveth the Son, and hath given all things into His hand" (John 3:35). He is revealed as the sovereign Administrator with the seven stars in His hand (Rev. 1:20); as the supreme Executor with the seven-sealed book in His hand (Rev. 5:7); as the stately Mediator, with the sacred censer in His hand (Rev. 8:3-4); and the sublime Adjudicator with the sharp sickle in His hand (Rev. 14:14). These are the same four official functions Christ claimed and exercised during His manifestation, as depicted in the four Gospels.

One of the choicest features of this fourfold unveiling is the demonstration of His loving-kindness, expressed in the manner in which He signs Himself at the close, "I Jesus." This constitutes one of the most perfect touches of His divine kindness.

After disclosing His numerous transcendent titles and tremendous honors with their indescribable degree of majesty and infinite range of immortal glory, He uses His best-known signature to authenticate His message to the churches. His exaltation to the position of highest eminence has not altered the character He displayed during His manifestation when He said, "I am meek and lowly in heart" (Matt. 11:29). He is the highest but is still the humblest, loftiest but lowliest, mightiest but meekest, greatest but gentlest, kingliest but kindliest.

He has not allowed the imperishable prerogatives and incorruptible potentialities of His glorious splendor to obscure His identity. His treasured signature, "I Jesus," enables us dimly to visualize the exhaustless mine of wealth, the incomparable worth, and the incalculable wisdom enshrined in His wonderful person. He supersedes our best-known superlatives, He surmounts our highest standards, He surpasses our greatest measurements, and no language can fully describe Him. "His Name is called The Word of God."

THE WATCHER

> Laban said . . . Mizpah; for he said, The LORD watch between me and thee (Gen. 31:45-49).
>
> Like as I have watched over them . . . to break down, and to throw down . . . so will I watch over them, to build, and to plant, saith the LORD (Jer. 31:28).
>
> Therefore hath the LORD watched upon the evil, and brought it unto us (Dan. 9:14).
>
> Behold a watcher and an holy one came down from heaven (Dan. 4:13,17,23).
>
> I watch, and am as a sparrow alone upon the house top (Ps. 102:7).
>
> Tarry ye here, and watch with Me (Matt. 26:38).

The first occurrence of the word "watch" in the Scriptures is associated with the familiar term, Mizpah, which means watchtower. Laban, the father-in-law of Jacob, used it in connection with a covenant of nonaggression, to conclude the settlement of a family quarrel. Centuries later the Lord informed Jeremiah that He had watched over Judah and Israel to afflict them but that He was about to alter His attitude, and watch over them to promote their welfare. Daniel in his intercessory prayer acknowledges that the Lord acted righteously in afflicting the nation, and had watched upon the evil imposed (Dan. 9:14). When King Nebuchadnezzer rehearsed his dream to Daniel, he described a watcher and a holy one he saw come down from Heaven, who cried aloud and said, "Hew down the tree" (Dan. 4:14). When Daniel prepares to interpret the dream he repeats this feature, that a watcher and a holy one came down from Heaven (v. 23). Let us recall that Christ is referred to as "the holy one" over thirty times in Isaiah's prophecy and thrice in the New Testament. Twelve months passed ere King Nebuchadnezzar experienced the fulfillment of his dream (v.29). This time it is stated, "There fell a voice from heaven, saying, O King Nebuchadnezzar, to thee it is spoken; the kingdom is departed from thee" (v.31).

How wonderfully and carefully the Lord watched over His people during the seventy years of captivity in Babylon. He was not unmindful of the difficulties they faced after their return to Jerusalem. As the Angel of the Lord He stood among the myrtle trees observing and supervising all that transpired (Zech. 1:10-16). He is ever watchful and mindful of His people. The Prophet Hanani told King Asa of Judah that "the eyes of the LORD run to and fro throughout the whole earth, to shew Himself strong in the behalf of them whose heart is perfect toward Him" (II Chron. 16:9). As an expression of the scrupulous care continually in exercise, Christ taught His disciples that the cheapest of the living sacrifices, a common sparrow, was not forgotten before God (Luke 12:6-7). The hymn that so many revel in today has the words in the refrain, "His eye is on the sparrow and I know He watches me."

Another aspect of Christ's watchfulness is recorded in what the teachers in the early church called the Gethsemane psalm. "I watch, and am as a sparrow alone upon the housetop" (Ps. 102:7). This verse pictures Him watching in lonely solitude under conditions that are illustrated by three birds: the lonely solitude of the pelican in the wilderness; the lonely separation of the owl in the night season; and the lonely submission in isolation of a sparrow upon a housetop. While at a distance (Luke 22:41), in the darkness (John 18:3), and in deep distress (Luke 22:44), He said to His disciples, "tarry ye here, and watch with Me" (Matt. 26:38). Then He went a little further, and fell on His face, and prayed. . . . And He cometh to His disciples, and findeth them asleep, and saith to Peter, "What, could ye not watch with Me one hour?" He who watches sympathetically over all His people, had no one to watch with Him when in the crucible of trial; wherefore the Father sent an angel to strengthen Him (Luke 22:43). He undertook a stupendous task when He entered Gethsemane, with the prospect of Golgotha before Him, but He did not relinquish or retract from it, although He had no human support.

From the very beginning of Bible history there is abundant evidence that the Angel of the covenant is the Watcher. Let us draw attention to four examples from Scripture. He was decidedly watchful and definitely mindful of Jacob's household and was fully aware of the discord that had arisen. When He set about to remedy the situation, he did not do so by a sudden intervention, but by a gradual process that assured a perfect result. Joseph's brethren had gone to Shechem with their flocks. Jacob decided to send his best-loved son to ascertain how they were faring. Joseph discovered the flocks had been taken to Dothan, near the caravan highway leading to Egypt. He arrived there at a time when his brethren were discussing his dreams. As he hove in sight, they determined a plan to foil the possibility of his dreams becoming true (Gen. 37:19-20). Their intention was to slay him, but Judah insisted it would be more profitable to sell him. In the nick of time the Ishmeelites arrived and the sale eventuated. They did not part with him until they reached Egypt. Potiphar,. a captain of Pharaoh's guard, purchased him, the very character of whose wife was the means of Joseph's imprisonment. The displeasure of Pharaoh and the incarceration of his butler and baker, their dreams and the interpretations given by Joseph, were all being carefully watched. The butler's promise to remember Joseph, when he was restored on Pharaoh's birthday, would not have promoted the divine plan had he kept his word. In God's time, after a dozen years had gone by, the assurances Joseph had received were realized. The Watcher had governed every movement at every turn of the way, so that Joseph was able to say to his brethren, "God sent me before you to preserve life" (Gen. 45:5), and full harmony was restored in the household.

We might rehearse the history of the nation. Their rigorous bondage in Egypt. The decree of death against the male children. Jochebed's determination to save her child. The placing of the little ark of bulrushes among the flags at the brink of the river. The notice taken by Pharaoh's daughter, the child crying, the wisdom of Miriam, and the wonderful result. The training and call of Moses and the message spoken by the one who had watched over every detail. "I have surely seen the affliction of My people which are in Egypt, and have heard their cry by reason of their taskmasters, for I know their sorrows and I am come down to deliver them out of the hand of the Egyptians" (Exod. 3:7-8). The Bible supplies a thrilling record of the nation's emancipation.

The following are functional expressions of His watchfulness as both Potter and the Purifier of silver. The potter is an eloquent witness, and supplies an excellent illustration of the watchful care that is necessary in the molding of a vessel from common clay. As a divine workman, the Lord has an eye for the architecture of the entire universe. He has marked out the highways of history and placed the massive pillars of great events in the structure of time. He has also a purpose for nations and an objective for the individual life. Clay is shapeless and will-less, whereas persons are not so. The image the Creator imprinted on man had been defaced and marred, but not erased. He has the power, the purpose, and the patience to make it again another vessel as it seemed good (Jer. 18:4). "Cannot I do with you as this potter? saith the LORD" (v. 6). Following the experience of new birth, the process of perfecting goes on under His watchful eye and almighty hand. "The righteous, and the wise, and their works, are in the hand of God" (Eccles. 9:1). He which hath begun a good work in you, will perform it until the day of Jesus Christ (Phil. 1:6), "It is God which worketh in you both to will and to do His good pleasure" (Phil 2:13). His object is to transform us into the same image as Himself, holy and without blame, so that when we see Him we shall be like Him. How much of our preservation and perfecting we owe to His watchful care.

Likewise He is the Watcher, sitting as a refiner and purifier of silver (Mal. 3:3). A refiner must not act carelessly when the precious molten metal is in the crucible. He is intent on realizing his objective, for he has a definite aim in mind. The metal has no voice to complain about the process, but we have. A young child that has no relish for soap and water may cry aloud when a kind mother is seeking to wash its body and make it clean. But the mother sings on, and completes the task, knowing full well the benefit the child will derive. Most of God's people are far too ignorant of the grand design the Master has in view in permitting sorrow and trial as a process for perfecting character. He knows what He is doing, and why He is doing it. He is observing the effects of His discipline with rapt attention, for it is all for our profit (Heb. 12:10). He perseveres in wonderful patience. His posture, as one sitting, signifies His settled resolve, which is prompted by ceaseless love, and promoted by tireless care. As an Almighty Saviour, He has bound Himself by an immutable oath to perfect His people and will see to it that the work is done. The reason for it all is to perfect us and present us before the presence of His glory with exceeding joy. When all is finished, His people will have been beautified in the beauty of holiness and the Father will be glorified because of the purity of infinite perfection established by His Son.

We may notice that in addition to His function as Watcher He is also the Weigher, for "by Him actions are weighed" (I Sam. 2:3). He it is who maketh the weight for the winds and He weigheth the waters by measure (Job 28:25). This measuring the waters by weight is reaffirmed by the Prophet Isaiah (40:12). If any reader doubts this statement, make the test from east to west and you will find water consists of two parts of hydrogen to one of oxygen the world over. Some one must have weighed it. When Daniel was called by the king of Babylon to read the mysterious writing that appeared on the wall of the banquet hall, he told the king the interpretation,

"Thou art weighed in the balances, and found wanting" (Dan. 5:27).

> Weighed in the balance and wanting,
> Weighed and found lighter than air.
> Weighed in the balance and wanting,
> Weighed — but no saviour is there.

More miraculous still is the fact, "The LORD weigheth the spirits" (Prov. 16:2). This is solely a divine function that no one else can fulfill.

THE WALL OF FIRE

> Therefore thus saith the LORD; I am returned to Jerusalem with mercies: My house shall be built in it, saith the LORD of hosts (Zech. 1:16).
> For I, saith the LORD, will be unto her a wall of fire round about, and will be the glory in the midst of her (Zech. 2:5).

From among the remaining features of our Lord's vocational functions, we select this one, "a Wall of Fire." This metaphor designates our Lord as having the ability to defend the city of Jerusalem against invaders and to protect the Temple from plunderers. The declaration is twofold, for it not only emphasizes the decision of the Lord to provide the protection for the city, by encompassing it as with a wall of fire, but expresses also His place of preeminence as being the glory in the midst of her. He acts as a rampart without to encircle and a radiance within to enlighten. He fulfilled both of these pledges, and safeguarded the Temple from the time Zerubbabel built it, until after He came to it as the true glory. Haggai, a contemporary prophet, predicted that this house would be filled with glory, the very same year in which Zechariah had his vision. This did not refer to a similar glory to that of the Temple built by Solomon, known as the Shekinah, for that was withheld from the second Temple, together with the ark, the tables of the law, the oracle, and the holy fire. These symbols were all to be replaced with the true substance and superior glory—Christ Himself.

The message of Zechariah, whose name means "remembered of Jehovah," has one pervading figure predominating in the entire prophecy. Herein we meet with the clear-cut and comely features of Messiah the Prince and Priest-King (Zech. 6:13).

His alertness is first revealed, He is seen watching, as the Angel of the Lord in shade of the myrtle trees (Zech. 1:11). The Hebrew word for myrtle is Hadassah, the bloom of the tree is a white five-pointed flower called "esther, star." Therefore the niece of Mordecai had both these names. Her people called her Hadassah, the Persians named her Esther. Archbishop Ussher stated that King Ahasuerus, of the book of Esther, was the Darius of Zechariah and Haggai, but that he could not give proof of it. Martin B. Anstey, of London, furnished the proof in his great work, *The Romance of Bible Chronology.*

The watcher among the myrtle trees is the sentinel of mercy, observing the attitude of the nations during the period of Haman's decree to exterminate the Jewish race. As the Angel of the Lord He thwarted the diabolical counsel, and wrought a God-honoring deliverance. There were no myrtle trees in Palestine until the returning remnant from the captivity brought them into the country.

We shall mention some of the portrayals of Christ without comment. He is the Armament as of fire encircling the city (Zech. 2:5). He is the Advocate assuring deliverance from the accusing adversary, Satan, standing at the right hand to resist (Zech. 3:1-2). He is the Anointed for kingly and priestly administration and intercession (Zech. 4:14). He is the authoritative King, sitting and ruling on His throne, and the approved Priest upon His throne. He is the Branch and the Builder of the spiritual temple (Zech. 6:12-13; Eph. 2:21). He is the abiding Lord dwelling in the midst (8:3). He is the acknowledged King, heralded with praise and also approachable, not as Alexander the Great, unapproachable, riding upon his white horse (9:8-9). Greece is mentioned in verse 13. He is the afflicted Shepherd who breaks the covenant, and is sold for the price of a slave (11:7-12). He is the Associate of God, "My Fellow," the word rendered "neighbor" eleven times in Leviticus. He is the accredited King, who will appear and make manifest His Kingdom in everabiding majesty.

Messiah is pictured in a score of figurative aspects in which He fulfills the various functional ministries and vocational services during the Persian control of the land (Zech. 1 — 8). The country was later brought under Grecian influence (9 — 10); and was eventually exploited by the Roman power, leading up to His manifestation and betrayal (11 — 14). The prophecy is like the column of Lord Nelson's great monument in Trafalgar Square, London; the tall shaft of the column bears aloft one conspicuous figure.

The Lord demonstrates His intense interest as a watchful sentinel. He describes His determined will to defend the city and Temple, both of which are to be rebuilt. He delivers the accused high priest from the power of Satan. He discloses to a discouraged remnant the secret of success in the rebuilding of the Temple: "Not by might [that is by the amassing of men and money], nor by power [referring to human decisions and determinings], but by My spirit, saith the LORD of hosts" (Zech. 4:6). Some were despising the day of small things (v. 10).

Notice this chapter opens with a vision of insignificant little lamps, but these are supplied from a source inconceivably large and lasting. The two anointed offices of Messiah, His superior Kingship and spiritual Priesthood, furnish a splendid guarantee to hearten the returned exiles for facing their task. Neither the replete resources of human wealth nor the resolute resolves of human wills could achieve such a work. He declares in Zechariah 5 that deliverance from captivity did not free the people from their responsibility in regard to obeying the law. The vision is a warning of the danger that would arise, after the Temple is rebuilt, of making it a center of commerce instead of a citadel of communion. This is what actually occurred over four hundred years later (Matt. 21:12-13), a method of merchandising was introduced such as they had learned in Babylon.

In chapter 6 He displays His sovereignty and sufficiency as Lord of all the earth. He is both the Branch and Builder of a greater temple. Here the pronouns "He and His" occur eight times in the space of two verses (12-13). Chapters 7—8 are associated with the fourth year of King Darius and conclude the account of Zechariah's ministry, which he received and exercised under the Persian power. In chapters 9 and 10, the prophet foretells, concisely, conditions and events that would pertain during the Grecian period, and contrasts the coming of Alexander the Great in military pomp and pageantry, and the coming of Messiah the King in majestic meekness. Chapters 11—14 predict the time of Roman dominion, which completes the fourfold character of Gentile administration as predicted by Daniel the prophet. While Gentile dominion lasts there will be no deliverance for the Jews (Zech. 11:6), "Out of their hand I will not deliver." Our main objective, under this final picturesque presentation of Messiah, is to meditate on the pledge He makes and the place He takes, encompassing the city as with a wall of fire.

In the first year of King Cyrus the proclamation was issued in keeping with Isaiah's prediction, for the rebuilding of the city of Jerusalem and its Temple (Isa. 44:28; Ezra 1:1).

The Temple was completed in the sixth year of King Darius; and those that wrought in the work were strengthened by the ministry of the Prophets Haggai and Zechariah (Ezra 6:14-15). In Solomon's day, with one hundred and eighty-three thousand workmen employed, it took seven years to build the Temple. Apparently, with less than one tenth of that number, forty-six years were occupied in the work of reconstruction (John 2:20). This period is often associated with King Herod's work of enlarging the Temple, but Herod did not reign that length of time.

Let us remember that during the early stages of reconstruction, Haman's rage and rancor, with its decree of doom, had spread throughout the entire Persian Empire and had brought distress to the Jews at Jerusalem. They doubtless began to wonder if there was such a thing as immunity or security from the danger of invasion. Were there not over sixty miles of thick, high, brick wall surrounding the city of Babylon, so well known to these exiles? Did this insure security, or deter King Cyrus from besieging and entering the city? Had not Jericho with its double wall, and mighty Nineveh with its massive bulwarks, suffered the same fate? Furthermore had not the renowned Temple built by Solomon been destroyed? Why then engage in such a project as rebuilding, if the same prospect of destruction lay ahead?

With these and other disheartening conditions assailing the minds of the people, how very necessary it was to be given a message of assurance. So the most wonderful declaration of protection and preservation, from the highest realm of authority is made to the bewildered remnant. "For I, saith the LORD," the pronoun is emphatic, implying, I Myself saith the Lord, "will be unto her a wall of fire round about." This constitutes an unscaleable, unbreachable wall of fire, scorching and consuming all who dare to design the destruction of the city. What an impenetrable and impregnable insulation is promised. "The Lord Himself!" The Almighty One, always alert and fully aware of all that transpires everywhere. What a caretaker! What a guardian! What a defender! Material ramparts are here superseded and security is based on a firmer foundation than stone masonry can provide. Faith in a God of unfailing faithfulness is the strongest fortress of the soul.

How startling and stimulating the thought that even in the sphere of material things, the very city they were rebuilding was to be entered by the blessed and only potentate Himself, who is none other than the King of kings and Lord of lords. Moreover, He would stand amid the spacious splendor of His own creation, in full view of this Temple they were reconstructing and say, without fear of contradiction, "That in this place is one greater than the temple" (Matt. 12:6). At that time the place of access to God was localized, limited, and circumscribed, but the mediation of Messiah has no boundaries, national, racial, tribal, or territorial.

Let us remember that the period of Jerusalem's defense was to exist for four hundred and ninety years. Messiah was to come, "For, lo, I come, and I will dwell in the midst of thee" (Zech. 2:10). This is confirmed during the Grecian regime, "Behold, thy King cometh unto thee" (Zech. 9:9). The

Prophet Haggai certified it, "The desire of all nations shall come: and I will fill this house with glory, saith the LORD of hosts" (Hag. 2:7). Malachi corroborates it, "And the Lord, whom ye seek, shall suddenly come to His temple" (Mal. 3:1).

He came, and part of the herald's message is, "Speak ye comfortably to Jerusalem, and cry unto her, that her warfare is accomplished" (Isa. 40:1-4). The city had been spared destruction even from Alexander the Great. He marched south and conquered Egypt, then he returned north and sacked Tyre (Zech. 9:8). Although he slaughtered many Tyrians only fifty miles from Jerusalem, sold others to slavery, ordering their dwellings to be destroyed, besides decimating their fleet of one hundred eighty ships, yet he did Jerusalem no harm.

Finally the One who had pledged protection, the Prince of peace, the Master of might, came to His own, and was not received. When He left the temple court He declared it would be demolished and left desolate (Luke 13:35). He wept over Jerusalem and declared her destruction. On the cross He prayed, "Father forgive them," and that generation was spared forty years ere their doom was sealed. When He withdrew from the city, all known forms of defense became obsolete, whether they be moats, mighty ramparts, mountain ranges, or marshaled armies.

We may sum up the irresistible charm of the Divine Protector as portrayed in this prophecy by recounting somewhat of the features revealed. Never before was preeminent sovereignty and perfect simplicity so beautifully blended (Zech. 9:9). His kingly majesty and kindly ministry were in direct harmony. He combined His lofty dignity with the discharge of lowly duty. He united His wonderful capacity of power with watchful care and patience. He linked Kinghood and Shepherdhood to govern and guide, and He joined Priesthood and Saviourhood to protect and provide. He merges the great bounty of His goodness with the genial beauty of His loveliness (Zech. 9:17). At great cost He opened a fountain for cleansing and ordained a purifying fire for refining (Zech. 13:1,9).

Y

THE YOKEFELLOW

Take My yoke upon you, and learn of Me; for I am meek and lowly in heart: and ye shall find rest unto your souls. For My yoke is easy, and My burden is light (Matt. 11:29).

I entreat thee also, true yokefellow (Phil. 4:3).

Awake, O sword, against My shepherd, and against the man that is My fellow (Zech. 13:7).

The designation Yokefellow may be applied to the Son of Man as indicating one of the vocations of His wonderful ministry. Christ applied the word *fellow* in the prophecy of Zechariah, as having reference to Himself (Matt. 26:31; Mark 14:27). Fellow is also rendered associate and companion; and in the book of Leviticus, eleven times the word neighbor is substituted. We are familiar with the use that is made of it in fellowheirs (Eph. 3:6); fellowhelpers (3 John 8); fellowservants, etc., and especially in the term "fellowship," which implies having all things in common (Acts 2:44-46; 4:32). Wherefore as Yokefellow, the Son of Man desires that we take His yoke. Very recently this came to my heart and mind as a real challenge, for Christ expresses it as an imperative command, "Take My yoke upon you, and learn of Me." What is the yoke like, to which Christ refers? If we do not know what it is like, how can we take it?

When challenged, a prayer request was made, which was answered in four words being impressed upon my mind. These were surrender, submission, subjection, and subordination. The enlightenment that followed threw a flood of new light on the service which the Son of Man rendered during the manifestation.

He was surrendered to the Will of God; submitted to the Word of God; subjected to the Wisdom of God; and subordinated to the Work of God. These four features are certified in the four records of the Gospel.

Matthew gives prominence to the Son of Man's surrender to the will of God. The words *will* and *wilt* occur therein one hundred times, and when the severe test came in Gethsemane, "He fell on His face, and prayed, saying, O My Father, if it be possible let this cup pass from Me: nevertheless not as I will, but as Thou wilt." He prayed the second time, "O My Father, if this cup may not pass away from Me, except I drink it, Thy will be done" (Matt. 26:39-44). He withdrew the third time, praying the same words.

The message by Mark makes it evident that in His preaching the Son of Man was submitted to the Word of God. "He preached the Word unto them" (Mark 2:2). "He taught them many things by parables. . . . Without a parable spake He not unto them. . . . With many such parables spake He the Word unto them" (Mark 4:2, 33-34). "He said to them, let us go into the next towns, that I may preach there also: for therefore came I forth" (Mark 1:38). "The Lord working with them, and confirming the Word with signs following" (Mark 16:20). In Mark's message only are these statements made.

Luke's Gospel portrays the Son of Man in subjection to the Wisdom of God. Herein the Spirit of God refers to wisdom more frequently than in the other three Gospel records combined. Five of its uses do not occur in Matthew, Mark, or John. God in His wisdom placed His Son under parental care, and He was subject to their control. At the age of twelve He knew far more than they did, and He could reason with the leading teachers. His parents found Him at the Temple, and He went down to Nazareth with them and was subject to them (Luke 2:51). Luke's Gospel record is the only one of the four that uses the word *subject.* The law enjoined this, "Ye shall fear every man his mother, and his father" (Lev. 19:3). This implies *revere them,* and is the same as the reverence that the Lord requires of us. "The fear of the Lord is the beginning of wisdom" (Prov. 9:10).

The Apostle John bears witness to the Son of Man as being subordinated to the work of God. Twenty-eight references are made to work and works in his message. Let us notice what Christ declared.

"My meat is to do the will of Him that sent Me, and to finish His work. . . . My Father worketh hitherto, and I work. . . . The works which the Father hath given Me to finish, the same works that I do bear witness of Me, that the Father hath sent Me. . . . I must work the works of Him that sent Me, while it is day. . . . I have finished the work which Thou gavest Me to do" (John 4:34; 5:17, 36; 9:4; 17:4).

Christ affirmed that both the words He spake and the works He wrought were the Father's; and of the two, the works contributed the more convincing witness (John 14:10-12).

Let us not lose sight of the fact that Christ became a Servant.

He said to His disciples "I am among you as He that serveth (Luke 22: 27), yes, a yokefellow, a fellowservant. The words *servant* and *servants* occur upwards of 960 times in the Scriptures; but He is greatest of all. "Behold My servant whom I uphold, Mine elect, in whom My soul delighteth" (Isa. 42:1).

Never before nor since has a person of such lofty honor stooped to such lowly humility in service to demonstrate the Father's love. What dignity has been conferred on us, that we should be called unto the fellowship of His Son Jesus Christ our Lord (1 Cor. 1:9). Do not forget that Christian fellowship is the result of a divine call.

The Gospels abound with evidences that the Son of Man was fully surrendered to the perfect will of God; completely submitted to the infallible Word of God; entirely subjected to the infinite wisdom of God; and resolutely subordinated to the foreordained work of God.

Some try to tell us that full surrender includes all. This is not so. Peter left all to follow Jesus (Luke 5:11), wherefore, when this subject was brought into prominence Peter was able to say, "Lo, we have left all, and followed Thee (Luke 18:28). Some months passed by and Peter received a command from the Lord, "Arise, Peter; slay and eat." He answered, "Not so Lord," and was rebuked. His attitude was not submission to the Word of God (Acts 11:8).

The meaning of the Greek word *koninonia*—fellowship—is best expressed by the words, "They had all things common" (Acts 4:32). The Father has made it possible, through the Son, for His redeemed people to have all things in common with Deity. We have been made "heirs of God, and joint-heirs with Christ (Rom. 8:17). Though rich... He became poor, that we through His poverty might become rich" (2 Cor. 8:9).

Take notice of two of the numerous things which Christ took voluntarily upon Himself with set purpose. He took on Him the seed of Abraham...to become a merciful and faithful high priest (Heb. 2: 16-17). Although in the form of God, He took the form of a servant. The word *form* has reference to an eternal state and, as used here, it implies He has become a Servant forever, in shepherdhood (Rev. 7:16–17), priesthood (Heb. 5:6-7). (See Luke 12:37). This is foreshadowed (Deut. 15:16-17).

Our Lord's teaching on service is very explicit. "Whosoever of you shall be chiefest, shall be servant of all" (Mark 10:44). As the one mediator, the man Christ Jesus, He gave His life a ransom for all (1 Tim. 2:6).

The four factors that comprise what Christ refers to as "My

yoke" gain new significance when considered in relation to the first man, the first Adam. To him God made known His will; and Adam disregarded it. He gave him the command of His Word; Adam disobeyed it. He made the covenant of His wisdom with him; Adam distrusted it. He committed the care of His work; and Adam dishonored it. This constituted the Fall.

The second man, the last Adam, when considering His Father's fourfold claim upon Him as a servant, could confidently say, "I do always those things that please Him" (John 8:29). This yieldedness was not a drudgery, but a delight (Psa. 40:8). His commands to us, "Come unto Me . . . take My yoke . . . learn of Me," are not to impose an undesirable, distasteful, heavy burden on us, but to provide a badge of fellowship.

We then are workers together with Him (2 Cor. 6:1). The first man Adam was made a living soul, the last Adam is a quickening Spirit. The first was given life; the last is the giver of life (1 Cor. 15:45). His command stands, "Take My yoke." He has left us an example that we should follow His steps.

When we consider the regal might of Christ as King, as revealed in Matthew; His legal right as Heir, as expressed in Mark; His moral merit as Priest, as portrayed in Luke; and His final verdict as Judge, as declared in John; who are we to disregard His governmental, judicial, sacerdotal, and creatorial powers; and deny Him our obedience and submission? Be not unequally yoked together with unbelievers (2 Cor. 6:14).

Z

ZAPHNATH–PAANEAH

And Pharaoh said unto Joseph, I am Pharaoh, and without thee shall no man lift up his hand or foot in all the land of Egypt. And Pharaoh called Joseph's name Zaphnath-paaneah (Gen. 41:44-45).
Without Me ye can do nothing (John 15:5).
Come, see a man, which told me all things that ever I did; is not this the Christ? (John 4:29)

Most readers are aware that the Hebrew alphabet consists of 22 letters, the Greek of 24, and the English of 26. None of the names or titles of Christ begin with the last letter in the English alphabet. Although this is so, some of His vocations are suggested and signified by the meanings of personal names that begin with the letter zee. This is very definitely the case in relation to the name Zaphnath-paaneah, which means "Revealer of secrets." But the secrets Joseph revealed to Pharaoh pertained to the present visible order, which is terrestrial and temporal; whereas the secrets Christ revealed relate to the invisible celestial realm, which is eternal, as well as having a bearing on the present. From the many statements Christ made during His ministry, as recorded by the Apostle John, the Spirit of God selected twenty-five, which He prefaced with double use of the word, "Amen, amen, I say unto you," which in the A.V. is rendered, "Verily, verily." Christ chose this method to reveal twenty-five secrets (See Deut. 29:29; Amos 3:7).

The writer's first impressions of the name Zaphnath-paaneah were received eighty-seven years ago, when ten years of age. While sitting at the breakfast table one Sunday morning, three of us who were the younger members of a family of ten, were discussing the Bible questions we had been given, to be answered in writing, as our homework. My father entered into the conversation by saying, "May I ask you a Bible question?" to which we all readily consented. Then here it is, said he:

Five A's, three H's, two P's,
Two N's, an E, a Z, and a T,
No name of nation, nor of place
I by these letters mean;
But if you will them rightly trace,
And put each letter in its place,
A word will then be seen;
And when you've searched the
    Scriptures round
It only once will there be found.

I immediately asked, "Dad, where is the answer to that found?" and received the reply: "If I tell you where it is, you will forget it. Find it out for yourself, and you will remember it through life." Leaving the breakfast table then and there, I ran up the stairway to my bedroom, opened my Bible, and turning to Genesis 2 began my search. Ere ten minutes elapsed I arose, ran to the top of the staircase and called out, "Dad, I've found it; it's in Genesis 41:45, Zaphnath-paaneah."

The life of the eleventh son of the patriarch Jacob is one of the most fascinating and captivating records in all history. The numerical construction of the Bible is outside the range of our present study, but suffice it to say that eleven is the number of election, and Joseph's life began and ended with it. He died at 110 years, which is ten elevens.

In the account given of Joseph's life we are furnished with a miniature foreshadowing of God's eternal purpose, which He purposed in Christ Jesus (Eph. 3:11); "For God has made known to us the mystery of His will, that in the new order of the fullness of times He might gather together in one all things in Christ, both which are in heaven, and which are on earth; (even in Him)" (Eph. 1:9-10).

In a time of widespread famine, Joseph brought about the unification of all the different classes of people in Egypt, by means of supplying natural bread. "In all the land of Egypt there was bread. . . . The people cried to Pharaoh for bread and Pharaoh said to all the Egyptians, Go to Joseph, what he says to you, do (Gen. 41:54-55).

How very significant that the words which Pharaoh made use of in reference to Joseph at the beginning of that branch of his work which unified Egypt, are the same as those spoken by Mary to Jesus at the commencement of His work. "Whatsoever He saith unto you, do" (John 2:5). This occurred in Galilee on the third day of Christ's ministry. The fact of the locality is confirmed by prophecy: for it was in Galilee of the Gentiles, "The people that sat in darkness saw a great light: and to them which sat in the region and shadow of death light is sprung up. From that time Jesus began to preach" (Matt. 4:16-17).

Wherefore, listen! Listen! Hearken to Zaphnath-paaneah the revealer of secrets. We must pass over the profound secrets He revealed during the first year and turn to the subject of Bread, which is mentioned seventeen times, and loaves four times in John 6.

A wheaten loaf, when made of whole wheat meal, contains a suitable combination of elements to sustain natural life. Analytical chemistry has given us a formula of the chemical content of human flesh, grain, and soil, each of which is made of similar elements. The Creator of all this is also the Revealer of secrets, who has told us that the Father giveth the true bread from heaven: which is the bread of God; therefore Christ in Person is the Bread of God. Said He, "I am the bread of life: he that cometh to me shall never hunger; and he that believeth on Me shall never thirst." "I came down from heaven, not to do Mine own will, but the will of Him that sent Me. And this is the Father's will which hath sent Me, that of all which He hath given Me I should lose nothing." Again He added, "I am the living bread which came down from heaven: if any man eat of this bread, he shall live forever (John 6:33-60). "The words that I speak to you, are Spirit, and are life" (John 6:63).

This bread does not consist of natural elements but is composed of Spiritual constituents: goodness, pureness, preciousness, righteousness, holiness, faithfulness, truthfulness, kindness, graciousness, loveliness, perfectness, meekness, winsomeness, friendliness, etc. This is one-third of the forty-two revealed attributes that characterize "the bread of God," "the true bread from heaven": "the living bread which came down from heaven": Christ Himself (John 6:32-33,51). Of the redeemed it is written, "We being many are one bread, and one body: for we are all partakers of that one bread" (I Cor. 10:17). This means partakers of righteousness, goodness, holiness, perfectness, etc. In other words, "We are made partakers of Christ, if we hold the beginning of our confidence steadfast to the end" (Heb. 3:14).

Let us ponder the splendor of what the true Zaphnath-paaneah reveals in relation to bread. Joseph, a man discreet and wise, was supplied with a prodigious sufficiency of resource to sustain millions of lives for seven years; this in itself is amazing. But we must enlarge the circumstances and expand the conditions when considering the ministry of the man named Moses, whom God assured of bread from heaven to nourish millions of souls for forty years (John 6:31). This was done in a sphere where there was no other source of supply: marvel of marvels! Now let us enlarge and expand in our thinking what has been already done, as we listen to the Revealer of secrets tell us who He is, what He is, from whence He came, and what He does. "I am the living bread which came down from heaven: if any man eat of this bread he shall live for ever: and the bread that I will give is My flesh, which I will give for the life of the world (John 6:51).

These words require and demand that we multiply and magnify all former magnitudes and mathematical calculations, and enter the realm of the infinite (Psa. 147:5). Visualize, if you will, One who tells "the number of the stars and calleth them all by name"; One who is all the fullness of Godhead bodily, who has the absolute sufficiency of resource to impart and sustain spiritual life to hundreds of millions: yea, a host that no man can number (Rev. 7:9). More so even for the eternal age! This is breath-taking and staggers the mind. A miniature illustration of it has already been given in this present temporal world. For "God that made the world and all things therein, seeing that He is Lord of heaven and earth, dwelleth not in temples made with hands; neither is worshipped with men's hands, as though He needed any thing seeing He giveth to all life, and breath, and all things" (Acts 17:24-25).

Every feature of the living bread is immortal, incorruptible, and immutable. These are three Bible words. The immortal cannot be marred or mutilated, and cannot decay or demise. The incorruptible cannot be cankered or corroded, and cannot be soiled or spoiled. The immutable cannot be increased or impoverished, and cannot be developed or depleted. The living bread is therefore imperishable, indestructible, and indispensable.

Will the objective of unification by means of this bread be reached and realized? Most surely it will. We have been told the end from the beginning, and from ancient times the things that are not yet done, saying, "My counsel shall stand, and I will do all my pleasure... I have purposed it, I also will do it" (Isa. 46:10-11). In order to achieve this end, five great problems require a solution, those of nation, race, class, creed, and sex. These five factors have become more acute than ever before, in the world today. Maybe this has been brought about by the various means of intercommunication that have been established. Statesmen are compelled to recognize the problems. Many attempts have been made, and are being made to rectify the condition of things. A League of Nations and the United Nations have endeavored to solve the national conflict.

Racial equality, of which movement the late General Smuts, a
former premier of South Africa, was president, has been advocated to
overcome the racial cleavage. Unionism and the forming of a worldwide labor union proffers a means of settling the class clash. The World
Council of Churches, with its ecumenical system, together with other
organizations, propose a way of ending the creed controversy. Mrs.
Pankhurst and her daughters in Britain became famous in heading the
suffragette movement, which demands equal rights for women in
courts, parliaments, pulpits, industry, and commerce to terminate the
sex contention.

All of these efforts have failed to provide a remedy; and
communism has no means of producing one. National distinction, racial
difference, social division, ecclesiastical disagreement, and sex disparity
need to be rectified ere unification can be established. This is altogether
beyond the ability of man to achieve. These five relationships are the
main cause of all the disharmony and disunity that exists. Human
nature with its carnal mind is at "enmity against God: for it is not
subject to the law of God, neither indeed can be" (Rom. 8:7). Man
needs a new nature; and this can be brought only about by a new birth,
which the Creator and Maker alone can undertake (John 1:12-13; 3:3).

God's great purpose which He has revealed is to unify, to gather
together in one the people of God (John 11:52; 17:22): "Gather together in one all things in Christ" (Eph. 1:10). Listen to the revealed
secret: "For as many of you as have been baptized into Christ have put
on Christ. There is in Him, neither Jew nor Greek, there is neither bond
nor free, there is in Him neither male nor female: for ye are all one in
Christ Jesus" (Gal. 3:27-28 Newberry margin).

Christ, the real Zaphnath-paaneah, wields the power to abolish
conflicting relationships and to establish amity for enmity, harmony for
discord, and unity for diversity. Four of the five great problems and
their removal are referred to, figuratively, in the message to the church
at Colosse; a message in which Christ is revealed in the magnificence of
His majestic supremacy. "Ye have put off the old man with his deeds;
and have put on the new, which is renewed in knowledge after the
image of Him that created him: Where there is neither Greek nor Jew,
circumcision nor uncircumcision, Barbarian, Sythian, bond nor free:
but Christ is all and in all" (Col. 3:9-11). Herein we find signified the
national conflict, creed controversy, race cleavage, and class clash all
rectified; conjoined also with sex contention (Gal. 3:28) which likewise
terminates. Therefore nation, race, class, creed, and sex have no diver-

gence in Christ.

Our Lord's teaching during the manifestation covered a very extensive range. He said to His disciples, "Behold, I have foretold you all things" (Mark 13:23).

When committing the memory of Himself and what he had done for a continual remembrance, He chose bread, the figure of Himself as unifier (Matt. 26:26). "For we are all partakers of that one bread" (I Cor. 10:17).

What a wonderful foreshadowing the life of Joseph is, of the unification which the eternal God has foreordained to establish in His everlasting kingdom!

"THOU REMAINEST"

THE ENDLESS EXCELLENCE OF EMMANUEL

In summing up this series of meditations on the munificent array of names, vocations, and titles which rightly belong to Messiah the Prince, together with the manifold personal glories that justly accrue to Him as the Son of God, we must draw attention to the declaration that is made on the opening page of the message to the Hebrews.

Herein the affinity of Christ as Prophet is announced, by virtue of His Divine Sonship, as the One who, in His dignity, surpasses the renown of all previous prophets. He expressed the final declaration of the everlasting name of Deity in all fullness, and exhibited the will of God in its faithfulness. The Spirit of Truth affirms, "God . . . has spoken to us by His Son" (Heb. 1:1-2).

The ability of Christ as Priest is affirmed. "When He had by Himself purged our sins, sat down on the right hand of the Majesty on high" (Heb. 1:3). The context makes known that in His character He excelled all former priests as Maker of all things, as Mediator for all mankind, as Maintainer in upholding the entire universe, and as Manifester of the Father. On this account, He completely demonstrates the glory of God and is the express image of His Person (Heb. 1:3).

The authority of Christ as a King is assured, for it is written, To the Son He saith, "Thy throne, O God, is for ever and ever: a sceptre of righteousness is the sceptre of Thy kingdom" (Heb. 1:8). Wherefore Christ's distinction, devotion, and dominion in their durability are age-abiding.

These three great essential offices of prophet, priest, and king, which in the purpose of God were established in the national life of Israel, culminated in Christ, whom they foreshadowed. He is the present and permanent holder of all three, and can never be suspended, surpassed, or superseded.

Because He is the famous Prophet of prophecy, He can never be displaced (Deut. 18:15,18; with John 6:14).

As the foremost Priest in perpetuity, He can never be deposed (Ps. 110:1,4; Heb. 5:6).

As the final King in prosperity, He can never be dethroned (Ps. 45:4,6; Jer. 23:5-6).

Features of the administration that were symbolical and typical in the ancient order of the old covenant, which dealt with things temporal and transient, have here advanced to their vaster values. In the realm of spiritual realities the true significance of the shadows found their full and final realization in the well-beloved and blessed Son of God.

He is invested with the insignia of Prophethood, the miter of Priesthood, and the scepter of Kinghood imperishably, incorruptibly, and infinitely. These great and glorious functions have found their full and final realization in the blessed and beloved Son of God.

But at this stage in the record it would seem as if all such intrinsically important issues reached were an insufficient proof of the sublime superiority of the Son's sublimity and sovereignty. Therefore we are directed to the existing material creation for additional confirmation. Not only do the three supremely important offices find their culmination in Christ, but in Him creation also reaches its consummation (Heb. 1:10-12). The entire universe was brought into existence for His personal pleasure (Rev. 4:11). Wherefore the Scriptures themselves furnish us with a prolific selection of the finest features of this fascinating cosmos, in order to express various phases of His personal characteristics and replete life. This fact supplies a definite reason for their existence, "For Thy pleasure they are and were created." In view of the multiform variety of figures made use of, we shall record but a few from the animate and inanimate spheres:

Color is called into requisition with its finest and fairest attractive beauty. The veil of the Temple was woven of blue, purple, and scarlet, suggesting Christ's threefold official rank (Exod. 26:31; Heb. 10:20). "Garments dyed red . . . glorious in apparel" (Isa. 63:1-2). "His raiment was white and glistening" (Luke 9:29).

Perfume is utilized to contribute its sweetest and strongest fragrance, "Thy name is as ointment poured forth" (Song of Sol. 1:3). "Thou shalt make it a perfume . . .pure and holy" (Exod. 30:35). The sweet spices, stacte and onycha and galbanum, with pure frankincense, suggest the inner virtues, graces, motives, and desires of the Lord in His royal Priesthood.

Jewels are selected, the costliest and comeliest, to portray His transparent purity and crystal preciousness (Rev. 4:3). These precious stones also express the loveliness of His fadeless beauty and the lastingness of His faultless glory. These fascinating features He imparts to His Bride (Rev. 21:11).

Fabrics are introduced which are made of the very choicest and cleanest of materials. Interwoven on the beautiful veil in colorful needlework were figures of the cherubim (Exod. 26:31). The curtains were made of fine twined linen (Exod. 27:9). The one expresses the reality of His nativity (Heb. 10:20), the other the purity of His divinity. Linen is used in Scripture to denote righteousness (Rev. 19:8,14). Righteousness constitutes the Redeemer's very nature, for He is "THE LORD OUR RIGHTEOUSNESS" (Jer. 23:6).

Metals, both pure and precious, are drawn upon to reflect His divine attributes. For instance, read Exodus 25, in which chapter gold is mentioned sixteen times in reference to articles representing Christ, His ministry, and His decreed administration (see Ps. 2:7-9; Rev. 1:15-16; also Mal. 3:3).

Rocks, the hardest and highest, are also given prominence, as if to display the stability and steadfastness of Christ (Ps. 61:2; Matt. 21:44). He is the Rock of Ages and abides forevermore (Isa. 26:4 margin; 32:1-2). He is likewise "The sure foundation" (Isa. 28:16). Christ is steadfast in His reliability as founder of the Church, He also stands fast in His responsibility as the sure foundation, reliable, dependable, and wholly trustworthy.

Stars are brought to bear on this matter, the biggest and brightest as we view them. Alceyone of the Pleiades cluster

and Venus of the day dawn (Amos 5:8; Job 9:9; Rev. 22:16).
His governance and guidance in such figures bespeak how
wonderful and worshipful Christ really is, for the stars in their
magnitudes and multitudes stagger the mind, but their Maker
and Maintainer is more marvelous than they. How imponderable His magnificence, how ineffable His brilliance.

Plants availed of for this same purpose are the topmost
and tenderest. He is the Plant of renown and the Tender Plant
(Ezek. 34:29; Isa. 53:2). These striking figures signify His
appointment to a station of lofty honor and His appearance in
a state of lowly humility.

Trees are included, the stateliest and smallest. Solomon
spake of trees, from the cedar tree that is in Lebanon even
unto the hyssop that springeth out of the wall (I Kings 4:33).
Both the cedar and hyssop were used with the sacrifice in
Num. 19:6. Christ combined in His character majesty and
meekness. Meekness is the majesty of divine might harnessed,
to minister to mankind.

Birds are more largely used to express features and
functions of the Saviour's ministering service. The selection
made ranges from the eagle, which soars highest, down to the
sparrow, which seems lowliest in bird life. The face of the
eagle, as revealed in association with the celestial throne, is a
figure of His lofty sovereignty (Ezek. 1:10).

In the ceremony for the cleansing of the leper, the
sparrow slain expresses His lowly submission during the
manifestation (Lev. 14:4; Ps. 102:7). In this connection
Christ is also likened to a pelican in the wilderness, a figure of
His lonely solitude (Ps. 102:6). Then again, the hen gathering
its chicks to guard them from danger portrays His lovely
sympathy (Matt. 23:37). The two cherubim with outspread
wings in the Temple sanctuary should be carefully considered
(I Kings 6:23-24). Beneath the point where the two inner
wings met, the golden mercy seat was placed. The numerous
references in the Psalms to those taking refuge under the
shadow of God's wings is a dramatic way of expressing what it
means to trust in the mercy of God for His care and comfort,
for deliverance and defense. (See also Ruth 2:12.) The mercy

seat represents Christ: "Christ Jesus: Whom God has set forth to be a Mercy seat (propitiation in AV) through faith in His blood, to declare His righteousness for the remission of sins" (Rom. 3:24-25).

Animals. Herein lies a wide range of symbolism from the lion which is wildest, to the lamb which is tamest. They set forth Christ in the might of His strength, prevailing, and the merit of His sacrifice, propitiating (Rev. 5:5; John 1:36; I John 2:2). Our Lord's glorious might and gracious meekness are correlated. As lionlike the Son of Man arrests the attention of three worlds—the celestial, terrestrial, and infernal. As lamblike He attracts affection. The stability of His Saviourhood and the suitability of His Shepherdhood combine in perfect harmony to set forth His sufficiency and sympathy.

Space forbids our dealing with the seven animals selected to show various features of the great sacrifice He made.

When faith is directed to Christ the material and physical things of this world are confronted with the moral and spiritual realities of the world to come. How brief and transient the present temporal shadows appear, when the soul becomes conscious of the value and virtue of the eternal substance. The vast range of display in the present visible creation, which has been so effectively used to portray the manifold perfections of the Son of Man, will have served the purpose for which it was ordained, and be folded up as an old garment (Heb. 1:12). In the Jewish economy, the objects and offices established in connection with the Tabernacle, the throne, and the Temple, including the bright colors of blue, purple, and scarlet were neither delusions nor human inventions, but divinely appointed shadows, specially given to forecast and foreshadow the true substance, which is Christ. When all else and everything else recedes, of Him it is written, "Thou remainest" (Heb. 1:11).

Christ remains age-abidingly in all the majestic magnificence of His magisterial, mediatorial, and ministerial glory, as declared and disclosed in Hebrews 8:1-6. Of all temporal things it is written, "They shall perish," but of the

Son of God the Word declares, "Thou remainest." He is forever regnant in royalty, resplendent in regality, and radiant in regency.

These statements are breath-taking! Awe-inspiring! They should startle and amaze us, and stir our souls to admiring wonder and adoring worship.

His Relationships remain undislodged
His Resurrection remains undeniable
His Repleteness remains underanged
His Resplendence remains undestroyed
His Resoluteness remains undaunted
His Raiment remains undefiled
His Riches remain undepleted
His Righteousness remains undeflected
His Resources remain undiminished
His Radiance remains undimmed
His Reign remains undisrupted
His Regency remains undisputed
His Reputation remains undamaged
His Return remains undefined

Each of these facts is worthy of comment, but their reality assures that on no account will there ever be any abatement or annulment of our Lord's sovereign administrative authority. The transcendent, triumphant throne of His everlasting kingdom is set at the preeminent peak of permanent power. In His superior regality, He wields the scepter of sovereignty. As the sublime summit of supreme strength, His reign in royal resplendence is far far above all principalities and authorities. He rules from the uttermost pinnacle of majestic might which is described as being far higher than the heavens (Eph. 4:10).

Christ is not only crowned King of kings, He is also designated Lord of lords and proclaimed Prince of princes. The everlasting covenant He established is forever certified (Heb. 13:20). The replete redemption He obtained is eternally ratified (Heb. 9:12). The merit of His mediative ministry is everlastingly magnified (Heb. 8:6). By virtue of His having rendered obedience unto death, the Father is transcendently glorified.

We learn from the Scriptures that myriads of angels, millions of perfected saints, and multitudinous hosts of the redeemed, revel in the realization that Christ the Lord:

outranges all other rulers
that He outweighs all other worthies
that He outpeers all other potentates
that He outshines all other sovereigns
that He outclasses all other conquerors
that He outmatches all other mediators
that He outnames all other notables
that He outrivals all other royalties
that He outsoars all other saviors
that He outvies all other victors
that He outruns all other runners
that He outbids all other buyers
that He outlasts all other leaders
that He outlives all other lovers.

Scripture supplies reference to verify every one of these facts. No person exists in any realm that is more amiable and affable in fellowship; or more desirable and durable in friendship; or more lovable and likable in companionship; or more admirable and adorable in lordship than He.

Let us not engage in debating the processes that must needs lead to the manifestation of the kingdom, but rather concentrate more attention on the character and competence of the King Himself. Let us meditate on His superior excellence and His sublime effulgence. Let us recall constantly His stately elegance, His superb eloquence, and His supernal eminence. All the attributes of Deity are beautifully blended and perfectly balanced in the kingly Son of Man. The fullness and fragrance of their combined comeliness express and exhibit His moral glory. The King Himself is preciously, permanently, and preeminently perfect.

All fullness abides and resides in the Son forever and ever. The attractive and captivating aroma that ascended to the Father from the amazing array of attributes, which constituted the very character of this altogether lovely One, met and merited the voice from Heaven that declared, "This is My Beloved Son, in whom I am well pleased." All Heaven unites in heralding forth His honor.

What are we to say respecting the quality of the love of this One of whom it is written, "Thou remainest"? He has asked that we set Him as a seal on the heart and arm, for love is strong as death (Song of Sol. 8:6). This fact has been verified, "For God demonstrates His love toward us, in that, while we were yet sinners, Christ died for us" (Rom. 5:8).

The treasure and measure of Christ's love is without a terminus.

The breadth and beauty of His love is without a boundary.

The heavenliness and holiness of His love is without an horizon.

The ocean fullness and faithfulness of His love is without a shore.

The constancy and continuancy of His love is without end.

The fervor and favor of His love flow on forevermore.

The benefits and blessings we derive from the reconciliation, which the Saviour secured for us by His sacrifice, are not as great as the indescribable, indestructible treasure that He is Himself, personally. This being so, the range and royalty of His love cannot be weighed.

The affection and attraction of His love cannot be appraised.

The preciousness and perfectness of His love cannot be priced.

The volume and virtue of His love cannot be valued.

The essence and excellence of His eternal love cannot be estimated.

The character and constancy of His perfect love cannot be conceived or comprehended, for His love surpasseth knowledge (Eph. 3:18-19).

To Him be glory forever and ever, Amen.

HEIR OF ALL THINGS (Heb. 1:2)

THE LION OF JUDAH PREVAILED (Rev. 5:5)

This scene is set in sight of Earth and Heav'n;
To myriad hosts, a challenge brief is given;
Who is worthy, to take this *sealed book,*
And loose its seals; within its contents look?

Although three worlds are seduously scanned,
No claimant stirs, to meet the great demand;
None qualified! this tragic state prevails,
In consequence, Earth's hopeful prospect pales.

A voice resounds, declaring to the court
Yon Victor stands, Who has in battle wrought
Deliverance; and won the right of claim,
Entitling Him to Earth's entire domain.

Of Judah's tribe, in David's royal line,
Whose sacrifice has met all claims divine,
He bound the foe established firm, God's reign
Will banish death and all the world regain.

Possessed in full of God's creative might,
With added weight of His redemptive right;
The Deeds are His Whose righteous claims prevail;
No power on earth His title can assail.

The world was His by right ere nature's birth,
For He held claim to everything on Earth;
But man had failed, when he was placed in charge,
And Satan gained complete control at large.

To regain Earth the rightful Owner came,
To buy all*back and vindicate His Name;
He paid in blood the ransom price complete,
Subdued the foe in absolute defeat.

Very costly the purchase He has made,
The price decreed His love has fully paid;
Well qualified to take Earth's *Title Deeds,*
His legal right, as Son and Heir, exceeds.

Christ has secured from under death's domain
The Universe, with title to retain
Earth's Government; Destroy both death and pain,
And righteously, forevermore, to reign.

Receive *Thy crown of Heirship* blessed Lord,
And spread Thy fame and glory all abroad;
Heir of the World and all therein contained,
Thy throne, Thy reign, God has for aye ordained.

C. J. ROLLS